WHITENESS IN THE NOVELS OF

CHARLES W. CHESNUTT

WHITENESS IN THE NOVELS OF

CHARLES W. CHESNUTT

MATTHEW WILSON

UNIVERSITY PRESS OF MISSISSIPPI / JACKSON

A letter from Witter Bynner to Charles W. Chesnutt is
quoted by permission of the Witter Bynner Foundation for
Poetry.
The unpublished material from the Charles W. Chesnutt
papers is reproduced by permission of John C. Slade and Fisk
University Library.
Chapter 6, "The Eccentric Design of Charles W. Chesnutt's
New South Novel, *The Colonel's Dream*," originally appeared,
in a different form, in *Prospects* 25 (2000): 365–89.
Chapter 7, "*Paul Marchand, F.M.C.* and the Strange
Alchemy of Race" originally appeared, in a different form, as
the Introduction to *Paul Marchand, F.M.C.* (Jackson: UP of
Mississippi, 1998).

www.upress.state.ms.us

The University Press of Mississippi is a member of the
Association of American University Presses.

12 11 10 09 08 07 06 05 04   4 3 2 1
∞
Library of Congress Cataloging-in-Publication Data

Wilson, Matthew, 1949–
  Whiteness in the novels of Charles W. Chesnutt / Matthew Wilson.
    p. cm.
  Includes bibliographical references and index.
  ISBN 1-57806-667-0 (alk. paper)
  1. Chesnutt, Charles Waddell, 1858–1932—Criticism and interpretation.
  2. Chesnutt, Charles Waddell, 1858–1932—Characters—Whites. 3. Human
  skin color in literature. 4. Whites in literature. 5. White in literature.
  6. Race in literature. I. Title.
  PS1292.C6Z94   2004
  813'.4—dc22   2003026568

British Library Cataloging-in-Publication Data available

TO MY PARENTS
EDWARD AND REGINA WILSON

Contents

Introduction

If the Negro author selects white America as his audience he is bound to run up against many long-standing artistic conceptions about the Negro; against numerous conventions and traditions which through age have become binding; in a word, against a whole row of hard-set stereotypes which are not easily broken up.

—JAMES WELDON JOHNSON
"The Dilemma of the Negro Author"

Searching the critical work of post-colonial critics, I found . . . very little expressed interest in representations of whiteness in the black imagination. Black cultural and social critics allude to such representations in their writing, yet only a few have dared to make explicit those perceptions of whiteness that they think will discomfort or antagonize readers.

—BELL HOOKS
Black Looks: Race and Representation

This study is an exploration of Charles W. Chesnutt's engagement with whiteness and with white audiences. It takes as its jumping-off point a claim of Chesnutt's and an argument by Toni Morrison. In accepting the Spingarn Medal from the National Association for the Advancement of Colored People in 1928, Chesnutt said that his "books were written . . . a generation too soon. . . . I had to sell my books chiefly to white readers. There were few colored book buyers" (*Essays* 514). Although Chesnutt stressed the selling of books here, my interest in this study is in Chesnutt's awareness of that white audience as he wrote fictions that he hoped to sell to them, a dilemma that has been articulated by Toni Morrison: "What happens to the writerly imagination of a black author who is at some level *always* conscious of representing one's own race to, or in spite of, a race of readers that understands itself to be 'universal' or race-free?" (xii). Acutely aware of that "universal" white audience, Chesnutt hoped to change the minds (and hearts) of those readers. He attempted to do this by working in recognizable genres and by representing both African American and, increasingly throughout his career, white characters and experience. However, he was attempting to do this in a period that led to the almost complete disenfranchisement of African Americans and that saw the hardening of racial lines. Hoping to see a withering away of the color line, he lived to see an even more rigid demarcation of it. As a result, throughout most of his writing career, Chesnutt was split—between his hope and his despair, between his conviction that racial attitudes of his white audience could be changed through appeals to reason (and through his use of sentimental strategies) and his experience that those same racial attitudes were entrenched beyond the possibility of change.

Charles W. Chesnutt was one of the first two African American writers to conceive of himself primarily as an imaginative artist and to write almost exclusively for an elite white audience. Along with Paul Laurence Dunbar, who wrote dialect poetry, plantation fiction, and white-life novels, Chesnutt was a second-generation African American writer. The first generation, writers such as Frederick Douglass and William Wells Brown, was primarily identified with the genre of slave narrative,[1] and, in the case of Douglass, with trying to prevent, after the Civil War, the "erasure from the national narrative of what the war had been about" (Blight 5), the fact that "race was . . . deeply at the root of the war's causes and consequences" (Blight 4). In other words, the origins of African American writing in the nineteenth century are polemical and found in the political urgencies of the antislavery crusade and subsequently in the attempt to preserve the emancipationist vision of the purpose of that war. Chesnutt, though, clearly conceived of himself as a writer of "literature"—more specifically, of imaginative literature that would keep alive Douglass's emancipationist vision in what was one of the darkest periods for African Americans.

As Dickson Bruce has pointed out, Chesnutt wrote at the "nadir" of race relations in America, "a deteriorating racial climate that even [Chesnutt's] best work had been powerless to affect" (185). Since the end of Reconstruction and the withdrawal of federal troops from the South following the election of 1876, African Americans had been progressively robbed of their political rights. As Chesnutt wrote in his 1903 essay "The Disfranchisement of the Negro," African Americans had been deprived of the right to vote throughout the South, and "the rights of Negroes are at a lower ebb than at any time during the thirty-five years of their freedom, and the race prejudice more intense and uncompromising" (*Essays* 187). In addition, as the lynchings of three African American businessmen in Atlanta in 1892 and the coup d'état/pogrom in Wilmington, North Carolina, in 1898 (the subject of Chesnutt's *The Marrow of Tradition*) demonstrated, African Americans in the South were not to be allowed to compete economically with European Americans. And finally there was the phenomenon of lynching itself: throughout this period, there was an explosion in the number of lynchings of African Americans, which peaked in 1892 with 156 lynchings throughout the United States, some 88 percent of them in the South. Joel Williamson has written that this "sudden and dramatic rise in the lynching of black men in and after 1889 stands out like some giant volcanic eruption on the landscape of southern race relations" (*Crucible* 117). Whites justified these lynchings through a social construction of African American men, especially mulatto men, as natural rapists of white women, and by imagining all African Americans as so low on the evolutionary scale that they were incapable of becoming part of American polity, because their blood was tainted by centuries of the supposed degradation that their ancestors had experienced in Africa. This fear of the contamination of blood led, of course, to more and more stringent prohibitions of racial intermarriage, something with which Chesnutt, a man of mixed-race ancestry, was concerned throughout his writing career.

In this period of hardening racial lines in the United States, white writers' fiction about African Americans attempted to keep African Americans in what was thought to be their "natural" place, and the primary genre that disciplined Others in this period was local color. Throughout the last two decades of the nineteenth century, there was an explosion of local color, or regionalist writing, in the United States, and one aspect of local color was the genre of the plantation tale, founded by writers such as Joel Chandler Harris and Thomas Nelson Page and practiced by a host of imitators.[2] These writers created a mythical, romanticized prebellum past in which kind and concerned masters took good care of contented slaves, and these freedmen then told the stories of their masters in the postwar era, expressing a proper nostalgia for slavery. As an old freedman says in Thomas Nelson Page's "Marse Chan" in what is a locus classicus of the celebration of slavery by those who had been oppressed by it, "Dem wuz good ole times, marster—bes' Sam ever see! Dey wuz in fac'! Niggers didn' hed nothin' 't all to do" (*In Ole Virginia* 10).[3] Of course, these tales did cultural work in the 1880s and 1890s, justifying the political and economic repression of African Americans, who were believed to have degenerated under the stresses of the freedom they were thought to be constitutionally incapable of appreciating or employing. If African Americans could be factored out of contemporary political realities through this kind of imaginative sleight of hand, then the work of sectional reconciliation could move forward, and in the literature of the plantation school (and even in mandarin novels like James's *The Bostonians* [1886]), reconciliation was accomplished through the device of sectional marriage: at the end of the narrative, a northern man married a southern woman, thus signaling a healing of the national rupture of the Civil War. In other words, in the fiction of southern (and most northern) writers, reconciliation was accomplished through reading African Americans out of the polity and slavery as a cause of the Civil War was repressed in the national memory.

One of the major cultural tensions with which Chesnutt had to contend as a writer was that he was producing his race fictions in a period when Americans wanted to forget what he insisted they remember, when the national consensus on race was one of active forgetting. The function of this national consensus on race can be illuminated by a passage from Ernest Renan's 1882 essay, "What Is a Nation?" Renan argued that a sense of collective national memory is often achieved by acts of forgetting: "Forgetting, I would even go so far as to say historical error, is a crucial factor in the creation of a nation, which is why progress in historical studies often constitutes a danger for [the principle of] nationality. Indeed, historical enquiry brings to light deeds of violence which took place at the origin of all political formations." Furthermore, while members of a nation "have many things in common, and also that they have forgotten many things" (11), those historical repressions allow national unity and purpose to emerge. In commenting on this passage, Amy Kaplan has written that Renan's ideas illuminate the process of forgetting that happened after the Civil War, which "writers and politicians actively 'forgot' as mutual slaughter and rewrote as a shared sacrifice for reunion. Also forgotten and reinvented was the legacy of slavery and the questions it posed of a contested relation between national and racial identity" ("Nation, Region, Empire" 242). In contrast, Chesnutt's activities as a novelist who insists on remembering what the nation would forget—the legacy of slavery—constitute a threat to national unity. From Chesnutt's perspective, there is a profound injustice in forging national unity by rewriting history in such a way as to erase African Americans from the national narrative.

Of course, as Frederick Douglass repeatedly pointed out, this national celebration of forgetfulness left out African Americans. Indeed, one could argue that while European Americans tried to forget African Americans, African Americans were unable to forget the trauma of slavery and its legacy, and Chesnutt was one of the few African American voices at the turn of the century with a potential national audience to continue to insist on an emancipationist vision, to insist on the importance of memory. In a period when white America wanted the unresolved problem that African Americans represented to disappear, in a period when there was a kind of compact of silence on issues of race, Chesnutt insisted, in all of his race novels, on the persistence of memory, a kind of countermemory that resisted the hegemonic national consensus.

Part of the story that I will tell in this book is the erosion of Chesnutt's faith in his fiction's ability to change that consensus by altering the hearts and minds of his white readers. In making this argument, I will be using as a touchstone one of Chesnutt's statements of artistic purpose from his journals. The passage was written in 1880, when he was twenty-one: "If I do write, I shall write for a purpose, a high, holy purpose. . . . The object of my writings would be not so much the elevation of the colored people as *the elevation of the whites*" (emphasis added, 139). Notice the almost imperial ambition here: he wants more than instrumental change; he wants to "elevate" those whites who are bewildered, lost in the morass of their own racism, and his position is something like that of a black missionary bringing enlightenment to the benighted (white) natives. From the beginning of his publishing career, then, he is in the "African American tradition, extending from Frederick Douglass forward, of insisting that talk of a 'Negro problem' missed the point and that the 'white problem' instead deserved emphasis" (Roediger, *Colored* 20). In diagnosing that "white problem," Chesnutt placed himself directly in a line of African American thinkers who "from folktales onward . . . have been among the nation's keenest students of white consciousness and white behavior" (Roediger, Introduction 4). As an analysis of Chesnutt's study of whiteness, this text should be seen not in terms of the recent development of the field of critical whiteness studies but in terms of studies such as Mia Bay's *The White Image in the Black Mind* and David Roediger's very useful anthology, *White on Black*, which have begun to describe the genealogy of African American studies of whiteness.

In the following chapters, I trace Chesnutt's development as a writer who, from the 1880s, was conscious—with his sketches in the comic magazine *Puck;* with the novella, *Mandy Oxendine* (1896–97); and with the novel that would eventually become *The House Behind the Cedars* (1900)—that his audience was predominantly white. In response to that awareness, Chesnutt chose to represent white experience, something he came to do increasingly in the three novels published in his lifetime. Although he felt it incumbent on him to represent African American experience and particularly the experience of mixed-race characters such as Rena Walden in *The House Behind the Cedars* and Janet Miller and her husband, Dr. Miller, in *The Marrow of Tradition,* he came to believe it necessary to present images of whiteness to his white audience, images that would denaturalize the privilege of that whiteness. As he increasingly represented white experience in his three published novels, his faith in his ability to "elevate" white folks (and in their willingness to be "elevated") eroded, and by the time of the last novel published in his lifetime, *The Colonel's Dream*, he shows how a "liberal" on the question of race is riven with contradictions and unexamined racist assumptions (and in terms of audience, the form of the novel is at war with itself and Chesnutt produces a text that embodies the extreme contradictions of his subject position in 1905).

In exploring whiteness in Chesnutt's novels, I examine how he was attempting to manipulate his white audience through his depiction of white experience. Certain characters—for example, George Tryon in *The House Behind the Cedars* and Colonel French in *The Colonel's Dream*—were meant to be surrogates for his white audience, and he hoped that his readers would follow and assent to the trajectories of their experiences. Other white characters, such as Major Carteret in *The Marrow of Tradition* and Fetters in *The Colonel's Dream*, were intended as counterstereotypes, as responses to the depiction of southerners in the fictions of white writers in this period. His exploration of whiteness also continued in the six novels that were left in manuscript at the time of his death.[4] In his two Harlem Renaissance novels, *Paul Marchand, F.M.C.* (1921) and *The Quarry* (1928), he looked at whiteness as a social construct by having each of his central characters discover, after having been brought up black, that he is biologically "white." In these rewritings of Twain's *Pudd'nhead Wilson* (1894), Chesnutt examined the arbitrariness of race ascription, but the novels are significantly different in their overall tenor. *Paul Marchand* is the most bitter of Chesnutt's fictions, and in it he has given up on his project of "elevating" whites, while *The Quarry* is quietly optimistic as he begins to reject his white audience altogether. The biologically white Donald Glover chooses to remain identified with his experience and his adoptive mother's people—he chooses to be a black man when he could have all the advantages of being white. Finally, Chesnutt examines whiteness from another angle—in the years from 1897 to 1903, he wrote three white-life novels (that is, novels that contain only incidental African American characters and that concentrate on depictions of white experience).[5]

Along with Paul Laurence Dunbar, who published three white-life novels, Chesnutt was among the first African Americans to work in this genre. In at least two of these novels, *A Business Career* (1898) and *The Rainbow Chasers* (1900), he imitates the forms of popular fiction and takes on the authority to write as if he were white, just as a myriad of white writers in this period took on the right to write in the voice of African Americans. However, the third of these novels, *Evelyn's Husband* (ca. 1903) is a critique of whiteness in the guise of a wildly melodramatic adventure novel.

Because of his engagement with whiteness and because of the cultural power of white writers who represented southern experience in this period, Chesnutt was acutely aware of the fiction of white writers and the genres in which they wrote. In fact, he was much more aware of their writing than the writing of his African American contemporaries, such as Harper, Hopkins, and Griggs. For example, in submitting a draft of a novella, "Rena Walden" (which would eventually become *The House Behind the Cedars*), to Houghton Mifflin in 1891, Chesnutt claimed that it was "the first contribution by an American with acknowledged African descent to purely imaginative literature" (*Letters* 75), and in 1928, in his speech accepting the Spingarn Medal, he was still making much the same claim: "I think I was the first man in the United States who shared his blood, to write serious fiction about the Negro" (514). Chesnutt apparently did not, until late in his life, read any fiction by African American writers (though I doubt that he could have been unaware of the fiction published in the *Colored American Magazine*). As a writer of counternarratives, he apparently felt that it was necessary to know how white writers were representing both white and African American experience. Because he wanted to write fictions with which he hoped his white audience would be initially familiar, I have tried to reconstruct the generic presuppositions that his white audience brought to his novels—for example, romance in the white-life novels, tragic mulatta fiction in *The House Behind the Cedars*, the historical romance in *The Marrow of Tradition*, and the New South economic novel in *The Colonel's Dream*. Even the first of his Harlem Renaissance novels, *Paul Marchand, F.M.C.*, harkened back to a novel by a white writer, George Washington Cable's *The Grandissimes* (1880).

In reconstructing Chesnutt's white audience through genre, I am trying to tease out what Jauss calls the "system of expectations that arises for
each work in the historical moment of its appearance" (22). Because
Chesnutt was always adapting popular genres, it is important to observe
that the popular novel fulfills "the expectations prescribed by a ruling
standard of taste, in that it satisfies the desire for the reproduction of
the familiarly beautiful; confirms familiar sentiments; sanctions wishful
notions . . . or even raises moral problems, but only to 'solve' them in an
edifying manner as predecided questions" (Jauss 25). In these novels,
though, Chesnutt's adaptations of initially recognizable genres resulted in
fictions of a distinctly "eccentric design"[6] in which ostensibly familiar
genres were turned against his audience, taking them into unfamiliar
generic territory, as if his manipulation of genre were a metaphor for the
unfamiliar representations of both black and white experience. However,
quite surprisingly, in the mid- to late 1920s, when he wrote his last novel,
The Quarry, Chesnutt had begun to read African American fiction, as his
lectures and the books in his library make clear. At the end of his life, in
response to a critical mass of African American book buyers, he began to
think about the fiction of the Harlem Renaissance and to envision his
audience as more racially mixed than in any of his other novels.

Even though Chesnutt finally acknowledged the fictional work of
African Americans, his subject position as a man of mixed-race ancestry
remained complicated throughout his life. Early in his life, Chesnutt wrote
that he had resolved to be a "voluntary negro" (quoted in Hackenberry,
Introduction xxiv), despite the fact that he was light enough to pass as
white. Chesnutt resisted the temptation to pass into the white world, but
paradoxically his subject position as a writer was not primarily African
American. Accepting the Spingarn Medal in 1928, he said that he wrote
"not as a Negro writing about Negroes, but as a human being writing
about other human beings" (*Essays* 514). In terms of his ethnic identity, he
chose to be an African American, but in his writing he strove for a universal subject position that he perceived as outside of race. As William
M. Ramsey has pointed out, Chesnutt wrote in 1904 that one should "exalt
humanity above race. The most diverse races resemble in more things

than they differ" (*Essays* 200). In this way, Chesnutt is the intellectual heir of Frederick Douglass:[7] both stress that humankind is one, as is its origin (that is, they are monogenesists rather than polygenesists). Ramsey makes much the same point when he argues, on one hand, that "Chesnutt's allegiance to the presence, legitimacy, and pride of the black family is undeniable, indeed a core generative force in his literary career. On the other, the broader human family also claims his allegiance, informing his vision for America" (41). That allegiance to family does not mean, however, that Chesnutt extended his sense of pride to race. He rejected the concept of race pride as part of the essentializing American racial binary. In other words, this is a study in the paradoxical subject position of Charles W. Chesnutt as a writer, and in the "complex double vision" (Ellison 131–32)[8] of the novels, a set of tensions that helped Chesnutt produce texts that still resonate today and remain the subject of a rich critical debate.

This is the first study to look exclusively at the full range of Chesnutt's novels. In *The Literary Career of Charles W. Chesnutt*, William L. Andrews examines fully only the novels that were published during Chesnutt's lifetime. Dean McWilliams, in *Charles W. Chesnutt and the Fictions of Race*, writes of the three race novels that were unpublished in Chesnutt's lifetime but ignores the white-life novels. In addition, McWilliams focuses on "the construction of racial identity" (xi), whereas I focus on the consequences of Chesnutt's awareness of his white audience. My study is also different from Eric Sundquist's *To Wake the Nations* with its discussion of Chesnutt's complicated relationship with African American vernacular culture. Until recently, the novels that Chesnutt left in manuscript have received scant critical attention. Of course, that critical task was made more difficult because those texts were, until recent years, available only in the Chesnutt Papers at Fisk University Library. But since all three of the manuscript race fictions have been published, the task of assessing all of Chesnutt's fictions has become easier. In addition, because the critical climate has changed, it is easier to assess the cultural work that Chesnutt is attempting in his three white-life novels. For me, these novels are not the embarrassments that earlier critics, like Andrews, have made them out to be but rather fascinating examples of Chesnutt working in popular genres in which he could let his imagination run wild, particularly in *Evelyn's Husband.* Because these novels have received almost no critical attention, I have chosen to begin with them, thereby highlighting Chesnutt's ambitions as a writer of white-life fictions and the ways in which he conceived of whiteness and his white audience.

This study began in my discovery of Chesnutt more than ten years ago, and I would like to thank those students who read Chesnutt with me at Capital College—Penn State Harrisburg and who shared my excitement at that discovery. My formal study of Chesnutt was initiated by an National Endowment for the Humanities Summer Seminar for College Teachers on "Slavery, Reconstruction, and the U.S. Civil Imagination" with Donald Pease at Dartmouth College. I would like to thank him and the other members of the seminar for their feedback on a draft of an essay on *The Colonel's Dream* that became the starting point for this project. In addition, the study was also furthered by two grants from the Capital College Research Council and one from the Institute for Arts and Humanistic Studies of Pennsylvania State University, grants that gave me access to all of Chesnutt's manuscript novels. I am also grateful to Dr. Patti Mills, Assistant Dean for Academic Affairs and Interim Assistant Dean for Graduate Studies, for a subvention from the Office of Research and Graduate Studies at Capital College to support the publication of this book. I would like to thank Capital College—Penn State Harrisburg for granting me sabbatical and William J. Mahar for supporting my sabbatical request. Beth Howse was extremely helpful in my several visits to the Chesnutt Papers at Fisk University, and I would like to thank John C. Slade for giving me permission to quote from Chesnutt's unpublished material. I also would like to thank my wife, Marjan van Schaik, and my colleague, Patricia Johnson, who convinced me to take the sabbatical that made writing this study possible. Finally, I would like to thank Gregg Crane, whose suggestions were invaluable and have made my analysis stronger and more cogent.

WHITENESS IN THE NOVELS OF

CHARLES W. CHESNUTT

[1]

Chesnutt's Racial Nonfiction

Theorizing Race

"It's not the Negro problem [James Baldwin] said to a sincere student questioner after a Harvard speech. It's the white problem. I'm only black because you think you're white."

Before I begin my discussion of whiteness in Chesnutt's novels, it is first necessary to provide a frame of reference: Chesnutt's theoretical pronouncements about race, over some fifteen years, from the beginning of his fiction-writing career until the publication of the last novel issued in his lifetime, *The Colonel's Dream* in 1905. Beginning with his racial nonfiction will allow me to use this chapter as a touchstone for Chesnutt's representations of whiteness in his novels and will facilitate my chronological analysis (with one significant exception) of his novels by connecting individual analyses to the issues raised by the racial nonfiction. To begin with a consideration of his racial nonfiction is not to claim, however, that Chesnutt is simply illustrating his ideas in his fiction; rather, there was a complicated cross-fertilization between his racial thinking and his fiction, in much the same way there was for a writer such as Ralph Ellison.

Judy Scales-Trent has observed that "white America expends enormous resources in school and in the media" to teach and maintain the color line (481)—that is, the "one-drop rule," what "anthropologists call . . . 'hypodescent' which means that the racially mixed people are assigned the status of the subordinate group," a system of racial classification that is unique to the United States (476). The result of policing the color line is that racial hierarchies remain in effect and the social and historical become naturalized. What Chesnutt called the "social fiction" (*Essays* 134) of race becomes the essentialized scientific "fact" of race with its inevitable binary of inferior/superior. In Chesnutt's view, in his final pronouncements of race, racism can only disappear when there are no longer "races" because the concept of race is always implicated in a power dynamic that supports the equation that black signifies inferior while white signifies superior.

There are three major pronouncements in the years he was most actively writing and publishing: "What Is a White Man?" (1889) in the *Independent,* the three articles entitled "The Future American" (1900) in the *Boston Evening Transcript,* and "Race Prejudice: Its Causes and Cures" (1905), a speech given to the Boston Literary and Historical Association (an abbreviated version of which was printed in *Alexander's Magazine*). Although these works are written over the course of fifteen years, there are a number of continuities among them as well as major differences, particularly in "Race Prejudice," a speech written at the end of a period during which Chesnutt had become increasingly pessimistic about his ability to affect his white readers and about white folks' willingness to change their attitudes toward African Americans.

I

"What Is a White Man," Chesnutt's first major nonfiction publication, appeared in the *Independent,* a national weekly that "printed some fiction and much comment on public affairs" (Mott, *American Magazines* 59). In the article, he established a position that he would sustain in both his fiction and nonfiction. He chose to focus on the "in-between people,"[1] those in the liminal category between white and black—that "very large class of the population who are certainly not Negroes in an ethnological sense" (*Essays* 68), the class of mixed-race people, of mulattoes. Although Chesnutt used this term, we must keep in mind its origins and its valence in racist discourse. Joel Williamson argues that because the "mule was the ubiquitous and important animal in the rural and premodern South" and because it was a "hybrid" with no mule ancestors and "no descendants," there was an association in southern minds between mules and mulattoes. They believed that "as the mule dies, so too dies the mulatto. The association with mules also carried the implication that the hybrid could be continued only by an artificial contrivance, by an unnatural act of mating that ought not and does not have to be, which, in fact, if we but know the truth, must be made to be by straining against the winds and tides of nature" (*New People* 96). At this time, as Williamson has pointed out, to maintain America's racial binary, racist ideologues were attempting to collapse any and all distinctions between mulattoes and blacks, and, in fact, the notorious one-drop rule was the final fruition of this effort. Given this insistence on the racial binary, "to merge white and black would have been the ultimate holocaust, the absolute damnation of the southern civilization. And yet that was precisely what the mulatto, by his very being, represented. He was the walking, talking, breathing indictment of the world the white man made" (95). But Chesnutt, in his response to racist discourse, like other African American writers in this period such as Frances Ellen Watkins Harper, employed the figure of the mulatto strategically.[2] Their "fair-skinned heroes and heroines . . . represent what for a brief while will look like the possibility of a breakdown of difference between black and white" (Michaels, *Our America* 55). At this point in his thinking, Chesnutt hoped that the third term—the mulatto, the white negro—would be able to split apart the binary of black and white, forcing the American racial imaginary to stop insisting on the rigid demarcation of the color line.

The strategy that Chesnutt used can be illuminated by Nancy Bentley's discussion of the figure of the mulatto in antebellum fiction, an analysis that applies also to its postbellum uses: "The Mulatto has a potentially disruptive position in the antebellum American novel. . . . The Mulatto figure was a scandal—not only a sexual but an intellectual scandal, confounding as it did the racial categories that were as fundamental to social life in the North as in the South" (197–98). Chesnutt pointed to this "intellectual scandal" throughout "What Is a White Man" by his use of irony. For instance, when he turned to examine the laws against interracial marriage, he remarked caustically on the necessity for such laws— "Nature, by some unaccountable oversight having to some extent neglected a matter so important to the future prosperity and progress of mankind" (*Essays* 71). At the beginning of his career, Chesnutt was arguing that America was already a miscegenated country, and a sign of that hybridity was the presence of the figure of the mulatto. But this position was exactly the opposite of the one taken by many white Americans. White folks, as Williamson has pointed out, thought of mulattoes as unnatural, "artificial contrivances" (*New People* 96). For them, "mulattoes became the living symbols not only of the defeat of the South but also of its great prewar sin—miscegenation" (Fredrickson 92). So what the white consensus excoriated, Chesnutt celebrated. While racist ideologues believed that mixed-race people would die out, Chesnutt argued that what distinguished America as a country was its race mixing.

In the face of a racial ideology that constantly policed the color line, wanted to maintain the fiction that it could not be crossed, and tried to maintain clear-cut distinctions between white and black, Chesnutt pointed to the fact that laws and judicial decisions throughout the United States acknowledged that persons of African descent were able to migrate into the white world. "As a general rule," Chesnutt claimed of his survey of these decisions, "less than one-fourth of Negro blood left the individual white. . . . Thus the color-line is drawn at one-fourth of Negro blood, and persons with only one-eighth are white" (*Essays* 69). Chesnutt's purpose here was twofold: first, he was using the scandal of the figure of the mulatto to show that whiteness is a permeable category (an idea he would develop at greater length in articles in the "Future American" series). Second, he was pointing to the difficulty that legislatures and judges had in defining what constitutes whiteness. When he discussed laws prohibiting interracial marriage, he quoted a Georgia law: "'the marriage relation between white persons and persons of African descent is forever prohibited, and such marriages shall be null and void.' This is a very sweeping provision. . . . A court which was so inclined would find no difficulty in extending this provision of the law to the remotest strain of African blood. The marriage relation is forever prohibited. Forever is a long time" (*Essays* 72). Even though most legislatures acknowledged that people of one-eighth African ancestry were white, Georgia at least still wanted to prohibit race mixing and to maintain the fiction of binary and unmixable races. This desire for an absolute binary, of course, anticipated the U.S. Supreme Court's decision in *Plessy v. Ferguson*, which imported plantation mythology from the literary into the heart of the legal system (Sundquist, *To Wake* 235). Summing up "the degradation of black rights that had occurred over the previous two decades," the decision also provided a framework for "American civil rights legislation and judgments for the next half century" (*To Wake* 237).

Although there seemed in the late 1880s to be a rough consensus about what constituted whiteness, Chesnutt made much of the inconsistencies inherent in the myriad of racial laws in the United States, and at the heart of his essay, he pointed to a contradicting standard for determining who was white. Most of the cases he discussed used a quasi-scientific approach by breaking descent down into proportions, but a South Carolina ruling pointed in another direction entirely. Chesnutt quoted some fifteen lines of this decision: " 'The line of distinction' " between mulatto and white, the Court wrote, " 'is not ascertained by any rule of law. . . . It is in all cases a question for the jury, to be determined by them upon the evidence of features and complexion afforded by inspection, the evidence of reputation as to parentage, and the evidence of the rank and station in society occupied by the party' " (*Essays* 70). In other words, if people looked white, if their parents were thought of as white, and if they were middle class, then they were white. Chesnutt was again pointing to the permeability of whiteness as a concept, but more radically he was attempting to undermine a generally accepted understanding in the late nineteenth century that race was based in science. The courts and legislatures, Chesnutt seemed to be saying, were confused: Is race a scientific fact determined by proportions of race mixing? Or is race determined simply by any African ancestry whatsoever? Or is race determined by what people think it is (if someone looks white, then he or she is white)?

In using this South Carolina Supreme Court decision as a touchstone, Chesnutt had carefully chosen his state and time. The decision that he quoted was written in 1831 (*Letters* 73 n.4) in one of the two states that was relatively liberal on the question of how to determine whiteness. (The other state was Louisiana.) South Carolina's unusual history on this question can be illuminated by a debate about how to define whiteness during the 1895 Constitutional Convention, which had criminalized interracial marriage. Of course, as soon as marriage between the races was criminalized, it became necessary to define legally who was white and who was black. One member of the convention proposed that in "such unions a negro should be defined as a person possessing 'any' Negro blood." George Tillman argued against this definition; if it were enacted,

> he declared, apparently to the astonishment of no one, some very respectable families of his Edgefield County would find themselves proscribed. These families, he argued, had given soldiers to the Confederate army. These men had served creditably, and it would be unjust and disgraceful to embarrass them in this way. Probably George Tillman's championship of this light fringe of the mulatto world spring from the fact that he had matured in that earlier age . . . in which . . . a man's status could not be decided by proportions of blood alone. Tillman was . . . a hangover from Carolina's racially loose and Latin past. (Williamson *New People* 93)

Subsequently, the convention changed the 1879 law that defined a Negro as anyone possessing a quarter or more of black blood, deciding on one-eighth as the new standard. Writing five years after this convention, Chesnutt resorted to an earlier 1831 law as his touchstone in an effort to hold onto remnants of a different racial past that was quickly being erased in the era of Jim Crow.[3]

Laying out this definitional dilemma in "What Is a White Man?" Chesnutt was anticipating the difficulties the courts would continue to have between 1878 and 1923 in determining, for purposes of naturalization, who was white. Ian Haney López has surveyed these cases in his brilliant book, White By Law: Legal Constructions of Race, and although these cases do not concern African Americans, who had been granted citizenship by the Fourteenth Amendment, the difficulties that the courts experienced in determining who was white clearly speak to the similar problems that they had in defining the whiteness of mixed-race Americans. The problem the courts faced in this period of vastly increased immigration, López points out, was a 1790 act of Congress that "restricted citizenship to 'white persons'" (1), a statute that remained in force until 1952.

In trying individual cases, the courts initially attempted to rely on science to answer the question "Who is white?" but they increasingly found science a definitional morass. For instance, in 1913, when asked to decide whether a Syrian was white, District Judge Smith rejected the scientific category of Caucasian and denied that whites could be thought of as Caucasians. "Nor could," López writes, "the term 'white person' be equated with other scientific concepts, for example that of the 'Aryan' race, 'one still more indefinite than Caucasian,' or that of an 'Indo-European' race, 'as sometimes ethnologically at the present day defined as including the present mixed Indo-European, Hindu, Malay, and Dravidian inhabitants of East India and Ceylon.'" Smith argued that it was impossible for "a very dark brown, almost black inhabitant of India . . . to rank as a white person" (73). Rejecting science all together, Smith resorted to an original-intent argument: white people were what the Founding Fathers meant—people from Europe. Most cases in this period either used scientific evidence or common knowledge, just as Judge Smith did when he rejected out of hand the possibility that a man who was "a very dark brown, almost black" could be white.

The judicial confusion about who was white was finally brought to an end by two U.S. Supreme Court cases heard in 1922 and 1923, in which the court held that "the words 'free white persons' are words of common speech, to be interpreted in accordance with the understanding of the common man." The Court rejected science in favor of common knowledge and in so doing "no doubt remained convinced that racial divisions followed real, natural, physical differences. The Court upheld common knowledge in the belief that people are accomplished amateur naturalists, capable of accurately discerning differences in the physical world" (López 8). In other words, if one is accepted, by common knowledge as white, one *is* white, exactly what the 1831 South Carolina law said about racial admixtures and exactly what Chesnutt argued throughout his lifetime. Chesnutt, though, has turned racial common sense and common knowledge on its head: the court says that everyone knows who is white, and Chesnutt will point to the many cases of peoples of mixed race who pass as white as evidence that commonsense knowledge is little more than a kind of wishful thinking on the part of white folks who will continue to police the color line to preserve an (illusory) binary racial system. In effect, Chesnutt is trying to demonstrate to his readers that the color line cannot be surveilled as rigorously as they think it can, and he is trying to undermine their essentialist conceptions of race.

After "What Is a White Man?" was published, Chesnutt received a letter from George Washington Cable that said that he had read the article "with care and great pleasure." In 1885–90, Cable was a kind of voice in the wilderness, a southern liberal on the question of race. He and Chesnutt had been corresponding throughout 1889, and Cable was "interested in coaxing Chesnutt to become his ideological ally" (*Letters* 21). Cable went on to say, "I have long thought of this branch of the question and have constantly and patiently watched opportunities to bring it forward. You know that all my earlier stories about quadroons really ask this question, 'What is a white man[?] What is a white woman?' I thought in my beginning that it was an initial question but believe now it is not, yet it is one that must have its place and time and value in the solution of our great question" (Cable to Chesnutt, 12 June 1889). Chesnutt must have been encouraged by the fact that he and Cable seemed to be thinking along the same lines, and it must have confirmed Chesnutt in his resolution to work, like Cable, on two tracks—to continue to write fiction but also to continue to intervene polemically on the race question.

II

Chesnutt's next major intervention in the conversation about race in America came in his three articles that appeared under the title "The Future American" in the *Boston Evening Transcript* in 1900. In the eleven years since "What Is a White Man?" had been published, his thinking about issues of race had become more complicated and more audacious. At the core of "The Future American" was the contention that the black race inevitably would be assimilated by the white, and from "a Negroid nation, which ours is already, we would have become a composite and homogeneous people" (*Essays* 125). Chesnutt argued that this process was already well under way, and the absence of any laws to discourage race mixing would "largely increase the flow of dark blood toward the white race, until the time shall come when distinctions of color shall lose their importance" (*Essays* 135). Chesnutt here offered as a cure for race prejudice the very thing that white Americans feared—race mixing—but instead of bringing about the degeneration of both races, he saw miscegenation as a kind of utopian solution to a problem that seemed otherwise intractable.

To gauge the audaciousness of Chesnutt's proposal, it is necessary to rehistoricize the virulent racism of the period. George Frederickson has written that virulent "anti-Negro propaganda . . . spewed forth in unprecedented volume around the turn of the [twentieth] century" (256), and "the 1890s saw an unparalleled outburst of racist speculation on the impending disappearance of the American Negro" (246). African Americans, in the racist imaginary, were bound to disappear because of their inherited racial characteristics made them unfit for the struggle for existence. They were believed to be more prone to disease than their white counterparts[4] and to have degenerated since the days of slavery. And the 1890 census appeared to offer evidence to support these conclusions because the African American population seemed to be increasing at a rate substantially lower than that of other ethnic groups. Furthermore, in the racist imaginary, as Paul Barringer argued in *The American Negro: His Past and Future* (1900) "the life history is the repetition of the race history," as if every individual recapitulated the evolutionary process of his race as a whole. Given the "'ages of degradation' in Africa," there was no way, Barringer posited, for education and acculturation to have had any effect on peoples of African descent. And so "reversion to type" was understandable. Lacking the discipline of slavery, "the young negro of the South . . . is reverting through hereditary forces to savagery" (quoted in Frederickson 253). Given this climate, Chesnutt's proposals in these three articles are quite stunning, as if he had taken the assumptions of the racist imaginary and turned them inside out. Rather than segregating African Americans both physically and imaginatively, Chesnutt argued for their integration not only into the body politic but also into the bodies of white folks. Rather than being a kind of infectious agent, their blood would become the surest way to escape the incessantly racialized American imagination.

While Chesnutt refused in these three articles to essentialize race, he also refused to confront scientific racism directly. Rather, he assumed that it had been superseded by more recent scientific explanations. He argued, for instance, that there was no such thing as a racially pure Europe and that "the secret of progress of Europe has been found in racial heterogeneity" (*Essays* 122). In place of scientific explanations for race, Chesnutt substituted an understanding of race as ethnicity: "I use the word 'race' here in its popular sense—that of a people who look substantially alike, and are moulded by the same culture and dominated by the same ideals" (*Essays* 123). In addition, he attempted to discredit many constituent elements of the American racial imaginary: he argued that what constituted common knowledge about race among Americans was little more than a recycling of what he termed "superstition"—folk beliefs that helped to preserve the American racial binary. For example, he rejected the belief that persons of mixed races were sterile (*Essays* 123). He also alluded to the belief that a "'telltale dark mark at the root of the nails,' is supposed to be an infallible test of Negro blood," rejecting it as "a delusion and a snare." Finally he rejected the belief in atavism—in terms of racialist discourse, "the reversion to type," or the belief that whether physically or morally, the remote African ancestor will always be revealed in the descendant. Specifically, he excoriated "the grewsome [*sic*] superstition that a woman apparently white may give birth to a coal-black child by a white father" (*Essays* 127), a commonplace in racialist discourse of the time.

In place of the explanations of scientific racism (and in place of so-called common knowledge about race), Chesnutt substituted a different understanding that was commonplace among African American intellectuals in the nineteenth and early twentieth centuries. Racial differences, Chesnutt wrote, can be accounted for by environment: "By modern research the unity of the human race has been proved . . . and the differentiation of races by selection and environment has been so stated as to prove itself" (*Essays* 122). Deploying this argument, Chesnutt was placing himself in the mainstream of African American thinking about race. As Mia Bay has demonstrated, almost all African American intellectuals rejected polygenesis in favor of monogenesis—that is, they emphasized the "the unity of the human race," in contradistinction to explanations that posited separate creations and thus separate essences. These intellectuals accounted for the differences in the races by emphasizing differences in environment. "Drawing on the environmentalist theories of human development propounded by great European thinkers of the Enlightenment, they argued that different environments rather than different origins were what distinguished the races of man" (Bay 220).

The logical extension of these environmentalist explanations of racial differences is that since "racial distinctions developed over time [they] were subject to further change" (Bay 221). Most often, this change was cast in terms of education and racial uplift: when African Americans had access to education and to a middle-class life, perceived racial differences would begin to erode. But Chesnutt made education just a stepping-stone on the way to total amalgamation: when African Americans' environmental deficiencies were remedied, all barriers to racial mixing would have fallen; when the races had sufficiently mixed, a "time shall come when distinctions of color shall lose their importance, which will be but the prelude to a complete racial fusion" (*Essays* 135).

The problem with this story is that Chesnutt seemed tacitly to admit the superiority of the white race by claiming that in the course of this amalgamation "the white race would have absorbed the black" (*Essays* 125).

Of course, this process of absorption was based on the relative proportions of African Americans and European Americans in the population of the United States in 1900, and through his scheme of amalgamation he was rejecting notions of racial purity on both sides of the color line. He was advocating a radical solution that would make racial distinctions disappear completely: "There would be no inferior race to domineer over; there would be no superior race to oppress those who differed from them in racial externals" (125). Chesnutt realized that as long as Americans insisted on the black/white racial binary, there was no way out of the binary of superior/inferior: the concept of race had to be expunged to get out of the trap of racial hierarchy,[5] and he could see no way of making race disappear except through the absorption of African Americans.

Still, a residue of racialist thinking remains in these articles, a residue that is implicit in the idea of amalgamation itself. When Chesnutt began this series of articles, he ridiculed the "popular theory" of what we might call white amalgamation—the combining of all of the "races" of Europe on American soil. In the popular imagination this would lead, Chesnutt writes, to a "perfection of type—no good American could for a moment doubt that it will be as perfect as everything else American. . . . [It will be] brought about by a combination of all the best characteristics of the different European races, and the elimination, by some strange alchemy, of all their undesirable traits—for even a good American will admit that European races, now and then, have some undesirable traits when they first come over" (*Essays* 121–22). Here again, Chesnutt's irony was at work, particularly in his use of the term "strange alchemy" to describe this process of white amalgamation. Yet later, in the final paragraph of the series, he seemed to support the operation of this alchemy when he wrote that the "white race is still susceptible of some improvement, and if, in time, the more objectionable Negro traits are eliminated, and his better qualities correspondingly developed, his part in the future American race may well be an important and valuable one" (*Essays* 135). Chesnutt's dilemma as a racial thinker came down to the phrases "objectionable Negro traits" and "his better qualities": better qualities were to be developed through the influence of improved environment (primarily through education), but I am not at all sure that the objectionable traits to be "eliminated" were products solely of environment. It seems as if Chesnutt were resorting to the kind of alchemy he scorned earlier in the series. Both the skin color and objectionable racial characteristics of African Americans were to be eliminated through amalgamation, and amalgamation would eliminate the objectionable racial characteristics of European Americans as well. The potential problem with Chesnutt's solution, as William M. Ramsey has pointed out, is that "it would seem to entail, if not *encourage*—the loss of distinctive black ethnicity through the flow of dark blood toward white" (32). Chesnutt's way out of this seeming erasure was through an investment not in the global idea of race but in the local idea of family and heritage, something much closer to the idea of ethnicity than the totalizing concept of race.

This ambivalence, as Bay points out, was typical of the thinking of nineteenth- and early-twentieth-century African American intellectuals. Even though their writing contained the most trenchant "denunciations of race as fallacy heard in nineteenth-century America, [they] never entirely rejected the idea of innate racial differences in their own thinking" (221). Chesnutt's confusions and ambivalences can be seen more broadly as cultural confusions, as the inability for anyone to escape racialist discourse in the nineteenth and early twentieth centuries. What Chesnutt was not ambivalent about, however, was the status of mixed-race people, something that remains consistent from his earlier essay, "What Is a White Man?" Chesnutt wrote in "The Future American" that "only a social fiction . . . makes of a person seven-eighths white a Negro; he is really much more a white man" (*Essays* 134). At this point, Chesnutt had not yet fully explored the implications of the phrase "social fiction." He fully developed that insight in his next major statement on the race issue, which came five years later.

III

Very much consistent with Chesnutt's previous pronouncements on the race problem in the United States, "Race Prejudice: Its Causes and Cures" continued to advance the environmentalist argument, but in this essay Chesnutt focused largely on the question of education. Assuming that race prejudice is a historical artifact, he argued that something constructed can also be altered historically, through the process of education. He also returned to the question of amalgamation, arguing again that should "strongly marked difference[s] . . . in physical characteristics . . . disappear entirely, race prejudice, and the race problem, would no longer exist" (*Essays* 231). In this essay and in his last two novels, *Paul Marchand, F.M.C.* and *The Quarry*, Chesnutt argued for a fluid account of race, as opposed to the American racial binary. As Walter Benn Michaels has argued in another context, if one rejects an essentialist and "scientific" account of race and substitutes for it the idea that race is culture, "if race really were nothing but a distinctive array of beliefs and practices . . . then people could change their racial identity" (*Our America* 133). When racial identity can be changed, one must also reject, in Chesnutt's view, essentialist accounts of racial pride:

> We have had preached to us of late a new doctrine—that of Race Integrity. We must so glory in our color that we must zealously guard it as a priceless heritage. Frankly, I take no stock in this attitude. It seems to me a modern invention of the white people to perpetuate the color line. It is they who preach it, and it is *their* racial integrity which they wish to preserve. They have never been unduly careful of the purity of the black race. I can scarcely restrain a smile when I hear a mulatto talking of race integrity, or a quadroon dwelling upon race pride. (*Essays* 231–32)

Chesnutt's contemptuous "smile" was a somewhat bitter acknowledgment that race pride was a trap. He believed that it helped to perpetuate America's invidious racial binary, and he saw "race purity [as] the latest argument for the oppression of the Negro in the South" (233). Beyond its tactical use in policing the color line, race pride violated his sense of "the unity of mankind" (215), the oneness of the human race: "But of what should we be proud?" he asked. "Of any inherent superiority? We deny it in others, proclaiming the equality of man" (232). A thorough Enlightenment universalist, Chesnutt rejected race pride on both sides of the color line, a position that might make him somewhat unsympathetic in our time; from his point of view, however, his conclusions were both logical and consistent with those of other black intellectuals of the period. As Ross Posnock has argued, like Sutton Griggs and W. E. B. DuBois, Chesnutt had emancipated himself "from the imprisoning rhetoric of authenticity with its inevitable racializing of culture" (*Color and Culture* 103) and had come close to being an "antirace race man" (5). In rejecting the concept of authenticity, he came very close in this speech to concluding that all constructions of race were social and legal fictions, that race was, in the words of López, "not a measured fact, but a preserved fiction" (102), that "race is entirely social. Race is nothing more than what society and law say it is" (103).

At the beginning of "Race Prejudice," Chesnutt echoed what he had written previously: the differences between races are "superficial and inconstant," and many people fail to see that these "purely fictitious lines and cleavages between races" are products of history and environment, preferring to see them "as something fixed and eternal" (*Essays* 215). On the contrary, Chesnutt claims, in a sweeping generalization: "I do not believe that the current notion of race has any logical or scientific ground" (214–15). Chesnutt here came as close as anyone in the nineteenth or early twentieth centuries to repudiating altogether the idea of race. In this foray into the polemical realm, he demonstrated the utter inconsistency of racialist thinking in the legal realm and suggested that race was a social construction with no basis whatsoever except in received opinion.

What is also new in this speech is Chesnutt's sense that he was articulating a vision of a raceless United States for the long distant future. In "The Future American," he had stressed that amalgamation would not happen quickly, and in this 1905 "discussion of race prejudice," he said, "I am seeking the long-time remedy" (234). The "structure" of racial antagonism had been "built up, beam by beam, stone by stone, so it must be torn down, stone by stone, beam by beam" (219). This deconstruction involved, in Chesnutt's view, the disappearance of "distinctions based on color"—in other words, the dismantling of the superior/inferior binary. To accomplish this goal, "all of us, white and colored, [must] resolutely shut our eyes to differences of color" (233). Racial antagonism, in Chesnutt's view, did not originate in different "essences" or different origins; rather, it was a historical product and as such could be dismantled only through the application of law and through adherence to the Constitution. As he wrote to Booker T. Washington in 1903, "I have no confidence in the friendship of the whites which is to take the place of rights, and no expectation of justice at their hands unless it is founded on law" (*Letters* 182), or as Chesnutt said publicly in "The Future American," the "Negro should let no right, great or small, go by default. He is either a citizen or not a citizen. . . . If he be a citizen, then he should be entitled, as an individual, without regard to his race or color, to every right that any man enjoys by virtue of his citizenship" (*Essays* 166). (Chesnutt's insistence on voting rights and equality before the law constituted his greatest public disagreement with Washington's policies.) Thus, in his nonfiction, Chesnutt was attempting a stern recourse to the law during the period when the Supreme Court was eviscerating the constitutional amendments passed after the Civil War. In this insistence on law and justice, Chesnutt was the heir of Frederick Douglass, who, Chesnutt wrote, "took [as] the only true ground for the solutions of the race problems of that or *any other epoch,*—that the situation should be met with equal and exact justice, and that his people should be allowed to do as they pleased with themselves, 'subject only to same great laws which apply to other men'" (emphasis added; *Frederick Douglass* 91).

But despite his insistence on justice, Chesnutt's dilemma as a racial thinker arises as the logical conclusion to his environmentalist position combined with his nascent racial abolitionism. Chesnutt wanted the concept of race, as it was understood in his time, to disappear. By 1905, he wanted two separate and unequal races to be replaced by one homogeneous, undifferentiated race, a position articulated in our time by writers such as Mia Bay and Paul Gilroy who "challenge the desirability of *any* racial identification, black as well as white" (Kolchin 169). If racial distinctions are to disappear through the combination of changed environment, education, and assimilation, then, we will have "given up the idea of race altogether" (Michaels, *Our America* 134). But Chesnutt, an heir to the intellectual traditions of the nineteenth century, cannot quite let go of racial essentialism (and Michaels asserts in any case that "there can be no coherent anti-essentialist account of race" [134]). This residual essentialism is clear in "The Future American" essays and returns in the surprising guise, later in Chesnutt's career, of a renewed emphasis on ethnicity and collective experience.

Throughout most of his novels and nonfiction writings, Chesnutt insisted that race was a historically produced social fiction, and the upshot was that he was "presenting race . . . in a way that confronted and destabilized the whole idea of whiteness" (Ramsey 41). In other words, in his first published fiction, Chesnutt used the liminal figure of the mulatto to try to destabilize the color line, but he abandoned the figure of the mulatto in subsequent novels to focus on white characters and white experience, insisting, as James Baldwin asserts, that the racial problem was a problem in the European American community (Durso). To highlight Chesnutt's engagement with whiteness, I will begin my consideration of his representations of whiteness by going out of chronology to examine his little-known white-life novels, in which he took on the authority to represent white experience to what he assumed would be primarily a white audience if the novels were published.

[2]

The White Novels

Melodrama and Popular Fiction

White America has a strong feeling that Negro artists should refrain from making use of white subject matter. I mean by that, subject matter which it feels belongs to the white world. In plain words, white America does not welcome seeing the Negro competing with the white man on what it considers the white man's own ground.

—JAMES WELDON JOHNSON
"The Dilemma of the Negro Author"

During the years he wrote his first published race fiction—the novel that eventually became *The House Behind the Cedars* (1900)—and apparently after he had finished his magnum opus, *The Marrow of Tradition* (1901), Charles W. Chesnutt was also working in another fictional genre altogether: he wrote a series of white-life novels (which only incidentally contain people of color) in popular genres. Chesnutt wrote the first two novels, *A Business Career* and *The Rainbow Chasers*, during the same years he worked on *Mandy Oxendine* (1894?–97) and *The House Behind the Cedars*. Houghton Mifflin rejected *A Business Career* in March 1898 (*Letters* 104 n.1) but apparently accepted *The Rainbow Chasers* before deciding instead to take *The House Behind the Cedars* (Helen Chesnutt 146). The third of the white novels, *Evelyn's Husband*, must have been written after *The Marrow of Tradition*: William L. Andrews notes that Witter Bynner[1] rejected *Evelyn's Husband* for McClure Phillips in 1903 (*Career* 131). From roughly 1897 to 1903, the years of his greatest productivity, then, Chesnutt was writing on two tracks—working on his race fictions and on his ostensibly nonracial fictions. In the hundred years since Chesnutt wrote them, these novels have remained in a critical limbo. Andrews is the only Chesnutt scholar to have mentioned them at any length, and he is quite dismissive: "Each of these undistinguished narratives had sprung from a similar motive—to write especially for the popular market—and each was concocted only after novel-length color line stories had failed to make headway either in the publishers' offices or in the bookstores" (*Career* 131). As Andrews argues, Chesnutt clearly was trying to gauge the expectations of his potential white audience and "to tailor a long work of fiction to the tastes of genteel readers" (*Career* 122). In these works, Andrews claims, Chesnutt failed "to find . . . that spark of conviction and serious purpose which appears" in his race fiction (*Career* 122).

A closer look at the correspondence shows, however, that Chesnutt's novels were not without interest to publishers. In rejecting *The Rainbow Chasers* for publication in *The Atlantic*, W. B. Parker wrote, "I have read 'The Rainbow Chasers' and have liked it—in fact have liked some parts of it very much. The homely sincerity of it—its entire freedom from affection and mere ornament of language give us genuine satisfaction" (Helen Chesnutt 141). Parker went on to explain why the novel would not work in serialization but concluded that "I am very sure, however, that Messrs. Houghton Mifflin would be glad to consider the publication of it as a book" (142). In rejecting *A Business Career*, Walter Hines Page wrote, "That 'A Business Career' may be a success—is not at all denied by Messrs. Houghton Mifflin and Company's conservative attitude towards it. You will doubtless be able to find a publisher, and my advice to you is decidedly to keep trying till you do find one" (Helen Chesnutt 92). Thus, Houghton Mifflin judged at least two of these white novels as commercially viable, with editors recognizing that Chesnutt had written narratives that reproduced elements of popular fiction. But as we have begun to realize in recent years, the use of popular forms—the adventure, the romance, and the melodrama—does not preclude the touchstone of serious purpose. In writing these white-life fictions, Chesnutt was trying to perform the same balancing act that he attempted in the race fictions—that is, to insure that his audience found itself on familiar generic territory while encoding a critique, in at least two of these novels, of gender and whiteness that would not alienate his readers.

Writing these white-life novels, Chesnutt was (along with Paul Laurence Dunbar) breaking relatively new ground.[2] From its beginnings, African American nonfiction writings had always represented the ways of white folks, but prior to the 1890s, no African American writers had written *exclusively* about white experience, and Dunbar and Chesnutt apparently were working on their first white-life novels at the same time (and Chesnutt owned copies of two of Dunbar's white-life novels, *The Love of Landry* and *The Uncalled* (McElrath, "Chesnutt's Library" 108)). Chesnutt's *A Business Career* was rejected in March 1898, while Dunbar's first white-life novel, *The Uncalled,* was serialized in *Lippincott's Monthly Magazine* in May 1898 and was published as a book later that year. (This novel was followed by *The Love of Landry* [1900], and *The Fanatics* [1901].) One review in particular of *The Uncalled* is revealing and helps contextualize the position of an African American attempting to write white-life fictions.[3] "*The Bookman* for December 1898 objected to the characters in *The Uncalled.* Claiming that Dunbar should 'write about Negroes,' the reviewer lamented that 'the charming tender sympathy of *Folks from Dixie* is missing' and asserted that Dunbar was 'an outsider' who viewed his action 'as a stage manager'" (Williams 174). At the turn of the century, critics, publishers, and white audiences were unwilling to listen to the voice of an African American who had stepped outside what they assumed to be his proper role—representing his own folks' experience and serving as a race spokesman. And whereas his contemporaries rebuked Dunbar for stepping out of his proper and subservient place, subsequent critics of white-life fiction also have been quite severe in their censures. For instance, in *From Apology to Protest: The Black American Novel* (1973), Noel Schraufnagel wrote about white life novels under the rubric the "assimilationist novel." Writers of these fictions believed "that the elimination of racial material will give the black writer a literary freedom that will allow him to concentrate on art rather than on protest." The African American author believed that "writing about whites" would free him "to explore any aspect of life that appeals to him. The fallacy of this argument, though, is in the mediocrity of the fiction itself. The black novelists were merely avoiding the issue that they were primarily concerned about, as evidenced by the fact that most of these writers produced racial protest novels of a superior quality" (99).

Schraufnagel saw any effort to write white-life fiction as an evasion of the duty of African American writers to protest, as a dodging of what they must always be "primarily concerned about." Addison Gayle wrote in similar terms about Dunbar's white-life fiction. For Gayle, Dunbar was not merely evading his duty but had become something close to a race traitor, having donned "the mask of white men, thus lending his own weight to the negative images which he despised, validating the arguments of those who championed the superiority of white images over those of blacks" (145). In contrast, Kenny Williams atypically celebrated Dunbar's freedom from the burdens of representivity: "In a period when the Negro novelist overtly concerned himself with race and by virtue of this wrote protest fiction, in a period when—in fact—a Negro was expected to be a 'spokesman,' Dunbar veiled what he had to say. . . . [O]ne must remember that at a given moment in American culture there was a novelist who looked upon race not as the controlling force of his artistic life but only as an incidental fact" (157). Taking another tack entirely, Roger Rosenblatt has written that *The Uncalled* "takes a steady and critical look at a white community, and despite its gentleness, in many ways it is the first successful protest novel in black fiction" (131). In the midwestern town where most of *The Uncalled* takes place, "Dunbar is portraying his perception of the white world. He is depicting a people, who, while pretending to adhere to principles of decency and to maintain an egalitarian world, efficiently and systematically stifle the freedom and honesty of an individual different from themselves" (136). The responses to Dunbar's white-life fiction illustrate a range of positions to which Chesnutt's white-life novels could have been subject: that African Americans have no right to write about white life; that African American writers are evading their duty to protest the conditions of American racism and that blacks who write exclusively about white life can be seen, from within the African American community, as acceding to white stereotypes; or that African Americans are veiling "what they have to say" and their accomplishments can be seen as evidence of their ability to escape the trap of America's racial binary.

I

All of Chesnutt's white-life novels, like Dunbar's *Love of Landry*, are romances, written in a period when "the romance became almost synonymous with the novel in the public mind and was the most popular form of reading matter" (Hart 183). In fact, as Grant C. Knight observed, "nothing stands out more clearly in our literary history than the remarkable vogue of light romantic fiction in 1894, 1895, and 1896" (88), the years just preceding Chesnutt's work on *A Business Career*. However, most early commentators on best-sellers (and this is the period during which the best-seller list was first developed) have talked in terms of escapism and reflection, arguing that the writers of popular literature tried to assess and then mirror back to the public its cultural common sense and to create an arena where readers could evade a pervasive sense of crisis—particularly economic crisis—during the 1890s. But in recent years, we have begun to see that popular fiction also performs the function of constructing cultural common sense, that the writers of romance and their audiences are actively rather than passively linked, that writers actively collaborate with their audiences to create fictions that shift, however marginally, the national imaginary.[4] It is, for example, no coincidence that both *A Business Career* and *The Rainbow Chasers* record a sense of economic unease: in the first novel, the family lives in reduced circumstances because of the failure of the father's economic interests, while in the second, the main male character, who has lived off the earnings of his stock, discovers that in one week his "property had lost two-thirds of its market value, and had ceased to be a source of income" (2). This unease might well be the result of the economically troubled 1890s—specifically, the depression of 1893. The stock market collapsed, "several railroads went bankrupt . . . 8,000 businesses and 360 banks (including 141 national banks) failed, and farm prices, depressed since the late 1880s, fell farther" (Painter 116). However, this unease did not have its sources in Chesnutt's immediate personal experience. His daughter records that his legal stenography firm did well throughout the 1890s—Chesnutt traveled for the first time to Europe in 1896 (Helen Chesnutt 74)—and "his business was growing so rapidly that he had much more than he could do and had to enlarge his office force" (81). Despite this success, Chesnutt clearly registered the national economic anxiety in his fiction, and the question to be asked about these two white novels is how romance intersects with that anxiety to satisfy his genteel audience.

Chesnutt's first two white novels are somewhat eccentric in their adaptation of the genre of romance. Dunbar's *Love of Landry* is, I would argue, much more representative than either of Chesnutt's narratives. Dunbar's novel, set in Colorado, consists of a typical love triangle: a rich young woman, after refusing her British suitor, goes west for reasons of health and falls in love with a mysterious westerner, Landry, who saves her life and who turns out to be a refugee from an old eastern family. The British suitor follows her to Colorado, where he bonds with Landry, and after a minimum of implausible impediments, Landry and the eastern young woman announce their intention to marry. Chesnutt's romantic plots, conversely, involve older men and younger women. Both of the first two novels, *A Business Career* and *The Rainbow Chasers,* end with the promise of marriage between the older man and younger woman, while *Evelyn's Husband* reverses that plot, and in its final chapter all the characters are sorted into marriage with appropriately aged mates. It is almost as if in these first two white novels Chesnutt were revising the plot of Howells's *Indian Summer* (1886) in which an older man of forty-one becomes engaged to a much younger woman, only to discover his mistake in an accident late in the novel, which concludes with his appropriate marriage to a woman of his own age. In Howells's novel, the impediments to marriage are the lack of understanding on the part of the younger woman and the sense of entrapment on the part of the older man, a knot that can only be untied in a moment of physical danger. In contrast, in Chesnutt's novels, the marriage plot is impeded by a series of elaborate misunderstandings that originate in the melodramatic topos of concealed knowledge. In both, those circumstances involve the financial failure of the fathers (both turn out to be criminals) and the subsequent fall of their families into genteel poverty; as a result of that poverty, both daughters have taken up stenography, Chesnutt's livelihood.

A Business Career is Chesnutt's adaptation of the working-girl novel, which was popular from 1880 to 1920. According to Christine Bold, the genre usually centered on "a poor factory operative, shopgirl, or mill worker who manages to resist the unwelcome advances of the wealthy, upper-class villain, yet is often forced—unwittingly—into an illegal marriage with him, and finally ends the novel marrying an upper-class hero who admires her for her personal virtues that transcend her humble background" (297–98). Chesnutt's novel is less sensationalistic; relatively straightforward in its plot, it is complicated in its misunderstandings. Stella Merwin has been brought up by her mother in the belief that her father had been defrauded by his onetime employee, Wendell Truscott, who went on to become a successful businessman in his own right. When Stella has the opportunity to go to work in Truscott's office, she does so under a pseudonym and under her mother's injunction to find in Truscott's papers the "truth" of her father's failure and to restore the family fortunes. However, Stella ultimately discovers that Truscott had done everything he could to save her father from his fiscal imprudence and that Truscott had, under the fiction of some investments rescued from her father's failure, supported the Merwin family since her father's death. Part of that support has gone to educate Stella, and when the novel opens, she has finished her junior year in college; being a practical girl, she has also just completed a course in shorthand. Stella is, then, a representative New Woman, a member of that generation of college women that caused much cultural anxiety in America at the turn of the century, anxieties as mundane as those about the effect of women's education and as hyperbolic as the debate about "race suicide" (college women were assumed to be less fecund than their uneducated sisters). For example, the English novelist Ouida wrote in the *North American Review* in 1894 that college education for women "can only be hardening and deforming" (614) and that the "publicity of a college must be odious to a young girl of refined and delicate feeling" (615). Chesnutt betrays no such anxiety about his college-educated heroine (in fact, his daughters were attending Smith College during the period when he was working on these two novels).

Stella's position as a New Woman is immediately reinforced by the presence of a businesswoman, Mrs. Paxton, who owns the firm where Stella learned stenography. Mrs. Paxton is a women's rights advocate, and she tries to dissuade Stella from marriage: "You're too good-looking to make a successful business woman. As soon as you've qualified yourself for independence, you'll throw yourself on the mercy of some man, who will crush all your higher aspirations and degrade you to the level of a mere housekeeper." She sees that Stella could, under the right circumstances, "take high rank in the sisterhood of progress. I feel that if I can just get you over the danger period, when a girl will marry any man who asks her, I can make you a noble exponent of the true doctrine that woman is man's equal, and can compete with him successfully in any sphere of intellectual or economic activity" (6). Stella goes on to demonstrate her competence while employed by Truscott, but she finds the world of business repellant. At first she thinks Truscott cold and unnecessarily brutal with his employees, and she is piqued because she seems to be nothing more than a "mere piece of office furniture—a modern business appliance, like the telephone or the telegraph. She had noticed that the men called the writing-machine and the operator 'typewriters,' indiscriminately" (158). As she continues in his employment, though, her attitude toward Truscott begins to change. Even though she was brought up to believe in his "villainy" and in the "fundamental baseness of the man" (81), she begins to feel the force of his personality: "She did not know whether it was the mere sex instinct of subordination, or simply the effect of a virile nature radiating an atmosphere of authority" (65). By the time she discovers the truth about him, she has fallen in love, thus demonstrating that Mrs. Paxton was only half correct when she said, "I'm afraid you're inclined to be romantic, Stella. . . . You'll find, my dear, that romance and business won't work in double harness" (113).

The romance plot allows Stella and her mother to resume their social position, but it also illustrates that romance and business *can* work in "double harness" because Stella has demonstrated to Truscott her faithfulness and worthiness (much as he had done over the years by supporting her family). Not only is she a very good stenographer, but she also discovers, at some personal risk, that the firm's bookkeeper had been skimming money. So while Stella enters and succeeds in the masculine world of business, Truscott makes a series of discoveries in the realm of sentiment. He realizes that he is not willing to marry the rich but older Matilda Wedderburn with whom he has been spending time. For instance, when he is about to propose, he looks at her and sees that she is getting "stout" and concludes that she "would soon be an old woman. . . . At his time of life, a woman fifteen or eighteen years younger than himself would make a more suitable wife. . . . He was good for twenty years more of vigorous manhood, and in half that time Matilda Wedderburn would be an old woman" (108). The younger woman is clearly the appropriate trophy wife for the successful businessman whose narrative is a version of a Horatio Alger story; her youth is of paramount importance to him, but so too is the fact that she *works* (he, of course, does not know until late in the narrative that she is working under false pretenses).

Stella's youth and her understanding of the world in which he operates make her attractive to him, but the narrative shows that her possession of cultural capital makes her a suitable mate for this successful businessman. For instance, she attends a performance of Victorien Sardou's *La Tosca* (1887) with Sarah Bernhardt in the title role. The play is given in French, which she, as a college-educated girl, has little difficulty following, but she "did not like the story of the play; much of it was repugnant to her pure, fresh mind. But the acting fascinated her" (43). The play is high, historical melodrama with two suicides, a scene of torture, and at its heart a sexual affair between two unmarried characters. Chesnutt carefully positions his heroine in this passage: she is traditionally high-minded, pure and moral, a guardian of traditional values, but she is not a prude; she can separate the immoral plot from the immortal acting. However, Chesnutt carefully shows that her taste is above that of the other employees in Truscott's office. She looks at the dime novels that the office boy reads and betrays an awareness of the development of the genre, of how these fictions have changed from depicting traditional characters such as Indians and scouts to more contemporary ones such as "detectives, card-sharpers, gold-miners, ball-players and prize-fighters" (117). While condemning the novels for their improbability, coarseness, and exaggeration, she also admires them: "the action was rapid and exciting; there was no padding; virtue always triumphed in the long run, wickedness was adequately punished, and the stories came to a cheerful ending" (118), a description that antici-pates Jauss's analysis of the function of popular fiction. In contrast to the guardians of morality at the time, Stella is not willing to condemn dime novels. Although she disapproves of their sensationalism, she also can appreciate other, more positive aspects of popular culture, an appropriate attitude for a woman who will marry a man who has risen from the people.

Of course, her attitude toward dime novels also is a kind of meta-commentary on Chesnutt's part, allowing readers to know in what genre he is working and what to expect from the conclusion of the novel. That genre has been defined by John Cawelti as social melodrama, "which syn-thesizes the archetype of melodrama with a carefully and elaborately developed social setting in such a way as to combine the emotional satis-factions of melodrama with the interest inherent in detailed, intimate, and realistic analysis of major social or historical phenomena" (261). Chesnutt knew well the novel's social setting of a stenographer working in an office, but inside that realistic package he was making clear that he was providing his readers with a somewhat untraditional romance plot, leav-ened with the yeast of several kinds of melodrama. One can see Chesnutt carefully adapting the genre he was employing, but the question remains whether he was doing any more than cynically wearing the mask of white-ness as he tried to write a novel that he hoped would become a popular success. Is he, in the words of Addison Gayle, donning "the mask of white men, thus lending his own weight to the negative images which he despised, validating the arguments of those who championed the superiority of white images over those of blacks?" (145). The novel almost entirely ignores the presence of African Americans (there is one reference to a popular Negro song, and Truscott's valet is a very dark black man), but I believe that Chesnutt saw his white novels in part as a way of escaping the burden of being representative by writing as if he were unraced. If he wrote his race fictions "not primarily as a Negro writing about Negroes, but as a human being writing about other human beings" (*Essays* 514), then he is doing much the same thing in the white-life novels. As he did in his polemical writing, Chesnutt assumed that he possessed the same rights as white folks; he assumed in his white-life novels that he had the right to represent white life, just as white writers had the right to represent black life. More importantly, though, Chesnutt believed that he did not necessarily have to criticize white life, that he could represent white life in a popular genre without having to assume the burden of racial critique.

However, one could also argue that in representing Stella as a version of the New Woman, he was employing a construct that he knew was historically white so that he could enter into an ongoing cultural conversation without engaging in overt racial representation or polemic. Cecelia Tichi has remarked, for instance, that "the idea of conscious choice in and of itself was a hallmark of the identity of the New Woman, who was very much a middle-class figure, since women lower on the socioeconomic ladder, laborers for decades as domestics and as factory operatives, were not at liberty to shape their lives according to such principles" (592). Of course, most African American women in this period were not middle class, and while they may have been concerned with their circumscribed choices, those choices were almost always configured in racial terms. Thus, in entering the ongoing cultural conversation about gender and about the New Woman, Chesnutt was attempting to find a utopian subject position outside of racialized discourse. Of course, in the nineteenth century, there was no such position (as the reviews of Dunbar's *The Uncalled* demonstrate), but in a way that was typical of his thinking, Chesnutt tried to find a middle position in this ongoing cultural conversation. He does not find the figure of the New Woman threatening, but he also believes that she needs to retain some of the traditional womanly virtues, a position articulated in another 1897 text, Lillian Whiting's *The World Beautiful.* This book has a chapter entitled "The Modern Corrina" about the career woman who is "identified with the professional or industrial world." According to Whiting, "in the increasing avenues of industrial labor opened to woman and preempted by them, . . . there is not one in which refinement, delicacy, and courtesy will not prevail over self-assertion, aggressiveness, selfishness, or rudeness." This woman's job is to "transmute falsehood to truth, irritability to pleasant speech, doubt and distrust to faith" (quoted in Tichi 595–96). Chesnutt's Stella Merwin inhabits the professional world without giving up her essential femininity, and after her marriage to Truscott she will do her best to ameliorate the rough business world her husband inhabits. She thus represents a compromise in a gender debate in the white world, a realistic figure in a romantic novel that is in no way critical of white folks or of whiteness. In this novel, Chesnutt is empowered by his enlightenment faith in the universality of the human character, and he tries to position himself as the universal and unraced writer.

Given Chesnutt's accomplishment in his first white-life novel, he stands outside of the tradition of white life fiction as articulated by Rosenblatt: "the general conception of the white world in black fiction is . . . that it is a weak, dull (colorless), and morally impoverished world, populated mostly by terrorized people who demonstrate their terrorized states of mind in their violence to others" (130). Rosenblatt argues that Dunbar's *The Uncalled* inaugurated this tradition in African American writing. Like Dunbar's *Love of Landry*, *A Business Career* does not depict such a terrorized and terrorizing white world, but Chesnutt is attempting to accomplish more than Dunbar did in *Love of Landry*, a romantic white-life novel that does little more than attempt to reproduce a popular genre of the day. Dunbar's novel is not "social melodrama"; despite Dunbar's personal experience of Colorado (he traveled there for health reasons), the novel offers the reader no scaffolding of realism and does not enter into an ongoing cultural conversation in the way that Chesnutt's does.

Chesnutt's second white novel, *The Rainbow Chasers*, is perhaps the most unusual long fiction in his oeuvre. The only novel to employ a first-person narrator and the only novel in which Chesnutt attempted comedy, *The Rainbow Chasers* became a venue (particularly in the first half of the tale) in which Chesnutt could mock his own occasional stodginess and Victorian high-mindedness. In *The Rainbow Chasers*, a number of men find Julia Gray, the main female character, attractive and want to marry her. And they all ask the narrator to intervene for them with her, while he is in the process of falling (unwittingly) in love with her himself. Before discussing the novel any further, however, I must note that this is the most problematic text in all of Chesnutt's manuscript novels. Chesnutt abandoned *The Rainbow Chasers* before he finished fully revising it, and he had not completely resolved the plot. However, the tone and the overall direction of the plot are clear in both versions,[5] as are Chesnutt's satiric intentions.

All of the male characters are rainbow chasers, pursuing illusions that they think will transform their lives. As the narrator says of one of his academic competitors (in a canceled passage), "The learned chemist was chasing the rainbow. How many people were chasing the rainbow—how few ever found the pot of gold" (158).[6] Mr. Quilliams, the narrator, is a man of science, a metallurgist, who conceives of himself, as he says in the first paragraph, as "a practical man, without a particle of foolish sentiment" (1). Because of that self-conception, he tends to satirize those men around him whom he sees as foolishly sentimental or as filled with illusions about their place in the world. Throughout most of the novel, he feels safely superior to the men who are pursuing Julia. He satirizes a self-important ward politician, a local carpenter, and a widowed clergyman, all of whom want to marry her. But as he satirizes them, he is also undergoing an education in sentiment as he falls in love with Julia, and the older man is brought out of the rarified world of his research through his love for her.

Julia Gray is another version of the New Woman, in many ways like Stella Merwin. Both have had to endure genteel poverty, and both are stenographers. But unlike Stella, who believed that she had to uncover a secret, Julia is hiding a secret, her father's past. Julia lives with the burden of the knowledge of her father's financial failure and his embezzlement, and in the final version of the novel she also has to live with the knowl-edge that he is a murderer. Unlike Stella, who has taken a summer job between her junior and senior years in college, Julia has dedicated herself to her work and to the restitution of the twenty thousand dollars her father stole. Quilliams admires her sense of obligation and honor but worries that she has taken on a burden that will prove crushing, one that she will never be able, no matter how hard she tries, to pay off. Quilliams, however, learns all this in stages: at first he is told by the crippled son that the father deserted the family; then Julia tells Quilliams that her father embezzled money from his firm and then ran away; finally, Quilliams learns that the father accidentally killed a policeman in a struggle while trying to escape. When he learns this fact, the actions of the other charac-ters suddenly look very different, and he reflects, "Justly or unjustly, the sins of the fathers *are* visited on the children. This, then, had been Julia's heaviest handicap—this weight of inherited obloquy" (147). The biblical allusion here is a point of contact between *The Rainbow Chasers* and the novel that was accepted in its place, *The House Behind the Cedars*, in which Chesnutt used the same biblical phrase: Rena "had yet to learn that the old Mosaic formula, 'The sins of the fathers shall be visited upon the children,' was graven more indelibly upon the heart of the race than upon the tables of Sinai" (*Cedars* 51). Mixed-race characters must pay socially for the sexual sins of their fathers; they are always marked by their differ-ence. Conversely, the daughter of an embezzler and cop killer, while mar-ginalized, labors under a handicap that is not insuperable. She can work to remove the dishonor from the family, and in the end she will have a happy marriage to Mr. Quilliams. Despite her father's crimes, Julia can still be a genteel heroine, a sister to Stella, both of whose fathers become criminals and ruin their families.

If there are certain similarities between the novels, *The Rainbow Chasers* is literally less monochromatic than *A Business Career* because Chesnutt introduces a major black character, George, Mr. Quilliams's manservant. Because of his financial reverses, however, Quilliams is forced, in the second chapter, to let George go. Although he is no longer employed by Quilliams, George continues to care for the man, teaching the cook at a local restaurant how to make Quilliams's favorite dishes and offering to work for Quilliams without pay. George approaches Quilliams on the street, and he sees that he is being found wanting: "His glance measured me from shoe to hat. I was immediately conscious that my trousers were not creased, that my shoes were inadequately polished, and that I had forgotten to shave that morning. George eyed me sorrowfully as he drew near. 'I'm 'fraid you ain't bein' looked after right, suh,' he said" (60). Although devoted to Quilliams, George sees him as a kind of big baby, unable to do even the simplest things for himself, and some time after this meeting, George goes as far as to secretly clean and press Quilliams's clothes. Quilliams's reflections on George's devotion to him, though, are instructive:

> "The faithful fellow loves me, and really imagines," I thought with a smile, "that I am in want. It is a curious conceit, and worthy of the simple African intellect."
>
> I am friendly to the colored race. My father fought to give them freedom. I sympathize with their higher aspirations, and would willingly see them attain, by worthy effort, to actual equality with the more favored race among whom their lot is cast. But personally, I must confess, I like them better as they are. The equality of all men is a beautiful theory; the unquestioned superiority of some is a comfortable fact. George was an ideal servant; I fear I should not have liked him quite so well in any other relation.
>
> But a Negro, I imagine, might think differently. There is everything in the point of view. (61)

Here one can see Chesnutt trying to suggest, even in a popular fiction, the validity of an African American interpretation of the world, but the suggestion is tendered with the clear understanding that the narrator shares his audience's cultural common sense about African Americans: he is superior, and George is, as he says later in the novel, "somewhat primitive" (152). But he is also willing to grant George a kind of equality based on friendship—"The very essence, it is said, of friendship, is equality" (152)—but despite this admission, Quilliams still paradoxically maintains his conviction of his superiority.

In these passages on George, Chesnutt is employing a minor African American character in much the same way that Dunbar did in *The Love of Landry*. In that novel, during the heroine's railroad journey westward, she and her father encounter a black porter who comes into their compartment to see if they need anything, and after he leaves the father reflects on black experience: "That man gets more out of life than I do. He has a greater capacity for enjoyment . . . You think it humiliates him to take a tip? . . . He courteously fleeces us, and then laughs about it, no doubt" (37–38). Later in the trip, the heroine asks the porter to call her father in such a way that the porter thinks something is wrong (in reality, she is excited at her first sight of prairie dog towns). When she and her father laugh over this misunderstanding, the porter "went back to his place, in disgust, no doubt with the thought in his mind that here was another instance of white people trampling on, and making a fool of, the black man" (46–47). Both Chesnutt and Dunbar try, in these white-life novels, to suggest the possibility that African Americans view their interactions with white Americans quite differently than white Americans do. But because these are popular fictions, these suggestions must be tendered only tentatively.

The presence of an African American character is only one of the major differences between *A Business Career* and *The Rainbow Chasers*. The latter novel is less rooted in social reality than the earlier one, less social melodrama and more pure melodrama. In fact, *The Rainbow Chasers* verges on becoming almost gothic: in the canceled version, the father kidnaps his own child, holding him for ransom; and in the final version, the father comes home to die, a repentant man, and his wife is cured of her blindness at the moment he recovers a sense of himself. In both versions, though, the novel shifts its tone toward the end; the genial double satire tends to disappear only to be replaced by the workings out of the melodramatic plot, the restoration of the family to their previous riches, and the workings out of the romance between Quilliams and Julia Gray. But what remains consistent is that Chesnutt (with the exception of the two passages on George) is writing, as he did in *A Business Career,* in a racially unmarked way. He is not, however, trying to enter into an ongoing social

debate as he did in *A Business Career*. He is doing his best to be an enter-
tainer, to write a novel that will satisfy his white audience, and given the
fact that Houghton Mifflin was willing to publish the book, he clearly succeeded. But from the perspective of a hundred years later, however, this is
the least successful and the least interesting of his white-life novels (just as
Dunbar's *The Love of Landry* is the least successful of his white-life novels). It is as if the same aspects of the novel that the editor at Houghton
Mifflin admired—its "homely sincerity . . . its entire freedom from affection and mere ornament of language" (Helen Chesnutt 141)—are what
make it the least engaging novel in Chesnutt's oeuvre. It is an interesting
experiment in first-person narration, an experiment in radically shifting
the tone of a novel that paved the way for his last white-life novel, *Evelyn's
Husband*.

II

While *Evelyn's Husband* contains certain similarities to the two earlier
white-life novels (like the older man/younger woman plot), it is one of the
most radical and baroque of Chesnutt's eccentric fictions. The novel, which
begins as a domestic comedy, is transformed into a wonderfully implausible adventure story in which conceptions of white manhood are at stake.
Edward Cushing is from an old New England family, independently
wealthy, without fixed occupation, and "past forty" (9). He believes that he
has fallen in love with nineteen-year-old Evelyn Thayer, the daughter of
Alice Thayer, a woman of his age. Evelyn has grave reservations about
marrying a man so much older, and she acts out on those reservations
on her wedding day by running away with Hugh Manson, thirty-two, an
up-and-coming architect who has risen from humble beginnings among
poor Kentucky whites and whom Evelyn sees as "undeniably fresh and
virile" (38). A year after Manson's marriage to Evelyn, he convinces himself through a series of delightfully improbable coincidences, that Evelyn
has run off with Cushing. Filled with his ancestors' desire for revenge, he
pursues Evelyn and Cushing to New York City and discovers that they are

apparently taking a ship to Brazil; Manson follows in another ship, which sinks in a hurricane. Blinded, he washes up on a desert island where, through another set of coincidences, Cushing (who takes the name Singleton) has also been shipwrecked. Because Manson is temporarily blind, he does not know that the man who keeps him alive is Cushing. They are eventually rescued and sail to Brazil, where Manson's sight is restored. Manson learns that his worst enemy is also his greatest benefactor, all the misunderstandings are unraveled, and Cushing, who, during his experience on the island, has realized his mistake in trying to marry Evelyn, declares his love for her mother, Alice. Everyone lives happily ever after.

If there is an analogue to *Evelyn's Husband*, it is Frank Norris's *Moran of the Lady Letty* (1898), a novel that Norris wrote in an attempt to produce a best-seller. Its initial setting is also the upper class, and the novel begins, "This is to be a story of battle, at least one murder, and several sudden deaths. For that reason it begins with a pink tea among the mingled odors of many delicate perfumes and the hale, frank smell of Caroline Testout roses" (1). The central character, Ross Wilbur, goes to a tea party, where he tells a girl who has just come out that a group of young girls, "girl in the aggregate like this . . . unmans me" (5). After leaving the party he is inveigled down to the San Francisco docks, where he is shanghaied onto a fishing boat, crewed by Chinese, bound for Baja California. As in Kipling's *Captains Courageous* (1897), Wilbur is toughened by his experience and begins to be transformed from a social dilettante into a "real man." Once the ship arrives in Baja California, the crew encounters Moran Sternersen, "a half masculine girl" (98), formed by her experiences at sea. Ross Wilbur and Moran seize the ship from the Chinese, and after a series of complicated developments, Ross discovers, in a hand-to-hand fight with another group of Chinese, his own atavistic self, "the primitive man, the half brute of the stone age" (214). In the same fight, he encounters Moran, who is filled with "bersirker rage" (219), and the two of them fight quite brutally until Ross throws her on her back and grinds one knee into her chest. "You've beaten [me], mate," Moran says, "you've conquered me, and . . . mate . . . I love you for it" (221). The fight restores proper gender roles: Ross has gotten back into contact with his primitive man.

His masculinity has been restored in the process of subjugating her, and she is transformed from an independent masculinized woman into a cringing female who makes no effort, later in the novel, to defend herself when attacked by one of the Chinese, and she dies whimpering for Ross to come to her rescue.

In their equally hyperbolic fashions, *Moran of the Lady Letty* and *Evelyn's Husband* participate in the discourse of beleaguered masculinity around the turn of the century. In broadly cultural terms, anxiety about masculinity, as Gail Bederman has demonstrated, could be seen in the concern about women's education and the falling white birthrate, in concerns about immigrants, in the rise of organized athletics in this period, in Theodore Roosevelt's displays of masculinity as hunter and Rough Rider, and, as Amy Kaplan has pointed out, in the celebrations of the recovery of American masculinity in the Spanish-American War and its immediate imperial aftermath. Kaplan quotes Senator Albert Beveridge asking in a debate over the annexation of the Philippines, "What does all this mean for every one of us? . . . It means opportunity for all the glorious young manhood of the republic—the most virile, ambitious, impatient, militant manhood the world has ever seen" ("Romancing" 660). Kaplan argues that the popular historical romances of the day—novels such as Richard Harding Davis's *Soldiers of Fortune* (1897)—function as "fictional equivalents of the Philippines . . . as a site where a man can reassert this 'militant manhood'" (660). The adventure novel itself can function as another such site, and in Norris's *Moran of the Lady Letty,* Ross returns transformed by his experience of violence; he now has a proper masculine desire to accomplish something in the world, a proper manly contempt for his previous life. Back in San Francisco, he says to his former society friends, "That sort of life, if it don't do anything else, knocks a big bit of seriousness into you. You fellows make me sick. . . . As though there wasn't anything else to do but lead cotillons and get up new figures!" (258).

Of course, we need to notice the unmarked marker: in this period, there is a crisis of *white* masculinity that also manifested itself in events such as the Wilmington, North Carolina, coup d'état/pogrom (which would become the basis for *The Marrow of Tradition*) and in the explosion of lynchings of African American men throughout the United States. Bederman has written that white Americans in this period were "obsessed with the connection between manhood and racial dominance" (4), a discourse that constructed African American men as brutish and primitive and white men as the epitome of civilized restraint. However, as we have already seen in the example of *Moran of the Lady Letty* and in the celebration of militant manhood, there also seems to be a countervailing idea that white men must demonstrate their manliness by their momentary recovery of what Bederman terms "the natural man," the opposite of "white man." "Where 'the white man' embodied civilized manliness, 'the natural man' embodied primitive masculinity. Lacking civilized self-restraint, the natural man acted upon his 'natural' impulses." Those "natural" impulses were seen in national press coverage of lynchings: reporters "continued to assert that 'masculine' impulses toward sex and violence, although savage and illicit, were 'natural.'" Modern men had, for the most part, successfully repressed the natural man, "but when they joined lynch mobs, they allowed the savage within themselves free reign. As . . . [a contemporary journalist] saw it, within every man, 'a savage is waiting to assert himself if only encouraged'" (72). What made the white man better than the natural man was the ability to suppress and repress, but that very ability then threatened the white man's racial dominance. As Theodore Roosevelt argued, a total repression of the natural man would make America into an effete nation, and the further consequences of that suppression would be the continuance of the falling white birthrate—in a term to which Roosevelt gave wide currency at the time, the consequence would be "race suicide." For cultural spokesmen such as Roosevelt, there was a terrible danger in losing contact with the natural man, but then too much indulgence of the natural man would mean that there was little to distinguish between the superior and inferior races.

As *Evelyn's Husband* begins, Edward Cushing clearly is close to being an effete dilettante; he does not possess the requisite masculine "seriousness." He studies medicine in college but finds himself revolted by the "prospect of daily contact with disease and deformity" (5). After traveling for a year, he enters Harvard Law School; he passes the bar exam but never practices law because he is too "fastidious" (10). He "deferred for a while longer the selection of a definite career" (10), and by the time of the novel's opening, he is somewhere older than forty with no employment, no purpose in life. He thinks, of course, that he has found that purpose in Evelyn Thayer, who has agreed to marry him more out of a sense of duty than out of any love she feels for him. At various points, she thinks of him as a father or as a "schoolmaster . . . in love with a pupil who has grown up in his school" (47). Evelyn desires to love "with a great, fierce, passionate, love, which would sweep her off her feet and compel her to do and dare all things for her beloved" (31). Knowing that she is not in love with Cushing makes her more than susceptible to Hugh Manson, a completely different model of masculinity. Unlike Cushing, Manson is a self-made man born in eastern Kentucky to a family of "poor whites" (51). They were not slave-holders, he says, and they lacked "pride of race, for they knew nothing of history; the specimens of white men around them were nothing to be proud of; there were no negroes among them" (51–52). While emphasizing their lack of race pride, Manson also insists on his people's investment in whiteness, and in telling the rest of his "romantic history" (51) to Evelyn, Manson emphasizes his "ancestry . . . white people . . . to whom art, science, history, culture—even comfort—are a sealed book, for want of the key of knowledge to unlock them, and we call ourselves civilized!" (52). He emphasizes that his people were liberated by the Civil War, and Evelyn thinks at the end of this story that Manson is "one of nature's noblemen, a self-made man" (56). Although a successful architect with a growing reputation, he is still enough of a child of eastern Kentucky to admire the manliness of his ancestors in their maintaining of a sense of honor through revenge and feuds.

We are meant to remember Manson's defense of revenge when he elopes with Evelyn on the day she is supposed to marry Cushing. In the aftermath of her desertion of him (almost at the altar), Cushing is publicly humiliated, and he becomes much more cynical about women in general. In fact, he is so humiliated that he goes abroad for nearly a year, and when he returns, "he made no calls, drove about in a closed carriage, and if perchance he met an acquaintance, turned his head away" (110).

In contrast, when Manson thinks that Cushing and Evelyn have run off together, he is filled with an almost atavistic desire for revenge, a return to a primitive "militant manhood":

> His state of mind was comparable to that of a red man of the forest, who, having seen his wigwam in ashes, his squaw and children butchered, and his winter stores carried off, merely draws his belt the tighter, sharpens his toma- hawk the keener, and sets out upon his evening's trail, finding in the anticipa- tion of revenge a bitter pleasure that replaces and in a measure compensates him for his ruined happiness. (147)

Later, after Manson has been castaway and lost his sight, his "passion for revenge" is said to be "like that of the ancient Greeks, whose shades, even after death had claimed their bodies, carried their earthly hatred with them into the gloom of Hades itself" (169). The contrast between the two men could not be more pointed: Cushing is demasculinized, and Manson is hypermasculinized; however, unlike the male protagonist of Norris's *Moran of the Lady Letty*, Manson has never been fully civilized and has never lost touch with "the primitive man, the half brute of the stone age" (214).

Manson's ability to follow through on his desire for revenge is compro- mised, however, by his blindness (he has previously met Cushing only in passing and when first hearing his voice on the island does not recognize it). The first words out of Manson's mouth after Cushing has said hello are, "Thank God! . . . a man, a white man, and an American" (194). When the narrator introduces the castaway Cushing, a few chapters earlier, he is also immediately characterized as a "white man" (171). Up to this point, Cushing's race has been unmarked; before this, his whiteness is taken for granted. Once transposed into the realm of adventure, Cushing's race needs to be marked, and that marking is a signal of how he will be trans- formed by his understanding (and rejection of) elemental passion. Before he became white on this desert island, Cushing considered himself "a fair type of the cultivated man" (187). He had had no great passionate experi- ence: "He had looked upon passionate love, with its offspring of jealousy, hatred and revenge, as something for the vulgar, who did not possess the resources of culture or the consolations of philosophy. His sudden passion for Evelyn had been his first awakening" (186), and his second awakening had been his desire for revenge on Manson after he eloped with Evelyn. Cushing "had rankled under a fierce and gnawing jealousy; he had felt the poison of hatred, the animal longing for revenge" (189). Now, stranded, alone with a man who conceives of himself as Cushing's mortal enemy, Cushing has to decide whether to let Manson die. After deciding that it would be inhumane to execute Manson through neglect, Cushing has to listen to Manson repeatedly explain his desire for revenge. To recover his white masculinity, Cushing has to be immersed in the primitive desire for revenge that he has repressed in himself.

As Cushing cares for Manson, the younger man is profusely grateful, and in the concluding chapters of the novel Chesnutt pulls out all of the stops in terms of hyperbolic, self-conscious melodrama. At various times, Cushing thinks of his experience as an experiment, as a "rare comedy" (216), and as a "tragic farce" (298), self-reflexive literary terminology that Chesnutt uses to alert his readers to the hybrid quality of the narrative. When Manson and Cushing are rescued, Chesnutt chooses to reunite the major characters in the novel in Brazil, which the narrator calls a "laboratory for fusing again into one race the various types into which primeval man had in remote ages become differentiated" (276), and Dr. Silva, the famous "eye man" who operates and restores Manson's sight, is said to be "a little off color, like a lot of the Brazilians" (270). Manson, who has been identified from the beginning as a white man, has his sight restored by a man who would be considered black in the United States, as if Chesnutt were rewriting the conclusion of *The Marrow of Tradition*, in which the African American Dr. Miller is invited to operate on a white child. Furthermore, it is also as if Chesnutt needed to conclude this drama of beset white masculinity in a country where whiteness and blackness are not seen as binary terms, because he wants to point to a fusion between the binaries of Cushing and Manson that removes them from the racial binary.

The terms of the fusion are rather obvious: Manson has had his militant masculinity tempered by Cushing's care, while Cushing now understands passion as well as the mistake he made in trying to marry Evelyn rather than the woman of his own age, Alice. When Cushing reveals that he and Singleton are the same man, Manson is unable to shoot Cushing, with whom he now shares a homosocial bond, "a love surpassing that of woman" (300). However, when Cushing, accidentally wounded, looks up to the faces of Evelyn and Alice hovering above him, Evelyn appears as little more than "the child whose guardian he had been so many years; while his head was resting upon a true heart, which had always beat for him" (304). In the end, the novel is more like Howells' *Indian Summer* than either *A Business Career* or *The Rainbow Chasers*. The older man–younger woman marriage does not come off, and all the partners are mated appropriately. More important, though, is the men's fusion of subject positions. Manson has purged himself of the "the primitive man, the half brute of the stone age" (Norris 214) and clearly will become a major American architect. (In his absence, Evelyn has saved his affairs from ruin and become, like Stella Merwin in *A Business Career,* "a good business woman".) The major change, though, is in Cushing: when he returns to the United States, he marries Alice and writes a book on South American capital cities. The book "attracted much attention, and an active interest in a presidential campaign, to the success of which he was held to have contributed, brought him an appointment from the administration as minister to Chile" (313). In a sense, then, his experience of becoming white rescues him from being a dilettante, and both Manson and Cushing return to being racially unmarked in the last chapters of the novel. So Chesnutt rescues one character from a crisis of white masculinity while the other is purged of his whiteness by undergoing the experience of being shipwrecked with his mortal enemy.

III

In his first two white-life novels, Chesnutt was not attempting to be critical of his potential white readers; rather, he used the romance plot to help assuage concerns about America's economic difficulties in the 1890s—the families in economic difficulties are returned to their proper classes and the daughters will no longer need to work as stenographers. Although these novels are different in their emphases—*A Business Career* a social melodrama, *The Rainbow Chasers* a comic melodrama—neither attempts to confront its audience. And while the latter novel might seem a more traditional romance, it does have a significant African American character and an unusual older man/younger woman plot. Although *A Business Career,* conversely, enters the national conversation about the New Woman, the novel does not seem to criticize whiteness or white life. By the time he wrote *Evelyn's Husband,* however, Chesnutt had already published two novels, including his magnum opus, *The Marrow of Tradition,* which not only included a clear critique of whiteness but also allowed Chesnutt to gauge, in its reception, the power of the racist imaginary, the power of whiteness. So when he came to write his final white-life fiction, it had a very different tenor from the preceding two novels in the genre. Chesnutt still retained the form of the romance, but he used his chosen form, as he did in his race fictions, for the purpose of critique. In examining Cushing and Manson as white men, Chesnutt created a position between opposite poles, between militant manhood and dilettantism, that suggests the possibility that whiteness could be changed and modified. Whiteness does not necessarily have to take the form of the militant manhood of the kind seen in the Wilmington coup/pogrom, nor are African Americans, by inference, limited to the subject positions ascribed to them in this period. The sight of the blind man who grew up poor white in the South can be cured by the doctor of African descent, but the fact of race does not count in Brazil, which is outside of our national racial imaginary. In a sense, Chesnutt in this last white-life novel begins the quest that he concludes only in his Harlem Renaissance novels—the quest for a position outside of race that does not deny family or evade the burden of history.

[3]

Mandy Oxendine

The Protocols of Tragic Mulatta Fiction

In contrast to his work in his white-life novels, in *Mandy Oxendine* Charles W. Chesnutt was writing more directly out of his own experience, and he was, for the only time in his career, relatively free of his audience's racial expectations, something of which he was clearly always aware in his subsequent race fictions. *Mandy Oxendine*, Chesnutt's first novel, was probably written in 1896 and was rejected by Houghton Mifflin in February 1897 (Hackenberry, Introduction xv). Charles Hackenberry, the editor of the 1997 edition of *Mandy Oxendine*, speculates that the novella "could have existed, in one form or another, as early as 1889" (xv). Clearly, then, Chesnutt was working on *Mandy Oxendine* concurrently with the first two white-life novels and with *Rena Walden*, which was eventually published as *The House Behind the Cedars* in 1900. He completed *Mandy Oxendine* before he received George Washington Cable's advice about writing for white audiences: "you must remember in your description of persons," he wrote, "that the greatest element of strength is to yield all the ground you honestly can to the possible prejudices of your reader" (25 September 1889). Atypically, Chesnutt did not attempt to take his potential white audience into consideration in *Mandy Oxendine*, which is, as William L. Andrews has written, "more resistant to popular notions of femininity and less willing to accommodate itself to the protocols of 'tragic mulatta' fiction than is *The House Behind the Cedars*"

(Foreword x). So *Mandy Oxendine* is, I think, an example of how Chesnutt conceived of a race fiction before he began his struggle with his white audience, before he began his extremely conscious manipulation of genre and racial characteristics.

His relative obliviousness to his white audience, however, did not mean that he completely ignored generic considerations. As Hackenberry has observed, the novel is bifurcated in its plot: the first part focuses, in a relatively realistic fashion, on the question of passing and on Tom Lowrey's experience of teaching in a rural southern school, while the latter part of the novel turns into a melodramatic murder mystery. To explain this bifurcation, Hackenberry points to an 1880 journal entry in which Chesnutt wrote that his ambition as a writer was "while amusing [his audience] to lead them on, imperceptibly, unconsciously step by step to the desired state of feeling" (*Journals* 140), and Hackenberry concludes that "in *Mandy Oxendine,* the entertainment comes in the form of a cliff-hanging plot" (Introduction xiii). Chesnutt's first novel, then, has its own eccentric design that points to artistic ambitions that were almost impossible to realize. How to write a popular race fiction that combines elements of realism and melodrama? How, simultaneously, to amuse and instruct his white audience? As both Andrews and Hackenberry have observed, Chesnutt's artistic solution to these ambitions in *Mandy Oxendine* is not very satisfactory, but the novella is a kind of test run, the first longer fiction in which he grapples with artistic questions that will preoccupy him throughout his writing of race fictions.

I

One way of approaching *Mandy Oxendine* is to think of it in terms of the more conventional *The House Behind the Cedars,* particularly in terms of his central female character, Mandy Oxendine. Unlike Rena Walden, the central female character of *The House Behind the Cedars,* Mandy expresses no reservations about her decision to pass as a white woman. Rena apparently never considered passing before the arrival of her brother, who had passed into the white world, and even after she had begun to pass, she had to be convinced of the propriety of her engagement to a white man. Conversely, when Chesnutt first presents Mandy, she is already in possession of her whiteness. She defiantly justifies her decision to Tom Lowrey, the mixed-race young man who grew up with her and loves her, when she says, "I wouldn' be a nigger, fer God made me white . . . an' I 'termined ter be what God made me, an' I *am* white" (23). Unlike the hesitant Rena Walden, Mandy never second-guesses her decision to pass, and she points to her appearance; she refuses to accede to the irrational notion of invisible blackness, the logical conclusion of the idea, being developed in this period, that any African ancestry whatsoever made people black regardless of their appearance. She realizes that she would have been hamstrung in her life, that a host of opportunities would have been denied her had she not claimed her whiteness. The narrator says that she had intuitively seen the "essential element of difference in the status of the two races she stood between; she felt that it was not learning or wealth, or even aspiration—but opportunity. . . . And so by becoming white she had stepped across the line of demarcation and into the freedom and light of opportunity" (31). A thorough pragmatist, Mandy's desire for opportunity includes attending a white school, but it is clear that she is not going to rise in the world, as Tom Lowrey hopes to, through education. From early in the novella, she knows that a woman's way out of the restrictions of her life is through marriage.

When Tom Lowrey first manages to talk to her, Mandy informs him that she is going to marry another man, "a gentleman; he is white, he is rich, he rides on horseback, he lives in a big house" (24). Lowrey's response is incisive:

> "Who is this fine gentleman that will marry a sand-hill mulatto?"
> "You fogit," she retorted, "I'm passin' for white—"
> "Who is this fine man on a horseback who will marry a sand-hill poor-white girl?" (24)

The parallelism here of "sand-hill mulatto" and "sand-hill poor-white girl" points to what Mandy does not know (or chooses to ignore): from a gentleman's perspective, there is little difference between the two. The line of class is almost as impassable as the color line, and the attentions of Robert Utley, her aristocratic white admirer, can be nothing but dishonorable. But for Mandy, Utley "represented that great, rich, powerful white world of which she dreamed, and to enter which since meeting him she had dared to aspire" (40). So her desire to enter more fully the white world and her ignorance of class distinctions cast her, from the beginning, in the role of a victim who thinks that her whiteness protects her from sexual violence. But Utley, the first of Chesnutt's degenerate aristocrats, is more driven by his libido than is Tom Driscoll in *The Marrow of Tradition*. The narrator notes that Utley "was not a man accustomed to curb his desires," and he is represented as a melodramatic villain when, after saying good night to Mandy, he mutters, "D——n, you my pretty, I'll have you yet" (55). The plot bifurcates at the moment when he acts on his desire and tries to rape her. He has tried to convince Mandy that his arranged marriage to an asexual white woman will never happen and that he loves Mandy: "He drew her close to him. 'Give me last, best proof,' he whispered. 'Be mine without reserve. Then I will know that you love me, and that you will not fail me.'" Mandy sees him unmasked and tries to escape. Responding with the language of high melodrama, she says, "Let me go . . . or I'll scream. I hate you and despise you." Equally melodramatic, he says, "'You shall not trifle with me.' He placed his hand over her mouth, and, as she struggled with him, he tried to draw her into the wood" (73). Mandy is saved from being raped by a male figure whom she is unable to recognize in the darkness of the woods, and Utley is killed in the struggle.

When suspicion of the murder falls on Mandy, she is arrested and takes full responsibility for the killing, saying, "I was too proud to be what God made me, too vain to be content with my lot. I didn't act right, an' my punishment is just" (89). But her punishment lasts only for a short time because in the complications of the cliff-hanging plot, the true murderer is revealed; she realizes the full extent of her love for Lowrey, and at the end of the novel, they marry. But in the final paragraph, which Robert

Nowatzki has said is the most interesting passage in the latter half of the novel (Review), the narrator entertains two possibilities for their future lives without foreclosing either. Whether they "went to the North . . . remaining true to their own people . . . or whether they . . . sought in the great white world such a place as their talents and virtues merited, it is not for this chronicle to relate" (112). Even though Mandy, in the stress of the latter part of the novel, asserts that passing is a sin, the final paragraph reinscribes Mandy's rather matter-of-fact, guilt-free attitude toward passing. From her perspective (and from that of the narrator), passing is seen as little more than one in a range of possible options. Chesnutt, though, simplified Mandy's options by giving her no family, with the exception of her mother (who is also white enough to pass): the two women "had left no near kindred behind to mourn their departure or to be hurt by their desertion" (28). By subtracting family considerations, Chesnutt made it much easier for Mandy to be completely rational in her decision to pass: unlike Rena from *The House Behind the Cedars,* Mandy has no family to make her feel guilty because of her separation from them.

Her guiltless rationality about passing would have been deeply problematic for Chesnutt's audience had the novel been published in the last decade of the nineteenth century. Indeed, Hackenberry has written that "one can only imagine the controversy *Mandy Oxendine* would have stirred up . . . had the editors at Houghton Mifflin decided to publish this slim novel in 1897" (Introduction xviii). According to the conventions of the time, tragic mulattas were to be anguished by the decision to pass and aware of the horror the idea of the corruption of pure white blood invoked among white folks. Mandy, of course, exhibits none of these characteristics; it is as if she is resolutely determined not to be tragic, and in that sense she is much closer to embodying Chesnutt's arguments in "The Future American" series than is any of his other characters except for John Warwick (Walden) from *The House Behind the Cedars.* But the figure of Mandy would not have been the only one to cause controversy had this novel been published at the time: Chesnutt's representations of his male, white characters would also have brought down critical condemnation.

As in his white-life novels, Chesnutt in *Mandy Oxendine* was representing a range of white experiences from the planter class through poor whites. In so doing, he created one white character in each class who desires Mandy. After failing to seduce her, Utley tries to rape her, and an itinerant preacher, Elder Gadson, becomes obsessed by her. It is also clear that a minor character, the white jailer, is going to try to have sexual relations with her. Utley is not only a stereotypical melodramatic villain, but most importantly he is the scion of the southern plantation class, who, according to the discourse of blood of the time, should have been the soul of rectitude and honor. But Deacon Pate tells Lowrey when he arrives in Rosinville that Utley is the antitype of the southern gentleman. Pate says that Utley rides a horse named Satan. "It's Satan ridin' Satan, ef all tales is true; fer day say young Mistah Utley is as fast as dey make 'em, drinkin', gamblin' an' rakin'" (7). Even though Chesnutt is mining the tradition of melodrama, with which his audience would have been deeply familiar, that melodramatic representation of Utley would have directly clashed with plantation mythology as well as with the relatively recent depictions of the planter class in magazines such as the *Century* and the *Atlantic*. As Tourgée wrote a few years earlier, "Our literature has become not only Southern in type, but distinctly Confederate in sympathy" ("South" 405).[1] Reviewers would not have been particularly pleased with Chesnutt's representation of a southern villain of the planter class or with the representations of lower-class white men driven by their libidos.

Elder Gadson, who is also sexually obsessed with Mandy, is from the lower class, and the narrator characterizes Gadson as a sort of "wandering John-the-Baptist" (47) and as "some ancient Hebrew prophet or some medieval monk" (49). When Gadson sees Mandy come to the mourners' bench, he is overcome with almost uncontrollable lust for her, and because of his naïveté and his relative unworldliness, "he did not know at first what had happened to him. He thought the thrill that shot through him was but an access of religious emotion, or a special outpouring of the Divine presence" (53). But Mandy knows that something is wrong when he touches her head while she kneels, and she conceives a strong "feeling of dislike and repulsion" (53) for him. Gadson is not, however, as dishonorable as Utley, offering to marry Mandy when she is in jail and to help her escape. But her instinctive dislike of Gadson is so strong that she thinks of him as "some hateful or harmful thing" (89). Both white men sexually desire her, and when she recognizes the force of that desire, she recoils. As Chesnutt conceived her, she is a conventionally moral young woman (like the heroines of Chesnutt's first two white-life novels), and when Lowrey implies, early in their reacquaintance, that she might have had sex with Utley, her response is that of a proper Victorian woman: "You ought to know me well enough, Tom Lowrey . . . to know that I am an honest gal, whatever my faults may be" (25). Despite her ignorance (willed or not) of the fact that the sons of the planter class do not marry "sand-hill whites," Mandy is not a Sister Carrie; she wants to be married. Yet it is almost as if her sexual desirability were overdetermined in the novel,[2] and to make that even more clear, the jailer intimates that he wants to have sex with Mandy, something she never learns. But the townsmen know his reputation, and one of them states that "Bill takes good keer ter collect the perq'isites er his office" (94), which apparently include sexual access to his female prisoners. Of course, the jailer's desire also heightens Mandy's beleaguered vulnerability in jail and provides motivation for Lowrey (improbably) to confess to a murder he did not commit in an attempt to exonerate Mandy.

This nexus of white desire focused on Mandy is quite remarkable and daring on Chesnutt's part, particularly because Mandy is a mixed-race woman who a potential audience would have seen as always already sexually desirable in contrast to the asexual white innocent to whom Utley was betrothed.[3] Mandy's effect on the men around her can be explained in part by context—as the narrator says, most the women among the sand-hill whites tended to be unappealing sexually, "listless . . . pale and anaemic for want of nourishing and varied food; and not infrequently yellowed from excessive use of tobacco; with lank figures and sandy hair, lack-lustre eyes and expressionless faces" (52). A passage such as this one, which would seem to be simple realistic description, becomes, of course, more complicated when one assumes that it was written by an African American. When a white writer, John Trotwood Moore, in *The Bishop of Cottontown*

(1906) had an African American character describe poor whites working in a cotton mill, the passage is meant to heighten the pathos of their unnatural exploitation. But when an African American writer did the same thing during this period, a whole different set of expectations came into play, ones to which Chesnutt seemed relatively oblivious.

Against a background of poor white women, Mandy stands out quite startlingly. When Lowrey first meets her again, she becomes angry with him, and the narrator gives a physical description. When she draws "herself up to her full height, . . . the statuesque lines of a noble figure, unspoiled by the distorting devices of fashion, were visible through a frock whose scantiness lent but little envious drapery to conceal them." Her hat falls back, "disclosing a luxuriant head of nut-brown hair, with varying tints and golden gleams as the light fell on it at different angles. By intuition or inspiration, she had gathered it into a Greek knot" (23). When the only subject positions available for the representation of black women in popular culture and in literary works were either the mammy or the hypersexualized black woman, Chesnutt faced a difficult problem in reception when he created a sexually attractive woman of mixed-race ancestry because his audience would have too easily fit her into the pre-existing cultural stereotypes for such women, stereotypes seen in Twain's Roxy in *Pudd'nhead Wilson* and in the heroines of Hopkins's *Contending Forces*. Chesnutt tried to shift the register by alluding to Greece and by calling attention to Mandy's "statuesque" qualities. Her figure recalls a statue, but her scanty clothes, paradoxically, call attention to her body, and her "nut-brown hair, with varying tints and golden gleams" would seem not to be racially inflected. Chesnutt created for these white men, for Lowrey, and for his audience the perfect white woman (albeit not a lady, as Utley's aunt points out to him). But race can never be read out of the audience at the turn of the century, and I would not be surprised if readers would have seen Mandy as little more than a very good imitation that reveals its hidden essence through the white men's desire for her.[4] For this audience, her sexual attractiveness would not have been evidence of her whiteness; rather, it would have been evidence of her more primitive nature, hidden under the veneer of her faux whiteness. As long as

Chesnutt buys into the binary of the sexualized/asexual women and one of them is of mixed-race ancestry, his audience will always interpret her in terms of preexisting racialist categories. The proper white woman obviously must be the asexual one, the statue that is "visibly unbending" (4). And if the intended is asexual, Mandy must be sexualized and thereby racialized in the white audience's eyes.

II

In his foreword to *Mandy Oxendine,* Andrews writes that the novel "is a prototype of a new brand of African American literary realism in the early twentieth century" (x), and this is particularly true in the first half of the novella, where Chesnutt mines his experience as a teacher in rural southern schools. No African American writer before him had represented so faithfully in fiction the conditions in southern black schools in the 1880s. Chesnutt's depiction of those conditions is unsparing but unpolemical. Through the experiences of Tom Lowrey, a character who must be in some degree an alter ego, Chesnutt describes the poor quality of his pupils' academic preparation. When Lowrey examines them, he discovers that only two or three of the students in the packed school "could read simple English taken at random, though most had learned some part of the spelling book. Of useful knowledge they were grossly ignorant" (17). Their previous teacher had been a firm adherent of beating knowledge into them (as were their parents), and the school year was only two months long (13). In these early chapters, Chesnutt's quiet depiction of these conditions is effective, in particular because the narrator is less intrusive and more willing to let conditions speak for themselves than in the rest of Chesnutt's fiction. The other set of conditions that the narrator depicts but does not comment on is the almost total separation of the races in the South of the 1880s. Lowrey sees white folks when he first gets off the train in Rosinville, but until Utley's murder, there is almost no contact between whites and blacks. It is a system of almost complete apartheid, in contrast to the reigning plantation paradigm, which is filled with contented blacks serving as a collective memory for white folks. In *Mandy Oxendine,* African Americans know full well what is happening among white folks but little interaction occurs. Emblematic of this relationship is what Lowrey sees when he arrives at a revival meeting to which African Americans have been invited. African Americans have a separate section reserved for them, and "while there was some conversation going on in subdued tones, there were no whites and blacks conversing together" (48).

At least in its first part, then, the novella could be characterized, as "a prototype of a new brand of African American literary realism" (Andrews, Foreword x), but when one reinserts Chesnutt's fiction into the time of its writing, the question of its prototypical qualities and its realism becomes much more vexed. In the dominant Howellsian strain, realism is anything but value neutral. As Susan Harris has argued, for Howells the "virtues of realism lay in the close delineation of ethnic stereotypes, not in the attempt to reassess the nature of human beings or to reconfigure white American's notions of what constitutes 'civilization'" (134). Chesnutt did not have such high ambitions for *Mandy Oxendine;* he was not trying to reverse the dominant, ethnographic gaze. But in an unassuming way, he was claiming the mantel of realism: he was, as he wrote to Howells a few years later, endeavoring to "to depict life as I have known it" (*Letters* 146). Yet how would his depiction of the life that he had known as a schoolteacher have been received in the late 1890s? For Chesnutt's audience, everything was racially inflected, and even his modest representation of conditions in a black school in South Carolina would not have been accepted simply as "realism."

First, the representation of conditions in this black school would probably have been received nostalgically. In discussing what Chesnutt writes about his teaching experiences in his *Journals,* Richard Brodhead observes that Chesnutt's descriptions of the rural school and of typical teaching practices are typical of "rural black schooling and the older national schooling which the professional grade school was superseding. Edward Eggleston's 1870 novel *The Hoosier Schoolmaster*" depicts a school much like Chesnutt's but "remembers this as a past feature of rural Indiana, something available to memory but since thoroughly reformed." One can conclude from Chesnutt's journal that "an obsolete education system already nostalgically recollected in the North was still in use" in the South (Introduction 10 n.8). If the school had been seen nostalgically, it would have been congruent with the larger nostalgia of the plantation tradition, of a past that was being superseded throughout the South. But that nostalgia would have been complicated by the issue of black education. If, on one hand, rural black education could have been seen as a heroic endeavor, an effort to make a whole people literate in one generation, many white Americans would also have seen it, on the other hand, as foolish, unwise, and unnatural.

As a way of trying to gauge the effect of Chesnutt's depiction of the schooling of African Americans, it is instructive to look at two articles published in the *Atlantic Monthly* in 1896–97—Booker T. Washington's "The Awakening of the Negro" and W. E. B. DuBois's "The Strivings of the Negro People." These two articles help measure what was considered to be culturally acceptable by one of American's major literary and social publications of the period and help contextualize the range of acceptable public debate. Washington's article is a brief for industrial education, including a vignette of the effect of a Tuskegee graduate on poor rural African Americans, who can be reached, Washington argues, only by "sending out among them strong selected young men and women, with the proper training of head, hand, and heart, who will live among these masses and show them how to lift themselves up" (323). In Washington's vignette, the Tuskegee graduate is much more than a teacher of children. Using "the three months public school as a nucleus for his work" (325), he helps the community by teaching the virtue of self-sacrifice, and as a result, because they cultivate their lands more effectively, these farmers can buy land and construct their own homes. "In a word, a complete revolution has been wrought in the industrial, educational, and religious life of this whole community," Washington writes. The people now have a "leader, this guide and object-lesson, to show them how to take the money and effort that had hitherto been scattered to the wind in mortgages and high rent, in whiskey and gewgaws, and concentrating them in the direction of their own uplifting" (325). By this standard, Lowrey distinctly falls short. He teaches his pupils effectively, but because he wants Mandy back, he makes none of the moves toward community building that Washington advocates. In that sense, Lowrey would be seen as an even less threatening figure than Washington's model Tuskegee graduate. (One could argue that the southern whites who held economic power would have seen even Washington's modest goals as threatening; whites clearly wanted to keep African Americans in economic submission and did not want the creation of a self-sufficient rural class.) Finally, when thinking about the figure of Lowrey, it is also necessary to remember that significant opposition existed in the South to any education of African Americans. As Mary Church Terrell wrote in 1904 in the *North American Review,* "Efforts are constantly making to curtail [sic] the educational opportunities of colored children" (863). She cites one state that prohibited schooling beyond the sixth grade, while in another state, the governor publicly opposed any education for African Americans. The figure of Lowery—the well-educated, middle-class African American man—is designed to be culturally unobtrusive. He attempts none of the community-building measures that Washington advocates, which would have brought him in some measure into conflict with local whites, and simply teaches his students and tries to win back the love of Mandy Oxendine.

However, as a representative of a newly educated black middle class, the figure of Lowrey would have been disorienting for Chesnutt's audience, which was used to a literary diet of subservient plantation blacks or, in the case of writers such as Thomas Dixon, black male rapists—big burly black brutes. Even by the 1890s, few black professionals existed, particularly in the South.[5] And Lowrey's cultural capital—especially exhibited in his standard English—would have been outside his audience's range of cultural reference. Like Chesnutt, Lowrey refuses, despite his appearance, to pass (when Lowrey arrives in Rosinville, Deacon Pate says, "Nobody wouldn't b'lieve you wuz colored, ef somebody didn' tell 'em" [4]), but Lowrey is uneasy with his liminal position between whites and blacks. The narrator says that Lowrey "very rarely went among white people. . . . [H]e was so nearly one of them that it always aroused in him a sort of dull resentment at being treated as an inferior creature" (45). Despite feeling

that he had been "robbed of his birthright . . . he had never felt the incli-
nation to give up his people, and cast in his lot with the ruling caste" (46).
In ideological terms, Lowrey is the closest of all of Chesnutt's characters
to being an alter ego, committed to his people but at a distance from them
because of his appearance and education, the same set of contradictions
that can be so difficult to understand in Chesnutt's journal. Like Chesnutt,
Lowrey is a "voluntary negro" (quoted in Hackenberry, Introduction xxiv),
a concept that would have been almost incomprehensible in the period, as
Chesnutt acknowledges late in *The House Behind the Cedars,* when Rena,
who is light enough to pass, is traveling with the darker Jeff Wain. As they
journey to the place where Rena is to teach, they are asked a number of
times why a white woman is breaching caste, not because she is traveling
with a black man but because she is eating with him and "sleep[ing]
beneath a negro's roof." When they explain that Rena is black, the "expla-
nation was never questioned. No white person of sound mind would ever
claim to be a negro" (153). Given the opportunity to claim one's whiteness,
as tabooed as that was in the period, the rejection of whiteness must have
seemed inexplicable.

In fact, Lowrey is a representative of the double consciousness that
W. E. B. DuBois discussed in his 1897 article in the *Atlantic Monthly,* but
Lowrey's is a very peculiar liminally inflected double consciousness. In
other words, DuBois says that "one ever feels his two-ness: an American, a
Negro; two souls, two thoughts, two unreconciled strivings; two warring
ideals in one dark body" (194). But because Lowrey (and Chesnutt) think
of themselves as in between white and black, their position is even more
painful—a double consciousness that sees double in both directions.
Caught in the middle, Lowrey sees the limitations of both the whites and
blacks on either side of him, and while he longs for the opportunities of
the white world, he throws in his lot with "his people" (46). As Chesnutt
wrote in an 1896 letter, "As for myself, I doubt whether I could call myself
much of a negro, although I have always been more or less identified with
the colored people. I am really seven-eighths white, but I have never denied
the other" (*Letters* 89). In a sense, then, Lowrey's decision not to claim his
whiteness, despite all of the taboos around passing in this period, would

have been seen as a kind of insanity, an inexplicable renunciation of economic and social opportunity in favor of a racial solidarity that would
have probably been seen by a white audience as both proper (no possible
pollution of white blood) and culturally opaque (because that audience
"knows" that all persons of African American ancestry would be white if
they could).

Exploring these complicated questions of identity in *Mandy Oxendine,*
Chesnutt is not really engaged by the larger context of African American
experience—of politics, history, or economic development. As in the
color line stories that he wrote at the same time and that would be
collected in *The Wife of His Youth* (1899), Chesnutt in this novella is
exploring questions of liminal identity in a resolutely eccentric form that
is not adequate to the complications of that experience. So he sends off
his two mixed-race characters into a future that he cannot (or will not)
imagine, in which they could take Tom's ideological position and like
Chesnutt work for their people or they could pass into the white world.
Not until more than twenty years later, in his second manuscript novel,
Paul Marchand, F.M.C., does Chesnutt return to the question of racial
identity. He does so in another eccentric form but one that is more
informed than *Mandy Oxendine* is by a theory of what constitutes racial
identity.

The House Behind the Cedars

Race Melodrama and the White Audience

I

When *The House Behind the Cedars* was published, it was clear that Chesnutt had paid more attention to his white audience than he had in *Mandy Oxendine*. In fact, his awareness of that audience dated back to the beginning of his career, when he published short stories and sketches in a variety of venues between 1886 and 1889. Some of the earliest work was published in local newspapers such as the *Cleveland News and Herald*, while other stories and sketches were published in national humor magazines such as *Puck*,[1] which had a circulation of ninety thousand during the years Chesnutt published there (Secor 219). Even in these early publications, Chesnutt obviously was aware that his audience was primarily white. That knowledge was further reinforced by the subsequent publication of his conjure stories in the *Atlantic*, which possessed "extraordinary literary prestige" (Price 261) during this period but had grown increasingly conservative. Having supported the Republicans and Reconstruction, the *Atlantic* had by the 1880s retreated into the national consensus about race. In these years, the "idea that civil equality might bring social equality for blacks provoked hostility both in the *Atlantic* and in the northern press at large" (Price 259). Chesnutt's awareness of the *Atlantic* as an arbiter of national taste and as a site of the representation of African Americans can be seen in his response, in a letter to Walter Hines Page, to one of the magazine's ubiquitous plantation tales published during this period. Chesnutt characterizes the dialect story as "one of the sort of Southern stories that make me feel it my duty to try to write a different sort" (*Letters* 120). From the beginning of his national exposure in the *Atlantic*, Chesnutt was aware of his white audience's expectations, and he wrote his plantation stories as a response to and a critique of that tradition. In the volume of plantation tales (*The Conjure Woman* [1899]) that he put together with the help of Page, Chesnutt deftly took his white readers' generic expectations and subverted them by satirizing the white narrator of the tales and by using the gap between the narrator and his wife as a way of exposing not only the horrors of slavery but also the difficulties of Reconstruction (and of the present) for African Americans. But as Kenneth M. Price points out, Chesnutt also ran the risk of being too subtle—the "subversion that avoided" the detection of the editor of the *Atlantic* "might also elude too many of the white readers he hoped to change" (266). Indeed, that was the reception of Chesnutt's stories: they were seen as extensions of what white writers had done in the genre, and he learned from the reception of his stories in the reviews[2] of the book that his critique had been invisible to his readers. He concluded that he might need to be more confrontational in his next work.

When Chesnutt decided to write a novel primarily for that white audience, he realized that he had to be less subtle but not so confrontational that he risked alienating his audience. In other words, he faced a complicated problem of genre and audience. Publishing short stories that his audience saw as falling into the genre of local color, he was perceived to be unthreatening, a curiosity, an African-American writing in a minor genre nostalgic for the "good ole times" of slavery, much like Paul Laurence Dunbar, who was also concurrently publishing plantation school stories. Deciding to write a novel, Chesnutt was explicitly claiming the right to write in a major form in what he considered a realistic mode. Despite the fact that the tragic mulatta genre was inherently melodramatic, he believed that he was writing realism, that he was presenting an aspect of African American life that had never before been sympathetically rendered in fiction. A very telling incident in this regard was the response of the editor of the *Century*, Richard Watson Gilder, to an early draft of what would eventually become *The House Behind the Cedars:* "somehow it seems to me," Gilder wrote to George Washington Cable, "amorphous— not so much in construction as in *sentiment*. . . . There is either a lack of humor in the author, or a brutality in the characters, lack of mellowness, lack of spontaneous imaginative life in the people, lack of outlook,—I don't know what—that makes them, as here depicted, *uninteresting*. I think it is the writer's fault, rather than the people's. The result seems to me a crude study, not a thoroughly human one" (28 May 1890). Chesnutt's response to Cable, as the editors of his *Letters* point out, was anger. "When Chesnutt expresses strong emotions in his letters, it is typically provoked by outrages perpetuated against the African American community. His feelings concerning his own situation are normally restrained" (*Letters*, 67 n.1). One gauge of his anger is that after he had written his original letter in a white heat, he revised it, making it more temperate (although he retained his first manuscript draft). In the revised letter, Chesnutt acknowledged that the characters are "amorphous," because the story "was written under the ever-present consciousness, so hard for me to get rid of, that a very large class of people consider the class the story treats of as 'amorphous.' I fear there is too much of this sentiment to make mulattoes good magazine characters" (65).[3] What must have especially galled Chesnutt was the implication that the "crude study" revealed that either the author or his characters were not "fully human." As a result of such a reaction from an influential editor, Chesnutt was forced to think about the effect of his writing on his audience, and he feared that he might not be able to write about what he knew because of the audience's racist preconceptions. In the middle of his letter, though, Chesnutt responded more directly to Gilder's criticism, quoting his statement that the characters have a "brutality, a lack of mellowness, a lack of spontaneous imaginative life, lack of outlook" and then making an historical and

environmental argument that "those are exactly the things that do characterize them, and just about the things that might be expected in them—
the very quality which government and society had for 300 years or so
labored faithfully, zealously, and successfully to produce, the only qualities
which would have rendered life at all endurable to them in the 19th century." This is clearly an argument from a position of realism, and
Chesnutt feared that he might have to resort to less realistic, more conventional, and stereotyped representations of African American characters, and he lamented that "I suppose I shall have to drop the attempt
at realism, and try to make my characters like other folks" (*Letters* 66).
In that last phrase, Chesnutt was responding to Gilder's approval of
Chesnutt's more conventional handling of the "black boy," who, Gilder
says, "is better, from a literary point of view" (to Cable 28 May 1890). The
irony was that Chesnutt (and Dunbar as well) was most successful with
his white audience when he was writing in the highly conventionalized
form of the plantation story, which was at an extensive distance from his
own experience as a middle-class autodidact. Writing *The House Behind
the Cedars*, Chesnutt positioned himself as an insider who tried to present
the lives of educated, mixed-race characters, and thus he created more
than a potential problem in his white audience's response to those unfamiliar representations.

As an insider, Chesnutt believed that realism was truth telling about
what he knew—the lives of mixed-race characters—and his endeavor had
been, as he wrote ten years later to William Dean Howells, "always to
depict life as I have known it" (*Letters* 146).[4] Chesnutt faced the problem
that realism, at least in its American incarnation, as Amy Kaplan has
argued, was not interested in helping readers understand or appreciate
the experiences of people who were radically Other. Instead, realism
wanted its readers to see that the Others on the margins were fundamentally no different from the white, largely metropolitan readers at the center. "Realism does not jar readers with the shock of otherness, it provides
a recognizable mirror of their own world. Realism . . . insure[s] that social
difference can be transcended in the medium of the commonplace.
Howells . . . envisioned realism as a strategy for containing social difference

and controlling social conflict within a cohesive common ground" (*Social Construction* 23). In a sense, the plantation tales of Chesnutt and Dunbar are more "realistic" than *The House Behind the Cedars* because they provide a "recognizable mirror" of the white readers' world, and Gilder responded to the draft of Chesnutt's novel with an instinctive dislike, a revulsion because the life depicted was too foreign, not sufficiently adapted enough to the audience's expectations of realism as a way of ameliorating rather than highlighting difference.

Chesnutt's essential dilemma as a writer of novels was made clear to him in his ten-year struggle with *The House Behind the Cedars*. He learned that "the literary door would be open to a black author to the extent that he helped maintain preferred fictions of racial life" (Brodhead, *Culture of Letters* 210). To have his race-problem novels be "widely read" (*Letters* 214) and to make a good living as a writer of fiction, Chesnutt struggled with the intractable problem of how to accommodate his white audience while remaining faithful to the life he knew. Chesnutt knew that the black middle class was not large enough to support writers of fiction, and so he needed to sell his books to white readers while emphasizing racial injustice. As he wrote to John P. Green in 1900, when *The House Behind the Cedars* was published, "I think you will understand how difficult it is to write race problem books so that white people will read them,—and it is white people they are primarily aimed at" (*Letters* 156). As part of his strategy to engage his white audience, Chesnutt assumed, as he had in writing his first two white-life novels, that he had the right to represent white experience, a consistent strategy in all three of the race fictions published in his lifetime. In *The House Behind the Cedars*, however, Chesnutt inserts his white character into the genre of the tragic mulatta narrative, and, like Harriet Beecher Stowe, he assumes that the only way to obtain justice for African Americans is to attempt to mobilize white readers' feelings. But those sentiments are to be mobilized not only through the dilemma of the tragic mulatta, Rena Walden, but also through the dilemma of the central white character. In generic terms, then, Chesnutt wants the reader to sympathize with both characters, an approach that gives the novel a unique dual focus.[5]

As I said in the previous chapter, *The House Behind the Cedars* is the most conventional of the three novels published in Chesnutt's lifetime in its willingness to accommodate itself to its genre, to what William L. Andrews has termed "the protocols of 'tragic mulatta' fiction" (Introduction ix–x), the racialized genre of the novel par excellence for a white audience at the turn of the century. Part of the reason for that conventionality is that Chesnutt worked on the novel for almost ten years under the title "Rena Walden" and during that time received a good deal of feedback. In fact, in 1885, at the beginning of the long gestation of what would become *The House Behind the Cedars,* Chesnutt was, as I mentioned in the previous chapter, corresponding with Cable, who was at the height of his notoriety as a polemicist on America's race problem. In an unpublished letter, Cable observed that Chesnutt had a

> chance to do something great in the grotesque, ludicrous, pathetic and barren conditions of colored society. You must remember that you are writing for white Americans and English—the most cultivated people of the world's most cultivated age.
>
> There is no danger that you will be supercilious or flippant. The danger is that in regarding these things with proper truthfulness and fraternal charity you will assert and ask too much of these qualities.
>
> Again, you must remember in your description of persons that the greatest element of strength is to yield all the ground you honestly can to the possible prejudices of your reader. (25 September 1889)

Chesnutt responded that he "cannot properly express my thanks to you for your wise and kindly criticism of 'Rena Walden.' . . . I am glad you think the story a good one in outline; I was afraid that it would suffer from the lack of white characters in it" (*Letters* 46–47). Chesnutt later decided that the novel did need white characters, and he added George Tryon, but I want to emphasize the double message Chesnutt got from Cable. Chesnutt never forgot the general advice to write always with the "the possible prejudices of your reader" in mind throughout his increasingly complicated relations with that white audience. The other part of the message—to which Chesnutt did not respond in his letter—concerns "the grotesque, ludicrous, pathetic and barren conditions of colored society." Chesnutt must have been ambivalent about this advice. His white audience expected such qualities in representations of African American characters, and Chesnutt must have realized how hard it would be to portray such lives without confirming the audience's preexisting stereotypes.

Since Chesnutt substantially revised "Rena Walden" several times, taking into consideration the responses of Gilder and Cable as well as the suggestion of the novel's editor, Page, the history of the composition of *The House Behind the Cedars* is complicated. There are at least five intermediate drafts of "Rena Walden," the first of which is only thirty-nine pages long (Sedlack 126). In the first few drafts, Chesnutt attempted to write, as he did in *Mandy Oxendine,* as if he could ignore "the possible prejudices" of his white readers. The voice that tells the story is "a sympathetic insider" (Andrews, *Career* 26), and the story begins. "I knew Mis' Molly in the years between 1866 and 1870" (quoted in Andrews, *Career* 26). Assuming the voice of a native informant, Chesnutt made no concessions to his potential readership, and the first-person narrator works less well than a third-person narrator as a mediator between his audience's expectations and the "amorphous" and "unnatural" experience he wanted to represent. Chesnutt was writing as if there had been a large community of African American readers who would be interested in his analysis of internalized oppression, of how "color consciousness *within* the Negro community ultimately destroys" (Sedlack 129) the central character, Rena Walden. Robert Sedlack has argued that the subsequent 1889–91 version of "Rena Walden" was "an attempt to awaken the consciousness of [white] America by showing that color consciousness *within* the Negro community destroys Rena." Sedlack claims that "any reflective reader would recognize the great moral evil of racial prejudice just beneath the surface," but I believe that this claim is ahistorical. Chesnutt's white audience would not have seen its prejudices reflected in Chesnutt's "oblique approach" (Sedlack 129). Rather, white readers would have Othered these characters and this dramatic situation, seeing in them confirmation of little more than "the grotesque, ludicrous, pathetic and barren conditions of colored society." Despite Cable's earlier advice, Chesnutt was still trying in these early drafts to depict the world he knew from the inside, without thinking of audience considerations.

All of the drafts of "Rena Walden" and *The House Behind the Cedars* focus on the possible marriage of Rena, a woman who is light enough to pass as white. In "Rena Walden" her suitors are the loyal Frank Fuller, who "has strongly marked African features" ("Rena Walden," quoted in Sedlack 127), and Washington Wain, who is "light brown" (128). Pressured to marry Wain because of his color and his presumed prosperity, Rena consents, only to discover after she is married that Wain is a fraud and a bigamist,[6] and she dies while trying to escape him. In *The House Behind the Cedars,* this narrative has been substantially modified—Rena never marries Wain, although he still pursues her, and he has been relegated to a subplot. Additionally, Chesnutt has shifted the overall focus so that "the question of crossing the color line" becomes "the predominant issue in Rena's life." As Andrews argues, the narrative shifts from a focus on "the destructive effects of color consciousness on intra-racial marriage" to a focus on "inter-racial romance" (*Career* 123). Furthermore, Andrews says that "what motivated Chesnutt to change his story so that the question of crossing the color line might become the predominant issue in Rena's life is not entirely clear" (*Career* 123). If one remembers Chesnutt's earlier engagement with Cable, I believe that the author's awareness of his potential white audience motivated this shift, and he introduced a new character, the young southern white man, George Tryon, to whom Rena, passing as white, becomes engaged.

As he reworked the novel, Chesnutt took his narrative into what would be recognizable generic territory for his white audience, a tragic mulatta narrative. This genre has been redefined by Susan Gillman as "race melodrama," a form that "focuses broadly on the situation of the black family—almost always of an interracial genealogy—and specifically on the issue of 'race mixture' as a means of negotiating the social tensions surrounding the formation of racial, national, and sexual identity in the post-Reconstruction years" (222). At the end of the nineteenth century, the central figure of race melodrama was always the light-skinned mulatta and her white lover, and the degree to which the figure proliferates in this period is astonishing. The figure of the mulatta who is indistinguishable from her white counterpart is found in major novels such as Mark Twain's *Pudd'nhead Wilson* (1894) and Pauline Hopkins's *Contending Forces* (1900) as well as in less well known novels such as Gertrude Atherton's *Senator North* (1900) and *Towards the Gulf*. In this period, the figure of the "white negro," a term Chesnutt used in his series of essays "The Future American" (1900), the mulatta who was indistinguishable from the "real thing" became a figure of powerful cultural anxiety for white audiences. As Nancy Bentley has argued, the "mulatto figure was a scandal—not only a sexual but an intellectual scandal, confounding as it did the racial categories that were . . . fundamental to social life in the North and in the South" (197–98); race melodrama, then, represents the double liminality of the woman who has no real place in either world once her "essence" is discovered. But what is new in generic terms is the way in which Chesnutt redirected the readers' attention to George Tryon, who became a surrogate for the white reader. By staging a long agon for Tryon, Chesnutt was attempting to mobilize his white readers' sentiments; by having readers experience what Tryon experiences, the author was attempting to mine and infiltrate readers' feelings.

The terms *mine* and *infiltrate* are a locus classicus for Chesnutt scholarship and are preceded by his statement about elevating whites: "The object of my writings would be not so much the elevation of the colored people as the elevation of the whites." He says that he would lead "a determined crusade" against prejudice, but he would not use force: "the subtle almost indefinable feeling of repulsion toward the negro, which is common to most Americans . . . cannot be stormed and taken by assault; the garrison will not capitulate; so their position must be mined, and we will find ourselves in their midst before they think it." He goes on to argue that it is the task of "the province of literature" to prepare the way for "social recognition and equality" and to amuse white readers while "lead[ing] them on imperceptibly, unconsciously step by step to the desired state of feeling" (*Journals* 139–40). One always needs to be careful when using such theoretical statements, which, all too often in Chesnutt scholarship have been employed in unnuanced ways, as if Chesnutt were simply a propagandist whose purpose as a writer was to illustrate his theories in fiction, as if the conclusions of the twenty-one-year-old neophyte writer were the same as those of the man who wrote his major works in his forties. Still, this passage is very revealing about Chesnutt's early aspirations. For someone who had not yet published a work of fiction, these are high literary and cultural ambitions. Putting himself into the tradition of abolitionist writers, he believed that the cultural work of "literature" was to "open the way" for African Americans by presenting sympathetic and unstereotypical depictions to his white audience. But there is a crucial difference between the two operative terms, *mine* and *infiltrate*. The first implies some level of violence: after all, a portion of the mined garrison must be blown up before it can be entered. But the implied metaphor of *infiltrate* ("we will find ourselves in their midst before they think it") is less violent and potentially more useful in how it forecasts a kind of cultural sneak attack through sentiment, an attack that parallels the entrance of mixed-race folks into the white world that Chesnutt chronicled in such essays as "What Is a White Man?" and "The Future American."

In positioning himself in the tradition of abolitionist writers, Chesnutt represented the difficulties of his liminally positioned mixed-race characters. Acutely aware of the separations suffered by families with members who chose to pass as white, Chesnutt hoped his readers could recognize that suffering as analogous to the separations suffered by families under slavery. Chesnutt's use of sentimental strategies, however, is more complicated than his predecessors'. In *The House Behind the Cedars*, Chesnutt, like Twain, satirizes the "romantic view of the world perpetuated by writers like Scott" (Thomas 182), particularly in the scene at the mock tournament where George and Rena meet. Brook Thomas argues that Chesnutt "tries to alter people's feelings" much like the women sentimentalists; for his strategies, however, "he relies as much on logos as pathos to do so" (182). Structurally, Chesnutt was working in this novel with a set of binaries— logos and pathos, rationality and sentiment—a tension enacted in the difference between the assertions that "custom *is* law" (23) and that "custom was tyranny. Love was the only law" (194). These binaries gave Chesnutt the opportunity to infiltrate his white audience's racial expectations by exploring both the reactions (those he considers sentimental and those he considers rational) of a nonideological racist such as George Tryon to the discovery that the woman to whom he is engaged is not white.

While Chesnutt chose to employ sentimental strategies, he also represented, unlike Stowe, the cost to subsequent generations of the "sins of the fathers," a phrase repeated at least twice in the novel.[7] Rena, Chesnutt writes, "had yet to learn that the old Mosaic formula, 'The sins of the fathers shall be visited upon the children,' was graven more indelibly upon the heart of the race than upon the tables of Sinai" (51). The fathers "sinned so lightly, after the manner of men" (21). In contrast, in the racist imaginary, the mothers are always to blame through their hypersexualization and the infection they carry in the taint of their blood. In such passages, Chesnutt was trying to reverse racist ideology: in the United States, where race mixing was criminalized, the sins of the fathers will reverberate forever, much like the law, quoted in "What Is a White Man?" that "forever" prohibited "the marriage relation between white persons and persons of African descent" (*Essays* 72). By criminalizing sexual activity that "Nature, by some unaccountable oversight [had] neglected" to prevent (*Essays* 71), whites had punished and would continue to punish their mixed-race children, not only through neglect but also by constituting them as having breached a boundary that whites wanted to pretend was impermeable. The children were not in any way personally guilty; rather, the fathers constructed a system that made those children always collectively guilty.

An advocate of racial mixing, Chesnutt focused his readers' attention in *The House Behind the Cedars* tactically on the sexual activities of the fathers. Because sexual attraction could not lead to marriage between people of different races, all mixed-race offspring, in racist ideology, were presumed to be illegitimate. American laws, Chesnutt writes in "What Is a White Man?" "made mixed blood a *prima-facie* proof of illegitimacy" (*Essays* 72), and the law delegitimated the children not only in terms of their parentage but also in terms of their being, as if they were a crime against nature. In fact, so tabooed did the racist ideologues wish the mixing of racial blood to appear to be that miscegenation was often imagined as analogous to incest. As one Mississippi statesman said in this period,

"The same law which forbids consanguineous amalgamation forbids ethnical amalgamation. Both are incestuous. Amalgamation is incest" (Saks 53). Of course, in conjuring up this taboo, this speaker ends up acknowledging not the inevitable difference in races but their metaphorical consanguinity: the incest taboo is in place to keep apart people who are related rather than separated by blood.

The sins of the fathers blight the lives of their mixed-race children as well as confound the lives of white descendants. In focusing on his central white figure, George Tryon, Chesnutt wanted to give readers the opportunity to witness the character's struggle with love and racism and to examine their ability to be sympathetic to the "illegitimate" characters, like Rena, who were a result of sins. In so doing, Chesnutt wanted to undermine, from inside, the ideology of the American racist imagination by showing that both white and black characters suffered and would continue to suffer the consequences of those sins as long as America's system of racial apartheid remained in place. Writing a generation after the end of the Civil War, Chesnutt, however, was more aware than writers like Stowe of the ideological boundaries separating white and black in America. For Stowe, sympathy led to political action, but, as for Howells later in the century, his sympathy was bestowed on "polite inferiors" (Howells, "An Exemplary Citizen" 195).[8] African American writers, however, were more aware of the ideological limits of white sympathy and of the class and caste barriers that separated the races. For instance, William Wells Brown, in his 1853 novel, *Clotel; or, the President's Daughter,* wrote about the white witnesses to the suicide of Clotel, the slave daughter of Thomas Jefferson: "she was a slave, and therefore out of the pale of their sympathy" (197). Chesnutt echoed this conclusion a year after the publication of *The House Behind the Cedars* when he wrote toward the end of *The Marrow of Tradition* about a mixed-race character, "The negro, by the traditions of [white] people, was barred from the world of sentiment" (271). In *The House Behind the Cedars,* Chesnutt's strategy was to use George Tryon as a waveringly sympathetic focalizer through which readers are brought, through the use of sentimentality and of race melodrama, to consider, at least momentarily, whether a nominally African American character could enter into the white readers' pale of sentiment. At the turn of the century, this kind of deployment of sentimentality, in the hands of an African American writer, did create a radicalized genre, particularly when the intended audience was white. In fact, Philip Fisher has argued that "sentimentality often marks precisely the point within accepted patterns of feeling and representation where radical revision is taking place" (93). Rather than letting his female characters be the locus of sentimentality, Chesnutt instead rather daringly made all his male characters experience feelings of sentiment, and he used those experiences, especially those of George Tryon, as a way of attempting to revise part of America's racial story.

II

In "The Future American," Chesnutt commented that "curiously enough the male octoroon has cut no figure in fiction, except in the case of the melancholy Honoré Grandissime, f.m.c." (*Essays* 126), a character from Cable's 1880 novel of the same name, and in the character of John Warwick Chesnutt was filling that lacuna. This absence had everything to do with how men of mixed race were represented in the racist imaginary in this period. Joel Williamson has cataloged some of these postbellum beliefs: mulattoes were "effete . . . both biologically, and ultimately, culturally." Southern whites believed that mulattoes "could not procreate among themselves beyond the third generation. Further, since mulattoes held themselves aloof from blacks, and whites shunned both blacks and mulattoes, there would be no new additions and soon no mulattoes at all. . . . Mulattoes, then, in the popular white mind were doomed to isolation and demise" (*New People* 94–95). However, as noted earlier, the mulatto was also a kind of scandal, an indictment, in Williamson's words, "of the world the white man made" (95). Thus, in this period, the policing of interracial sexual relations became of paramount importance, because its issue, a mulatto, was thought to be a crime against nature. George Fredrickson has observed that in this period, "the worst outrages" against white women were attributed to mulattoes and that this "was clearly one way of reconciling the traditional stereotype of black docility with the image of bold and violent offenders against the color line which was central to the new propaganda" (278). In other words, the hybrid, the mulatto, became a way of explaining the changes in African American behavior since the end of the Civil War, for if African Americans were essentially timeless and unchangeable, another way had to be invented to explain what were seen to be radical changes in behavior.

Ida B. Wells noted at the time that white men often used the cry of rape as a way of both policing and disguising the voluntary nature of the sexual contacts between black men and white women, because voluntary sexual contact would undermine racist stereotypes. Within the racist imaginary, the only way sexual contact could be represented was in terms of force; racist ideologues wanted to make the possibility of a white woman being attracted to a black man both unimaginable and unrepresentable. For instance, Thomas Dixon's *The Leopard's Spots* (1902) made absolutely clear how the racist imaginary could slide from equal political rights to equal social rights to intermarriage and how the figure of the mixed-race male, with his social and educational ambitions, was a figure of high cultural anxiety. This can be seen in the portion of Dixon's novel devoted to George Harris Jr., the son of Eliza and George from *Uncle Tom's Cabin*. In the racist imaginary, his education led inevitably to his desire to marry the daughter of his white patron. Even though George says he is the "equal in culture" to Mr. Lowell, the father of the white girl he wants to marry, Lowell tells him that the idea of intermarriage is "nauseating, and to my daughter it would be repulsive beyond power of words to express it!" Lowell clinches his argument by showing George the door and thundering, "I happen to know the important fact that a man or woman of Negro ancestry, though a century removed, will suddenly breed back to a pure Negro child, thick-lipped, kinky-headed, flat-nosed, black-skinned. One drop of your blood in my family could push it backward three thousand years in history" (397–98). The infection of African blood (and its concomitant reversion to type) was theorized as atavism and was then used as a way of justifying the prohibition of sexual contact between

African American men and Euro-American women, and the mulatto was seen as most prone to cross racial lines.

Chesnutt's mixed-race character, John Warwick (Walden)[9] seems absolutely free from this fear of reversion to type. He is a racial conundrum, a "white negro" who has grown up with a knowledge of his own liminality and his paternal heritage: a bookcase that is, Richard Brodhead writes, "the primal scene for the Walden children . . . the bookcase . . . stands for their absent white father, the place where they read his literary classics" (*Cultures* 207) and where access to literature fuels his desire to escape the limitations of the racialized world in which he finds himself. By sheer force of will, John convinces a local magistrate, Judge Straight, who in a "moment of sentimental weakness" (79–80) allows John to read law. In the face of John's insistence that he is white in spite of his mixed-race ancestry, the judge looks up a statute that gives John the warrant he needs to pass as a white man, the 1831 South Carolina law discussed in "What Is a White Man?" As the judge says, since John has "all the features of a white man, you would, at least in South Carolina, have simply to assume the place and exercise the privileges of a white man" (114–15). Taking advantage of this law, John moves to South Carolina and during the Civil War marries the daughter of a "good family," who dies after giving birth to their son.

As John tells this story to his sister and mother during a clandestine visit to them, they find that it has "the charm of an escape from captivity" (15), and that comparison is more telling than they realize. His story, in their view, could be a high romantic tale of capture and providential escape, or it could be like an escape from the captivity of slavery. Although he has escaped the disadvantages of his ancestry, his decision to pass is made at a high cost to him and to his mother and sister, the same cost that escaped slaves paid and one to which the narrator points in this exchange between John and his mother. She says, "I thought I'd lost you forever," and he responds, "'I couldn't live without seeing you, mother,' . . . He meant it, too, or thought he did, although he had not seen her for ten years" (12). From the beginning of the novel, Chesnutt pointed to the anguish of the mother, abandoned and unacknowledged because she was unable to pass, and the necessary withering of the affections of the separated son. Warwick (Walden) does feel, however, a momentary "blind anger" that he must sever all family ties to become white, but he also quickly banishes that thought as "pure sentiment" (20). He has lived his life by "principles of right and reason" even though his individual principles were "at variance with what society considers equally right and reasonable" (19). His decision, then, involved a devaluation of sentiment, of feeling in favor of "argument, of self-conviction. Once persuaded that he had certain rights, or ought to have them, by virtue of the laws of nature, in defiance of the customs of mankind, he had promptly sought to enjoy them" (53–54), even though the cost of that enjoyment was nearly permanent separation from his family.

Sedlack has shown that the character of John Warwick (Walden), like George Tryon, came rather late in Chesnutt's revision of "Rena Walden," and Sedlack sees John as providing, in structural terms, the "necessary bridge between the world of Rena Walden and that of George Tryon" (130). (In other words, John is needed to introduce Rena to George.) If John bridges the white and black worlds of the novel, he also provides a instructive contrast to George, who finds it more difficult than John to live his by "principles of right and reason." Unlike John, Tryon reasons from a position of racist rationality,[10] while John's rationality is antiracialist; both, as characters, have the same effect on the women around them. John separates himself from his mother, annealing his sense of affection, and George attempts to do much the same thing when he discovers that Rena is passing as white. Thematically, then, Chesnutt equated these two characters, who struggle to differing degrees with what they consider rationality and sentiment. In staging this struggle, Chesnutt extended the effect of the tragic mulatta genre to the privileged white male character, and he hoped that his audience would feel sympathy for Tryon. Part of the strategy of that genre (in its antiracist versions) was to demonstrate to the white audience that given the proper education and upbringing, the mulatta—the white negro—was no different from the white reader, and what she felt (whether the loss of a child, as in Stowe, or the stifling of ambition) was no different from what putative white readers would experience in similar circumstances. However, with these two male characters, Chesnutt was showing that they were internally almost identical in terms of a masculinist view of the world in which masculine rationality overruled female sentiment. Of course, Chesnutt was critical of both of these men for sealing themselves off from sentiment, and despite the similarities between Chesnutt and John Warwick (Walden), Chesnutt established a certain ironical distance between himself and John. In representing John's decision to pass, Chesnutt explored the consequences of the denial of family history and connection, a choice Chesnutt refused to make in his life. He was aware that mixed-race families were most often constructed on white denial: the white fathers refused to acknowledge their mixed-race children. Passing was also predicted on a similar denial—the denial of the African American family left behind and its heritage, which must be shunned to prevent any accidental racial revelations.

Warwick (Walden), who says that he has been almost completely successful in banishing sentimental considerations except in this single visit to his hometown, claims that in coming home he has yielded to a "sentimental weakness" (19),[11] but he also has an instrumental reason for seeing his sister and mother after such a long separation. He wants to ask his sister to live with him and care for his motherless child. Chesnutt wanted his readers to be aware of the human cost of annulling sentiment, not only in John's separation from his family but also in his separation from almost all human feeling, except for that regarding his son. In contrast to John's utilitarian view of passing, his sister, Rena, is filled with doubts, which only grow when she decides to marry George Tryon. He, on the other hand, has no doubts, either about her as a white woman or about his love for her, but Tryon instinctively draws the color line when he reads an article in a contemporary "medical journal" that argues, from a position of scientific racism, for the impossibility of race mixing. This "scientist" argues that "negro blood," no matter how "diluted," will always "revert to the African type, [and] any future amalgamation of the white and black races . . . would therefore be an ethnological impossibility; for the smallest trace of negro blood would inevitably drag down the superior race to the level of the inferior" (71). Lest we think Chesnutt was exaggerating for effect here, it is important to remember that ideas such as these were accepted orthodoxy in the late nineteenth and early twentieth centuries. As Nancy Leys Stepan and Sander L. Gilman have observed, "In studying the history of scientific racism, we have been struck by the relative absence of critical challenges to its claims from within mainstream society" (73). In its heyday, the "concepts within racial science were so congruent with social and political life . . . as to be virtually uncontested from inside the mainstream of science" (74). The article that Tryon reads, though, moves beyond science and concludes with a peroration in which the southern man is enjoined to "maintain the supremacy and purity of his all-pervading, all-conquering race, and to resist by every available means the threatened domination of an inferior and degraded people" (71). Tryon concludes that this seems to be "a well-considered argument, albeit a trifle bombastic" (71). Tryon's judiciousness here is a sign that he is not a racist ideologue, a notion that Chesnutt reinforced in a subsequent chapter by introducing another white character, Dr. Green, who obsesses about the "negro problem" as in this sample of dinner conversation: "The negro is an inferior creature; God has marked him with the badge of servitude, and has adjusted his intellect to a servile condition. We will not submit to his domination" (92). This statement has the tone of George in the earlier "Rena Walden," where he was characterized, Sedlack has observed, as a "loud, blustering bigot" (131); however, in *The House Behind the Cedars*, Tryon is more moderate, and Dr. Green is the hyperventilating racist. Chesnutt was trying to make Tryon more sympathetic to a northern white audience that would have found Green's level of unabashed bigotry to be slightly embarrassing and would have been more comfortable with George's understated, more gentlemanly, less overly ideological racial prejudice.

Tryon was a representative of Chesnutt's white audience, which saw the position of white supremacy as rational. Such racist rationality, though, concealed a deep-seated irrationality that can be uncovered in Chesnutt's reference to the reversion to "the African type" in the article that Tryon reads. This phrase conjured up for Chesnutt's white readership a nightmarish vision articulated by a character in Dixon's *The Clansman* who says that the African lived in an undifferentiated time out of history.

He "stole his food, worked his wife, sold his children, ate his brother, content to drink, sing, dance, and sport as the ape!" The African is further characterized as a "creature, half-child, half-animal, the sport of impulse, whim and conceit . . . whose speech knows no word of love, whose passions once aroused, are as the fury of the tiger—they have set this thing to rule over the Southern people" (292–93). Attitudes such as these were exactly the kinds of naturalized, essentialized prejudices that Chesnutt, as a writer attempting to affect a white audience, needed to take into consideration— the nightmare vision of the inevitability of racial hierarchy and the sense of violation involved in any action that breached that "natural" hierarchy. The anxiety of that breach was acute during Reconstruction, the era in which both *The House Behind the Cedars* and *The Clansman* are set, and in both the cause of anxiety was the rule of blacks over whites—political rule in one case and racial, almost genetic rule in the other. Chesnutt also found Tryon's use of the term *argument* to describe the racist "scientific" article to be quite ironic because the word concealed something more uncontrollable than rational conviction, something that was revealed when Tryon discovered the truth about Rena.

Through a series of coincidences, Tryon and Rena end up in the town where Rena was raised and where she cannot pass, and she is revealed to him as a colored woman. When she confronts Tryon, she sees "a face as pale as death, with staring eyes, in which love, which once had reigned there, had now given place to astonishment and horror" (94). As Rena subsequently says to her brother, Tryon "looked at me as though I were not even a human being" (120). In seeing her instantaneously slide from one order of being to another, Tryon faces the fundamental instability of appearances within the racist imaginary. Although racists insisted that they could infallibly tell when anyone had any admixture of black "blood" (as the Supreme Court implied in its 1922–23 decisions defining whiteness), their anxiety of course resulted from the fact that they were unable to do so, either by external signs or by behavior, because in this period the one-drop rule had rendered race as potentially invisible. The sexual transgressions of the fathers, then, haunted their sons in the nightmare of the simulacrum, the white negro.

Sedlack argues that Tryon's response to the discovery that Rena is black "makes him an odious figure" (133), quoting the following lines: "The full realization of the truth, which followed speedily, had for the moment reversed his mental attitude toward her, and love and yearning had given place to anger and disgust" (95). Chesnutt, I would argue, did not want his white readers to see Tryon here as "odious" or his actions here as "unnatural" or in any way out of the ordinary. To mine and infiltrate the ideological assumptions of those readers, Chesnutt first needed to represent a response with which they would sympathize—Tryon's completely understandable horror at the simulacrum. After the horror has been represented, Chesnutt can undermine it through Tryon's agon, his shiftings between racist rationality and sentiment. Although we, as readers, may have difficulty understanding the depth of his revulsion, his response in literary terms is rather mild. For instance, in Gertrude Atherton's *Senator North*, published in the same year as *The House Behind the Cedars*, a white man, Jack Emory, unwittingly marries a black woman who is passing. In a letter, he writes that his first response to the knowledge of her ancestry was that "I hated, I loathed, I abhorred her." He writes that he has not forgiven her, and "although the thought of her awful hidden birthmark still fills me with horror and disgust, I know the weakness of man." Even though their marriage carried no legal force in Virginia, he is afraid that if he stays with her, she might ask him to remarry her in the North, and he fears he might give in. "And rather than do that, rather than dishonor my blood, rather than do that monstrous wrong, not only to my family but to the South that has my heart's allegiance . . . I am going to kill myself" (245). Both characters—Emory and Tryon—feel horror and disgust, but Emory's actions provide an instructive contrast to what Tryon experiences after his discovery of Rena's race. Emory acknowledges his profound ambivalence, and to prevent himself from weakening, he commits suicide.

Tryon's horror is displaced into a dream a few nights later that is central to Chesnutt's exploration of America's racist imagination: "In all her fair young beauty she stood before him, and then by some hellish magic she was slowly transformed into a hideous black hag. With agonized eyes he watched her beautiful tresses become mere wisps of coarse wool, wrapped round with dingy cotton strings; he saw her clear eyes grow bloodshot, her ivory teeth turn to unwholesome fangs" (98). This image recurs even more explicitly in Hopkins's *Hagar's Daughter* when a New England white man who is about to discover that his intended is black says that the "mere thought of the grinning, toothless black hag that was her foreparent would forever rise between us" (271). This image of the "black hag" (almost a racial gothic) points to an extreme level of cultural anxiety.[12] The woman who is revered and desired, who is the epitome of the virtues and beauties of whiteness, can turn in an instant into her opposite, that which is despised and loathed, and her beauty and virtues are seen as the merest of shells, a veneer that is always threatening to break off and reveal the presumed bestiality beneath. So the rationality of racist argument cracks at this moment to reveal a fundamentally irrational fear of pollution, a pollution that can occur in the sanctum sanctorum, the marriage bed. As Tryon thinks, a "negro girl had been foisted upon him for a white woman, and he had almost committed the unpardonable sin against his race in marrying her" (96). In nearly committing a "sin," the sin of the fathers, Tryon was about to "pollute" the "unsullied" blood (96) he had received as his heritage from his ancestors, and although blood for us exists as a "fictitious" figure of speech (Saks 40), for whites in the late nineteenth and early twentieth centuries, blood was a vehicle that carried not only what we might think of as genetic heritage but also cultural heritage. In giving Tryon these responses, Chesnutt is burrowing into racist common sense, and the effect on his white audience would have been normalizing. The audience would have found none of Tryon's responses here outrageous and would have sympathized with his horror, disgust, and confusion.

For Tryon, at this point, the American consensus on race trumps love, and in his self-understanding, he is simply being rational in resolving to "banish her image" (97) from his mind—that is, to banish the image of Rena as white woman. He discovers, however, that rationality cannot so easily annul sentiment, that sentiment possesses its own counter force that has its sources not in custom, the narrator says, but in "the laws of nature[, which] are higher and more potent than merely human institutions, and upon anything like a fair field are likely to win in the long run" (99). His internal struggle between custom and the laws of nature, between love and racist rationality, is prolonged and intense. At one point, overcome by sentiment, he rushes off to see Rena. He "was in a state of mind where any sort of a fairy tale would have seemed reasonable," and he "almost" wished that he could bribe someone to tell him that she was not "the descendant of slaves,—that he might marry her, and not have before his eyes the gruesome fear that some one of their children might show even the faintest mark of the despised race" (138). At this point, then, Tryon has dispensed with racist rationality to such a degree that he is willing to marry a Negro, but he remains somewhat deterred by the possibility that his children will exhibit the visible signs of degradation, the fear that Chesnutt dismissed as superstition in "The Future American." What Chesnutt thought of as superstition, however, many white Americans saw as firmly grounded in rationality, a possibility confirmed by the scientific theory of atavism, a reversion and degeneration of one's children.

Atavism in theory and practice is represented quite clearly in the interesting, little-known novel *Towards the Gulf,* which was published anonymously in 1887 and has been recently attributed to Alice Buckner (see Fick and Gold). The main character unknowingly marries a mixed-race woman who also does not know of her ancestry but who reverts to type in many ways, among them in her playing of Gottschalk's "Danse des Negres" (220–21). Her son reverts even more dramatically: he steals, he lies about stealing, and he has a racially marked "inability to think long or seriously of any one thing" (306). The only solution that the novel can envision is the death of both the wife and the son. In enacting the theory of atavism, *Towards the Gulf* demonstrates that "the mulatto's white appearance notwithstanding, one can tell the difference: black identity reveals itself" (Fick and Gold 31). Arrayed on the other side of this question is Howells, who thought of himself as a good liberal on the race question. Contesting the theory of atavism, the central character in *An Imperative Duty* (1893) (which is known to have been in Chesnutt's library [McElrath, "Chesnutt's Library" 100]), Dr. Olney, rejects, from a competing scientific point of view, the possibility of atavism, which he defines as the "reversion to the black great-great-great grandfather" (161). He claims that the "superior" types will inevitably expunge the "inferior," and he accounts for the concept of atavism's hold on the popular mind of white America by likening it to the thrill of something that is only on the "verge" of a mere possibility, a kind of superstition.[13] Olney and Howells fail, however, to question a fundamental tenet of racist ideology—that the white race is superior. The white race, Olney claims, "must absorb the colored race . . . obliterate not only its color, but its qualities. The tame man, the civilized man, is stronger than the wild man; and . . . in those cases within any race where there are very strong ancestral proclivities on one side especially toward evil, they will die out before the good tendencies on the other side." Olney concludes with the astonishing observation that all of this will happen because "vice is savage, and virtue is civilized" (161). Although Olney is enlightened in rejecting atavism as a theory, he simply turns racial theory on its head—for him, the superior will expunge the inferior—and with this theory he illustrates racialized discourse's tenacious hold on white Americans.

This racialized discourse, however, takes a particular form in the American racial imagination. Like the speaker in Dixon's novel, who can only imagine two possibilities—rule by whites or rule by blacks—Howells's character can respond only with a binary opposition—either black blood will degenerate white, or white blood will improve and help the evolution of blacks. We can also see here the radical difference between Howells and Chesnutt on the question of amalgamation: Olney (and Howells, I believe) still believed in racial essence ("very strong ancestral proclivities"), whereas Chesnutt was an environmentalist. Howells saw amalgamation as a way to expunge the wildness and evil of the black race; Chesnutt saw amalgamation as an instrumental way to expunge the binary of black/white, inferior/superior.

For a white audience enmeshed in racialized discourse, Tryon's fear of atavism—of genetic struggle—was palpable and acute. However, on his first return to Rena, he rejects this fear in favor of the power of sentiment: "if he should find it too hard to leave her—ah, well! he was a white man, one of a race born to command. *He would make her white. . . .*

If, perchance, their secret should be disclosed, the world was wide.... He would not let his darling die of grief, whatever the price must be paid for her salvation" (emphasis added; 140). Unlike the author of *Towards the Gulf,* Chesnutt does not allow his character to think at this moment about reversion to type, about atavism. He is willing to pay "whatever the price must be paid for her salvation" because he can now imagine that being black is the equivalent of being condemned to eternal damnation. When he returns to Rena's hometown, he discovers her at a dance at her mother's, an event he does not know that she is attending only reluctantly; even worse, he sees her dancing with "a burly, grinning mulatto, whose face was offensively familiar to Tryon" (149). (This is Jeff Wain, who, the reader learns later, lives near Tryon and has married one of his former slaves; Tryon knows of Wain's disreputable character.) Tryon leaves in a fury, concluding that "he had seen her with the mask thrown off, a true daughter of a race in which the sensuous enjoyment of the moment took precedence of taste of [*sic*] sentiment or any of the higher emotions" (150). He attributes her success in passing to "the monkey-like imitativeness of the negro" (150). Once again immersed in the assumptions of racist rationality, Tryon concludes that she is "not even a human being" (120), a phrase that echoes what Rena saw when he first discovered her race. Far from being his social equal, she is merely a bad copy, incapable of feeling true sentiment. At this moment, then, the American racist imagination provides an implicit answer to the caste and education argument that Chesnutt advanced in "The Future American" that the only thing that distinguished blacks from whites was lack of education and African Americans' concomitant inability to rise into the middle class. For Chesnutt's intended audience, African Americans were capable only of imitating the forms of whiteness; their "civilized" behavior was merely a hollow shell. Having seen Rena dancing with a "burly" mulatto (language that was sexualized in Chesnutt's time), Tryon resorts to the theory of atavism; he believes he has seen her reversion to type. Beneath this shell, Tryon thinks, the "dark ancestral strain" (151) is always lurking, and it will inevitably reveal itself, "if not in the wife, then in her children" (150), and if not in appearance, then in behavior. For Tryon, "every wayward impulse of the children, every defect of mind, morale, temper, or health" (151) would have been attributed to the reversion to the black blood of their ancestors. In this world of potential racial nightmare, Tryon would always feel the necessity to police his wife and children for an outbreak of their ancestry, and the cause for such an outbreak would be his—he would become, in his own eyes, the sinning father. At this moment, then, Chesnutt has reimmersed Tryon in the assumptions of American racism, and Chesnutt's intended audience would have perceived Tryon's responses here as natural, no matter how hyperbolic they may seem to us.

After seeing what he believes to be Rena's "essence," which will inevitably transform her into the toothless black hag, Tryon thinks he has finally conquered his "weakness . . . a sickly sentimentality to which he recognized now, in the light of reflection, that he was entirely too prone" (150). He concludes that "he had definitely banished" his vision of Rena "from the realm of sentiment to that of reason" (156–57). In fact, in his rediscovery of racist rationality he experiences a righteous anger at the fraud that has been perpetrated on him, and he uses a revealing metaphor to describe his state: "The more he dwelt upon the subject, the more angry he became with those who had surprised his virgin heart and deflowered it by such low trickery" (169). Tryon agrees, at this point, with John Warwick (Walden) that "masculine" reason is always preferable to "feminine" sentiment, that in the descent into sentiment men inevitably become feminized. Tryon feels as if he had experienced a kind of rape; his heart was "surprised . . . and deflowered." He has no way of expressing the degree of his outrage other than to resort to startlingly sexualized language in which he—the white man—becomes the victim, the emotional equivalent of all the white women who were alleged to have been victimized and raped by black men in this period.

Since the form of the novel is melodramatic, we as readers realize that "feminine" sentiment will once again assert its force, but before discussing that final reassertion of sentiment and the banishment of rationality, I would like to further underline the effect on Chesnutt's white readers of Tryon's seesawing between the sentiment of love and the rationality of racism. Tryon is so honorable that he apparently never moves beyond the binary to the third option available in the racist imaginary, the option that he marry his white fiancée and try to convince Rena to be his mistress,[14] the situation in which her mother lived and the situation in the founding narrative of this tradition, Lydia Maria Child's "The Quadroons." Although there is at first some ambiguity about his intentions, by the end of the novel Tryon is again willing to marry Rena. After he and Rena exchange letters, he remains convinced that he "could never marry her," but he is also happy that he has not proposed to Blanche, the white woman who is patiently waiting for him. In a state of radical ambivalence, Tryon is trying to convince himself of the impossibility of marriage to Rena: "He could not marry the other girl, of course, but they must meet again. The rest he would leave to Fate" (177). By the end of the novel, he has come out on the other side and is willing not only to think the unthinkable but to do the undoable. He feels as never before "strongly drawn to the beautiful sister of the popular lawyer," being "driven by an aching heart toward the same woman . . . placed, by custom, beyond the pale of marriage with men of his own race. Custom was tyranny. Love was the only law. . . . There were difficulties—they had seemed insuperable, but love would surmount them." Like a romantic hero, he is now ready to "give up the world for love" (194). Once again Tryon has concluded that racist rationality is unnatural, and he rebounds to sentiment and nature, stating that "custom was tyranny. Love was the only law" (194). Chesnutt wanted the ringing affirmation of love's paramount status to be balanced against Judge Straight's assertion from early in the novel that "custom is stronger than law—in these matters custom *is* law" (23). The statements that "custom *is* law" and that "love was the only law" encapsulate the trajectory that Chesnutt wanted the reader to follow with George Tryon. At the beginning of his experience with Rena, Tryon no doubt would have subscribed to the first assertion as a natural, commonsense belief. By the end of the novel, though, he is in the position of John Warwick (Walden) at the beginning of the novel: both reject custom as tyranny, but whereas Warwick (Walden) rejects it in favor of his ability to cross the color line and rise in the world, Tryon rejects it in favor of love and human connection. The process through which Tryon goes to come to the conclusion that custom is an arbitrary tissue of conventions sanctioned by history and is anything but natural and rational was intended to bring white readers along with him, "imperceptibly, unconsciously step by step to the desired state of feeling" (*Journals* 140). Tryon's experience has allowed him to realize that when custom becomes tyranny, any good American has the right to revolt against it, and his declaration of independence is his newfound faith in sentiment, in the power of love.

In having Tryon reject custom, Chesnutt wanted his white readership to see that love that leads to marriage between persons of different races was a process, as he wrote in "The Future American," that "has already been going on ever since the various races in the Western World have been brought into juxtaposition" (*Essays* 126). However, since custom is grounded in history, Tryon, were he to break radically with it and marry a black woman, would be forced like John Warwick (Walden) to give up his family, his history. Tryon realizes that if he were to marry Rena, he would have to "take her away where they might be happy together" (194–95), to a utopian space outside of history.[15] His action would be a kind of domestic lighting out for the territories. Marriage to Rena, however, would mean that he would have to repudiate his family and his history by exiling himself, as do Howells's characters, Dr. Olney and Rhoda (who is part black), when they emigrate to Italy (where Rhoda is "thought to look so very Italian that you would really take her for an Italian" [234]). William E. Moddelmog has argued that Tryon's decision to marry Rena "constitutes no solution at all" because his "willingness to step outside the law—to overlook Rena's black heritage for the sake of 'love'—offers a solution to the 'race problem' grounded not in the 'value' of blackness, but in its invisibility" (62). Although Rena's ancestry would have to be concealed, the potential effect on Chesnutt's white audience would still have been revolutionary: like John, Tryon is willing to risk what contemporary science tells him is a certainty—atavism—and he is willing to stay in America and amalgamate his white blood with hers.

Despite all his good intentions, Tryon's resolve to marry Rena is belated. When he returns to her house, she has died, almost as if Chesnutt had realized that in the racial climate of the turn-of-the-century United

States he could only tentatively suggest the possibility of amalgamation in fiction. In other words, Chesnutt knew that he gained more tactical advantage with his white readership by not having Tryon marry Rena. Chesnutt chose not to confront his audience with the fact of an interracial marriage, and in so doing, he allowed the possibility for the audience to mourn along with Tryon. In keeping Tryon focused on the binary possibilities, Chesnutt was pointing to a site, in Fisher's terms, of "radical revision" of his audience's expectations. Each time that Tryon entertains the possibility that love and marriage might overcome racism, that sentiment might drive out rationality, Chesnutt is using sentimentality to make permeable the boundaries that the racist imaginary wants to insist are impermeable. Each time he banishes the nightmare vision of the toothless black hag as irrational, he opens up a space for what the culture considers unthinkable, a racial "amalgamation" that is a matter of course. Hopkins finds this matter-of-fact amalgamation in British Bermuda in *Contending Forces*, and Chesnutt argues for it in "The Future American," where he says that race amalgamation is already taking place and will continue to do so as long as "the processes of nature are not too violently interrupted by the hand of man" (*Essays* 125). Of course, Chesnutt realizes that this interruption is exactly what has been written into law throughout America in this period, but he sees these legal proscriptions as deeply unnatural, as part of the effort, through legislation, to make amalgamation impossible and "to degrade the Negro to a distinctly and permanently inferior caste" (*Essays* 133).

Significantly, when Tryon rejects racist rationality in favor of sentiment, he brings another discourse into play—a specifically Christian one, a language of conversion that hearkens back to earlier women sentimental writers. He asks whether "God [would] have made hearts to so yearn for one another if He had meant them to stay forever apart?" Hopkins's white male character in *Hagar's Daughter* resorts to the same language of conversion when he decides to marry a "white negro." After the mixed-race woman dies, the central white character "questioned wherein he had sinned and why he was so severely punished" in the loss of the woman he almost married. The punishment for both these men is to be deprived of their lovers, but Chesnutt demonstrated for his white readership a way out of what he described in *Marrow of Tradition* as "a sort of *impasse*, a blind alley, of which no one could see the outlet" (238–39). Sentiment, then, has done its radical work because when African Americans are no longer barred from the world of sentiment, the work of ideological revision can begin. Early in *The House Behind the Cedars*, Chesnutt wrote that "one part of the baleful heritage of slavery [was] that it poisoned the fountains of human sympathy" (79). Chesnutt found in this novel that what could restore those fountains and act as an antidote was what was most tabooed: love and marriage between men and women of different races. But the possibility of another amalgamated generation can only be suggested in *The House Behind the Cedars;* the genre of the passing novel gains its particular cultural force from the impossibility of a mixed-race marriage and the death of the heroine. Rena must die, and only in her death can George Tryon plumb the depths of his sin. He had earlier thought that the unpardonable sin would have been to marry her; he now realizes his unpardonable sin is to have "ruthlessly spurned and spoiled the image of God in this fair creature" (194). The children, Tryon and Rena, pay for the sins of their fathers, and only through sentiment can white readers fully realize, in the words of Hopkins, that "the sin is the nation's" (*Hagar's Daughter* 283).

III

Central to Chesnutt's attempt to "infiltrate" his white audience is his demonstration of the process, through John and Rena, of becoming white. But before discussing the novel's enactment of whiteness, it is first necessary to situate the novel historically. *The House Behind the Cedars* opens "a few years after the Civil War" (1), and that period is critical because it allowed Chesnutt to represent the process of becoming white within the parameters of what was then existing law. When Judge Straight quotes to John the same South Carolina Supreme Court decision that Chesnutt had cited in "What Is a White Man?" the judge is referring to an

1831 decision. That decision was superseded by an 1879 law in which the legislature decided that anyone with one quarter or more of black blood was Negro; in 1895, that proportion was reduced to one-eighth. So Chesnutt has chosen a historical window between 1865 and 1879 when the 1831 decision was still in effect. He is hearkening back to a period less racially repressive than his readers' present, and he is trying to recover a part of the past that was being erased by the more rigid enforcement of the color line in the era of Jim Crow.

In this interregnum, John can pass into the white world. At the opening of the novel, he is a successful lawyer and plantation owner, and the only possible threat to his success is his African American family. As the narrator says about John, "No one would have acknowledged sooner than he the folly of his visit" (19) to the family from which he has been separated for ten years. If his black family is his point of maximum vulnerability in his new life, then his strange response to his first sight of his sister makes sense. Suspecting who she is, he follows her around their hometown, almost like a stalker, and he sees that she is "strikingly handsome, with a stately beauty seldom encountered.... The girl's figure was admirably proportioned... 'A woman with such a figure,' thought Warwick, 'ought to be able to face the world with confidence of Phryne confronting her judges'" (5, 6). The repetition of the word *figure* in a novel of this period is telling. Such language calls attention to the physicality of the mixed-race woman in a way that would be taboo for a (white) lady. For instance, the narrator in Ignatius Donnelly's *Doctor Huguet* (1891) feels free to comment on the "large" breasts of the mulatta, Abigail (47), as well as on the "full-breasted wenches" (180)—the African American prostitutes at the local house of ill repute, something he signally does not do with the narrator's white fiancée. This language sexualizes Rena in John's eyes from the moment that he sees her, and his classical reference reinforces that sexualization. Phryne was Greek hetaera (courtesan) famous for her nudity. It is said that she was the model for Praxiteles' Cindian Aphrodite, the first major female nude sculpture in the ancient world, and she is also (in)famous for her "confidence ... confronting her judges" (6) when accused of a capital charge. When her lawyer saw that the case was

going badly, he "laid bare her bosom" and the jurors felt "such superstitious fear of this handmaid of Aphrodite . . . they refrained from putting
her to death." She was "more beautiful in her unseen parts. Hence one
could not easily catch a glimpse of her naked" (Athenaeus 185–87), particularly when, in ancient Greece, her nudity is a sign of her not being a wife
or daughter of a Greek citizen, a sign of her inhabiting a liminal status
between wife and common prostitute. Why, then, is John using a classical
allusion to imagine the sight of his sister's bared breasts? Eric Sundquist
claims that "the novel's necessary unfolding of racial sins . . . implies
that, as in Faulkner's world, only an act of incest could finally protect
the family secret" (399). If, in the words of that Mississippi statesman,
"Amalgamation is incest" (Saks 53), then incest between the amalgamated
is the final refuge, the only sure way in which mixed bloods can be concealed. Sundquist argues that "John feels 'something more than brotherly
love' [44] for Rena, a love motivated by her 'Greek sense of proportion, of
fitness, of beauty' [44]" (399).[16] Her Greek stateliness signifies for John
that she could pass for white, for "if she had been homely or stupid, he
would never have disturbed her in the stagnant life of the house behind
the cedars" (44). Her beauty can give her entrée into the white world, but
her intelligence seems to insure for him that she can learn how to become
white, just as her brother has done.

To make her white, John sends Rena off to boarding school, and she
makes her first public appearance at a mock tournament straight out of
Walter Scott. Attending this tournament is Frank Fowler, Rena's childhood protector, whom the narrator describes as "a dark brown young
man, small in stature, but with a well-shaped head, an expressive fore-
head, and features indicative of kindness, intelligence, humor, and imagination" (25).[17] Frank's view of Rena is instructive. He says that if before we
passed she was an angel, now "she looks lack a whole flock er angels" (34).
When Rena comes home to nurse her ailing mother, he feels that she has
grown even more remote: "If Frank felt the difference in her attitude, he
ascribed it to the fact that she had been white, and had taken on something of the white attitude toward the negro; and Frank, with an equal
unconsciousness, clothed her with the attributes of the superior race" (87).

From Frank's point of view, Rena "had been" white (thus illustrating the fluidity of the concept of race within the African American community), even to the extent of taking on a tinge of condescension toward black folks. In terms of Chesnutt's white audience, his acknowledgment of her superiority (even as a mulatto) would of course make cultural sense, but Chesnutt was emphasizing how whiteness can be learned, how it can be enacted. But a skeptical white reader might say that the behaviors of whiteness can be learned, but whiteness can only be imitated, that Rena is a forgery. Chesnutt's answer, like that of his contemporaries Hopkins and Frances E. W. Harper, was to make Rena a paragon; never for a moment is she allowed to deviate from a high standard of middle-class propriety. When Tryon discovers her racial identity, she further reinforces her middle-class status by returning to the African American community to become a teacher in a rural school.

But why it is necessary that Rena fail to pass successfully? I argued earlier that one reason for her failure is generic: in terms of his audience, Chesnutt was less interested in her dilemma than he was in Tryon's, for he wants primarily to affect his readers through his central white character. SallyAnne Ferguson, though, has argued that Rena has to die because of Chesnutt's unacknowledged racism. In terms of his polemical writings, Rena is a failed "Future American," and Ferguson contends that Rena's "greatest fault" is that "she remains psychologically black while trying to pass," retaining "her black qualities after complete acceptance in the white world," which sets her "at odds with Chesnutt's theory of racial development." Instead of marrying white, she "retards the evolutionary process that leads to higher black status in society. Rena, therefore, commits a crime against society when she fails to pass. . . . Her crime—refusal to miscegenate—makes her elimination inevitable. Because Rena does not stop being black, she dies" (78, 82). Ferguson makes much of Rena's ignorance and associates it with what Ferguson terms Rena's psychological blackness, and Ferguson points to the fact that the unraveling of Rena's white identity is a result of her superstition. For instance, Rena has a dream, several nights running, that her mother is sick, and as a result of that dream she returns to her hometown, where Tryon learns that she is black. Ferguson states that Rena's "superstitious ignorance—a stereotypical characteristic of blacks" (78) is what motivates her to go home to her mother, but Chesnutt was very careful to qualify her actions. "No lady in Clarence, perhaps," he writes, "would have remained undisturbed by a vivid dream, three times repeated, of some event bearing materially upon her own life" (62). The word *lady* is racially encoded with the missing adjective *white* in front of it. Thus, rather than acting like a stereotypical black woman, Rena is acting like any woman, black or white, under the impulse of the dream, and rather than castigating her for her inability to cast off her psychological blackness, Chesnutt wants the reader to see that Rena is no different from the genteel white ladies of Clarence.

Ferguson, however, goes even further in her analysis of why Rena fails to pass, pointing to the binary of John and Rena: John, as discussed earlier, is rational and unsentimental; "Rena, on the contrary, seeks a deep, personal fulfillment from a white man that reaches beyond the conventional trappings of race and economic and social success to touch on the soul" (79). Ferguson then says that what Rena craves exists only in the black world of the novel, but I think Ferguson has inverted things. She assumes that John is "the novel's standard for black success" (76), but I think that Chesnutt is quite critical of John and his rejection of family and the feminine world of sentiment (and of his decision to pass, which Chesnutt refused to do). Rena's desire for "deep, personal fulfillment" allies her with Tryon, who, at the end of the novel, acknowledges the supreme force of sentiment. Rena has to die not because she is black and ignorant but because of American history, which had tabooed, against nature, marriage relationships across racial lines—because in postbellum America custom has become law.

If, in failing to pass, Rena is the example of the weight of history that confounds her relationship with Tryon, her brother is the counterexample. In contrast to the feminized Tryon, John is the masculinized man who disappears from the novel because he will never descend to sentiment again, and his disappearance signals his final absorption into the white world and his abandonment of his sister. He obviously will never see his mother again, nor will she ever see her only grandson. But there is also a sleight of hand involved with John's son. Chesnutt has smuggled past his white audience Albert, the son of John Warwick (Walden) and his nameless white wife of good family, almost as if Albert were the answer to Tryon's horror of children that might reveal the characteristics of Rena's "degraded people" (150). John apparently feels no necessity to police or monitor his son for evidence of the "dark . . . strain" of his ancestry. Atavism as a concept does not exist for John, and he is practicing the kind of amalgamation about which Chesnutt wrote in "The Future American" series and hoped would become a matter of course when "distinctions of color shall lose their importance" (*Essays* 135). Ironically, though, one of the distinctions that is no longer in force at the end of the novel is the conceptual category of *mulatto*. As Walter Benn Michaels has pointed out, the novel chronicles the passing of that class: "in *The House Behind the Cedars* [mulattoes] are becoming extinct" (*Our America* 54). Rena dies; John and his son pass into the white world, leaving not a trace; and only John and Rena's mother and Jeff Wain remain. It is as if Wain had become the symbol of the collapse of the class of mulattoes as a separate category, of their absorption into either side of the racial binary. The unintended result, then, of the novel's extinction of mulattoes is the erasure of that class as a strategic marker, the belief among writers of Chesnutt's generation of "what for a brief while will look like the possibility of a breakdown of difference between black and white" (Michaels, *Our America* 55).

At the time of the events of the novel, that utopian future has not arrived, and John's success at passing is predicated on concealment (the same kind that Dr. Olney and Rhoda in Howells's *An Imperative Duty* practice in their expatriation) and on the same lack of knowledge to which Judge Straight alludes in his ruminations about the mixing of racial bloods, "much diluted [or] sedulously concealed or vigorously denied or lost in the mists of tradition, or ascribed to a foreign or an aboriginal strain" (79). The knowledge of concealed ancestry accounts only in part for Tryon's decision, after Rena's blackness is revealed, to collaborate in John's concealment. Tryon writes to John, "I need scarcely assure you that I shall say nothing about this affair, and that I shall keep your secret as though it were my own. Personally, I shall never be able to think of you as other than a white man, as you may gather from the tone of this letter" (103). Even in the first shock of his discovery, Tryon takes a quite unexpected position. Dr. Green, were he in Tryon's place, would have had no hesitation in "outing" John with a self-righteous alacrity. For Tryon, John has successfully passed into the white world, and Tryon is willing, even at this point in the novel, to acknowledge that racial boundaries are fluid. But, of course, he can acknowledge John's abstract right to his whiteness because John does not threaten to pollute Tryon's Anglo-Saxon blood, as Rena does. Like Judge Straight, Tryon is somewhat liberal on this question, and he later acknowledges that in "the past centuries of free manner and easy morals . . . there must have been many white persons whose origin would not have borne too microscopic an investigation" (127). So the representative of the white audience does not contest John's right to his whiteness, and this presages Tryon's declaration toward the end of the novel that he will make Rena white (140). In the end, whiteness, at least for the mixed-race characters and for Tryon, is a social fiction, and Chesnutt hoped that readers had followed him to this conclusion because it breached the racist imaginary and allowed for movement in a system in which racist ideologues demanded firm and absolute demarcations between black and white.

Throughout the novel, then, Chesnutt carefully followed Cable's advice, taking the potential reactions of his white audience into consideration. By suggesting through Tryon's grief the possibility of a utopian space to which Americans could be brought by racial amalgamation, Chesnutt was measuring the historical impossibility of what he would propose a few months after the publication of *The House Behind the Cedars* in "The Future American" series—that the only way out of the binary of racial superior/inferior was racial mixing. And no matter how much success Chesnutt achieved in bringing his white readers into a sympathetic relation with Tryon and Rena, Chesnutt was also forced to admit that there was no such utopian space. In the United States of a hundred years ago there was no way out of the racial trap, and someone—John Warwick (Walden), Tryon, or Rena—would ultimately be forced to disown family and history.

IV

If Chesnutt was successful in his efforts to show the permeability of whiteness in this novel and to counter stereotypes of mulattoes in the figures of John and Rena, he was much less successful with the figure of Jeff Wain, the mulatto who pursues Rena in the latter part of the novel. When Rena returns to her mother's house after being cast off by Tryon, she meets Wain, who is said to be quite well-off, with a plantation, live-stock, a horse and buggy, and a gold watch and chain (131). In appearance he is "light brown . . . the broad mulatto type [with] straight black hair" (133). Rena goes off with him to teach in a local school and discovers that his farm is mortgaged and that he actually owns very little. In addition, she learns that Wain had abused his wife "most shamefully" and that she had abandoned him and her family. Rena begins to suspect "a lurking brutality" (165) in him, a suspicion that was proved true when he "threw his arms suddenly about her waist and smilingly attempted to kiss her." Wain, the narrator is at pains to point out, "had merely meant to declare his passion in what he had hoped might prove a not unacceptable fash-ion" and thus is astonished by her response: she is "speechless with fear and indignation" (166). Since she knows that Wain's wife is alive, "Wain's former conduct took on a blacker significance" (174). In other words, she sees Wain as a kind of sexual predator; she suspects that he has lured her to teach in the local black school so that he can possess her. Of course, his motivation is never clear; the audience perceives him only through her, but her final vision of him is telling. At a crossing of paths in a wood, she sees in one direction George Tryon; in the other, "advancing confidently, . . . she saw the face of Jeff Wain, drawn, as she imagined in her anguish, with evil passions which would stop at nothing" (181). Although the nar-rator is careful to attribute her characterization of Wain to her "anguish," she nevertheless conjures up the possibility of rape.

   Structurally, one can see why Chesnutt needed Wain—the author employs a male figure for each of the social positions theoretically open to Rena: Tryon for the white world, the faithful Frank Fowler for the black world, and Wain for the mulatto world.[18] The question is what effect

Wain's character has on Chesnutt's white audience. Why did he feel it necessary to make Wain a stereotypical villain? Moreover, he is not just any villain, but a mulatto one, and this representation is potent for Chesnutt's audience. And finally, why does he feel it necessary to conjure up, however provisionally, the specter of rape? John Mencke has cataloged some of the qualities associated with male mulattoes in this time, and overwhelmingly they were associated with "moral depravity." One contemporary white writer "insisted that the mixed-blood was 'notoriously sensual, treacherous, and brutal'" (125). Another white writer "cursed the mulatto as the very embodiment of immorality. Mulattoes were possessed by an 'innate depravity' as a result of their conception in the sinful union of a white man and a Negro. How could any sort of moral sense develop in a creature born out of a 'lustful debauch'?" (126). As discussed earlier, Fredrickson has observed that during the time when Chesnutt wrote, "the worst outrages" against white women were attributed to mulattoes (278), and from this perspective, the character of Wain is written formulaically: he is the "burly, grinning mulatto" (149) that Tryon sees when he discovers Rena dancing, the threatening mulatto who proliferates in literary and popular culture representations in these years.

In trying to make sense of Wain's function in the novel, Darryl Hattenhauer argues that the figures of Rena and Wain balance each other. By countering "the melodramatic image of Rena Walden as goodness with the image of Jeff Wain as evil, [Chesnutt] negates both the stereotype of the mulatto as naturally depraved and the image of the mulatto as naturally subservient" (32). I think that Hattenhauer underemphasizes the cultural power of the image of the mulatto beast. It is such a nightmare image (particularly to the extent to which the innately depraved mulatto is identified as a rapist) that it threatens to overbalance Chesnutt's complex structure of audience manipulation. By conjuring up this figure, Chesnutt ran the risk of having his readers see John and Rena as so atypical and unbelievable (in the face of what they would consider Wain's typicality) that his elaborate manipulation of his white audience might implode because his readers might respond to the brother and sister as nothing more than irreal fantasies. If Wain is balanced by anyone in the novel, it is not Rena but her brother, John, who is, like Wain, a mixed-race male character, but John in no way cancels out Wain's cultural force. Chesnutt's audience probably would have seen Wain as a realistic representation, while John would seem too idealized, too far removed from any representation of a mixed-race man that the audience had ever encountered.

Wain disappears from the last two chapters of the novel, but I think his influence lingers as an unresolved problem for Chesnutt. It would seem as if in Wain, Chesnutt were remembering Cable's more problematic advice to exploit "the grotesque, ludicrous, pathetic and barren conditions of colored society" (Cable to Chesnutt, 25 September 1889.) But this may be one place where Chesnutt's concessions to the prevailing literary conventions, concessions to the "preferred fictions of racial life" (Brodhead 210), did him and his work a disservice. He needed a melodramatic villain, and the reading public was already familiar with the leering black rapist of the sort found in Sarah Barnwell Elliott's "An Incident" (first published in 1898 in *Harper's*). The unsuccessful rapist is presented, at the end of the story, as a figure of the "awful problem" (40) of race in America. In confirming, through the figure of Wain, the existence of that awful problem, Chesnutt miscalculated the figure's effect on his audience. Even though Wain was pursuing a woman of mixed racial ancestry, the effect on the audience was going to be complicated because part of the argument of the novel is that Rena can and has become white. In fact, one could argue, almost perversely, that Wain becomes a sexual predator *because* he perceives Rena as white. His reaction when he meets her is instructive in this regard: Rena enters the room, and "Wain stared a moment in genuine astonishment, and then bent himself nearly double, keeping his eyes fixed meanwhile upon Rena's face. He had expected to see a pretty yellow girl, but had been prepared for no such radiant vision of beauty as this which now confronted him" (134). If Chesnutt convinced his audience about the fluidity of whiteness and of racial identity, he was also paradoxically indebted to the stereotype of the sexual predator to reinforce his conception of that fluidity. He needed Wain's sexual rapacity to make his point about racial definitions, but the figure of Wain then worked in the opposite direction to reinforce dominant racial ideology and to confirm what the audience believed that it already knew. Wain thus provided Chesnutt with an inescapable dilemma, almost as if the novel demanded a rapist, who, for reasons of audience accommodation and structure, could not be white. Wain is ultimately a figure out of a plethora of southern fictions of this period—the rapists in Dixon's fictions spring to mind—and Chesnutt found this figure out of racial melodrama both too strong to resist and too difficult to adapt. In the end, the figure of Wain goes a long way toward canceling the force of the rest of the novel—both John and Tryon are atypical in their life choices, in their willingness to undermine current racial orthodoxy; Wain simply confirms that orthodoxy.

In his correspondence, Chesnutt wrote very little about what he was attempting to accomplish in the novel, and he typically was ambivalent in what he did say. In a letter about advertising for the novel, Chesnutt wrote that he did not know anywhere in the United States where "the story of a colored girl who passed for white would tend to cause any great rush for the book." He said that he hoped the book would "sell *in spite of* its subject, or rather, because of its dramatic value apart from the race problem involved. I was trying to write, primarily, an interesting and artistic story, rather than a contribution to a polemical discussion" (emphasis added; *Letters* 149–50). A few paragraphs later, he continued, "I hope that the book may raise some commotion, I hardly care in what quarter, though whether, from the nature of the theme, it will, I don't know. I published recently a series of articles in the Boston *Transcript*, on the same general subject, which brought me a number of interesting letters" (150). Chesnutt seemed to want to have it both ways: the story both is and is not a "contribution to a polemical discussion"; it is simply "interesting and artistic" when divorced from "the race problem involved." This ambivalence seems to speak to the double nature of Chesnutt's ambitions for this novel. He was trying to tell the general audience a good story, one that was generically familiar but was new in terms of its dramatic milieu, but he also wanted the novel to be a subversion, in many ways, of current racial ideology, a contestation of America's formulation of the binary nature of race. This dual focus, of course, is the same strategy he used in *The Conjure Woman* stories, which can be read simultaneously as both confirmation and contestation of the plantation tradition. Most curiously, though, Chesnutt seemed to believe that his audience could separate itself from issues of race ("I rather hope it will sell in spite of its subject"). Chesnutt had to maintain, at this point in his career, a belief in the potential impartiality of his audience—as if readers could abstract themselves from the matrix of American racism and read the novel purely as an engaging fiction. The final interesting aspect of Chesnutt's ruminations in this letter is his desire to "raise some commotion," a sentiment echoed in a November 1900 letter to his wife. He quoted a favorable review and went on to say, "If this keeps up, the book will be a genuine success, and my next book a howling success" (Helen Chesnutt 155). Perhaps the novel, as Andrews notes, was too conventional in generic terms to create his desired commotion, and if he had been hoping for a controversial success with *The House Behind the Cedars,* he was ultimately disappointed. By 1904, the novel had sold fewer than thirty-three hundred copies (*Letters* 214 n.4), and his daughter reported that "although the book had gone into its fourth printing . . . Chesnutt was not satisfied; he had hoped for a much larger sale" (Helen Chesnutt 157). Almost as if making up for this novel's failure to stir his audience, Chesnutt's next novel, *The Marrow of Tradition,* would indeed create some "commotion" as he moved to confront more directly his white audience.

[5]

The Marrow of Tradition

Living to Tell the Tale

Every phase of the southern white view has been ably presented in fiction, and I thought it only fair that the Negro's side should be given a hearing.

—CHARLES W. CHESNUTT

Charles W. Chesnutt clearly failed to create the "commotion" for which he had hoped with *The House Behind the Cedars,* perhaps because he met his readers' generic expectations too well and, as with *The Conjure Woman,* his subversions of genre were invisible to those readers. When he turned to his next fiction, *The Marrow of Tradition* (1901), he tried to create a commotion by moving from representing the relatively distant past to depicting a recent historical event: in Wilmington, North Carolina, on 10 November 1898, an elected city government was overthrown, and African Americans were terrorized and killed by their fellow citizens in an extremely well planned operation that was part coup d'état and part pogrom.[1] In choosing to be more confrontational with his white audience in this novel, Chesnutt had begun to change his conception of that white audience and what he was trying to accomplish with them. Although he was still trying to elevate his white readers, he now sought to do so by presenting them with a counterhistory that he hoped would help them remember what they had been taught to forget.

In February 1971, some seventy years after the events on which Chesnutt based his novel, "Wilmington, North Carolina, trembled on the edge of race war." All of the elements of the race riots of the 1970s were in place: National Guard troops on the streets; snipers firing at police; white vigilantes driving around the city and shooting at African Americans. In the midst of the riot, a white Methodist minister "called a meeting of black and white parents to see whether something could be done to bring peace and find a pathway toward racial reconciliation." During the meeting, the African American parents made "bitter references to 'what happened' and 'what caused all this,'" references that obviously puzzled the white parents in the audience. The minister finally intervened and asked the African American parents, "'When you say, "what caused all this," what are you talking about?' . . . At first, the black parents refused to believe that he [and the white parents] did not know what they meant. Finally, one black mother paused to point in the direction of the Cape Fear River." And she said, "They say that the river was full of black bodies" (Tyson and Cecelski, "Introduction," 3).

Long after the events of that November day, the dynamic of remembering and forgetting persisted across the color line, a dynamic that Chesnutt was at pains to illustrate in *The Marrow of Tradition*. Although the novel has been called one of "the most significant historical novels in American literature" (Sundquist, "Introduction" vii), very little critical work has been done on the novel as a historical fiction. In this chapter, I will be recontextualizing, historically and generically, *The Marrow of Tradition* to try to recover the expectations that Chesnutt's white audience brought to the novel, expectations that had been conditioned both by the reporting of the events in Wilmington in the national press and by the genres of the historical novel and the historical romance. Aware of the popularity of these genres, Chesnutt thought of this novel as a magnum opus, writing to his publishers that he wanted *The Marrow of Tradition* "to become lodged in the popular mind as the legitimate successor of *Uncle Tom's Cabin* and the *Fool's Errand* as depicting an era in our national history" (*Letters* 162).[2] Chesnutt's hopes that this novel would help define a particular historical moment in the popular imagination, however, were disappointed. In a year that saw six novels sell at least 150,000 copies and nine others sell 100,000 copies (Hart 183) and that saw Frank Norris's *The Octopus* sell 33,000 copies (Starr x), *The Marrow of Tradition* sold a grand total of 3,276 copies (Chesnutt, *Letters*, 172 n.4). Reviews in the North were at best mixed (William Dean Howells termed the novel "bitter"), while the reviews from the South were almost uniformly negative. For a writer whose desire was to "mine and infiltrate," this was either a major miscalculation of his audience or evidence of a fundamental shift in attitude toward that white audience.

I

The November 1898 events in Wilmington were widely reported in the national press and remained present in the memory of Chesnutt's audience when *The Marrow of Tradition* was published some three years later. To appreciate Chesnutt's accomplishment and his dilemma in this novel, it is first necessary to examine what happened in Wilmington and how it was reported in major newspapers and magazines.

The long-term origins of the events lie in the election of 1894, which a coalition of Republicans and Populists won throughout North Carolina, ending a period of nearly twenty years in office for the Democratic Party. This coalition was often referred to as the Fusion Party; *fusion* also "had [a] colloquial usage as a term for miscegenation" (Sundquist 409), an unfortunate pun that kept white folks constantly aware of the implicit connection in the racist imagination between political rights and social rights, between the vote and interracial marriage. After the 1894 election, the situation in Wilmington, which had a black majority (11,324 to 8,731), changed quite drastically. Not only did the Democrats lose their political appointments, but African Americans "held considerable political power." Three out of ten members of the board of aldermen were African American, as was one of the five members of the board of audit. "Other public offices held by blacks included justice of the peace, deputy clerk of court, superintendent of streets, and even coroner. The city had two black fire departments and an all-black health board" as well as "a significant number of black policemen and . . . the mail clerk and mail carriers" (Prather, "We Have Taken" 16). In addition, President William McKinley appointed an African American, John Campbell Darcy, as collector of customs of the Port of Wilmington, a job that paid almost four thousand dollars a year at a time in which the governor, "conservative editors often reminded the white public" made only three thousand dollars (Prather, "We Have Taken" 17).

In addition to this conspicuous political and civic presence, Wilmington's African Americans possessed economic clout. For example, the restaurant and barber trades were almost entirely in African American hands. There were more African American boot and shoemakers than European Americans; one of four fish dealers and three of nine butchers and meat dealers were African American, and African Americans were present in significant numbers among Wilmington's other trades and craftsmen (Prather, "We Have Taken" 17). From the perspective of Booker T. Washington, Wilmington was an example of what he had been advocating: the elevation of African Americans through economic uplift. By providing goods and services to the communities that they lived in, African Americans would gradually become accepted by the white community. But Washington's optimism was misplaced.

Wilmington's Democrats formed a group, the Secret Nine, that conspired against the legally elected Fusion city government. The group's objectives were both political and economic: to overthrow the government and replace it with Democrats and to eliminate African American economic competition. In concert with a vicious white supremacy campaign throughout the state, one "unparalleled in American history" (Prather, *We Have Taken* 55), the Secret Nine resorted to the standard argument, going back to Reconstruction, of "negro incapacity" (Foner, *Reconstruction* xx). For instance, one commentator in a national journal, *The Independent*, listed the various offices held by African Americans in Wilmington and concluded, "It is probable that not one of these was qualified to fill his office" (M'Kelway 1490). However, the Secret Nine also used the press to conjure up the image of blacks dominating whites as in

an illustration from the *Raleigh News and Observer*, "The New Slavery" (see figure 1). A tiny white figure, with his hands folded in prayer, implores a gigantic Sambo figure, overdressed with a diamond in his shirtfront. What is even more disturbing about the image is that it seems to be a black figure in blackface, as if the illustrator had to exaggerate the blackness and absurdity of the figure and the only way to do so was to double its blackness. Over the head of the beseeching white figure are the words, "Fusion Office Seeker." In addition, the Secret Nine manufactured a crime wave to scare all whites, no matter what their political affiliation, into racial solidarity. This crime wave, as Laura F. Edwards has written, "was a Democratic creation, whipped up by sympathetic editors who continually printed incendiary reports in an effort to woo white votes. Many reports were fabrications. Some were only loosely based in fact. And others turned black 'insolence' into criminal behavior" (130).

Incapacity and crime clearly did not resonate deeply enough in the white racial imagination, so the Secret Nine brought into play the most potent weapon in their arsenal: the black rapist. "This figure gave the Wilmington racial massacre of 1898 its force; it haunted white women's dreams and pushed white men to reach deep inside themselves to fan a rage that became murderous" (Gilmore 74). The Democratic press seized on an editorial by Alexander Manly, the editor of the city's African American newspaper, the *Daily Record,* which was written in response to a speech of Rebecca Latimer Felton, a Georgia reformer and activist in the United Daughters of the Confederacy, urging southern men to "'lynch a thousand times a week if necessary' to protect white women from black men" (Prather, "We Have Taken" 23). Manly's response as it was reported in the white Democratic press, figures in *The Marrow of Tradition* and consequently needs to be quoted extensively:

> We suggest that the whites guard their women more closely, as Mrs. Felton says, thus giving no opportunity for the human fiend, be he white or black. You leave your goods out of doors and then complain because they are taken away. Poor white men are careless in the matter of protecting their women, especially on the farms. . . . [O]ur experience among poor white people in the country teaches us that women of that race are not any more particular in the matter of clandestine meetings with colored men than the white men with colored women. Meetings of this kind go on for some time until the woman's infatuation or the man's boldness brings attention to them, and the man is lynched for rape. Every negro lynched is called a Big Burly Black Brute, when, in fact, many of those who have thus been dealt with had white men for their fathers, and were not only black and burly, but were sufficiently attractive for white girls of culture and refinement to fall in love with them, as is very well known to all. (quoted in Prather, *We Have Taken* 72–73)

The *Wilmington Messenger* reproduced parts of Manly's editorial every day from 23 August until the election, using capitalization to emphasize its message: "OUR EXPERIENCE AMONG POOR WHITE PEOPLE IN THE COUNTRY TEACHES US THAT WOMEN OF THAT RACE ARE NOT ANY MORE PARTICULAR IN THE MATTER OF CLANDESTINE MEETINGS WITH COLORED MEN THAN THE WHITE MEN WITH COLORED WOMEN" (quoted in Kirshenbaum 12). The Democratic press, however, did not quote the rest of the editorial, in which Manly argued that white men had to learn sexual "purity" and that "it is no worse for a black man to be intimate with a white woman than for a white man to be intimate with a colored woman. . . . [Y]ou cry aloud for the virtue of your women while you seek to destroy the morality of ours. Don't think ever that your women will remain pure while you are debauching ours" (quoted in Prather, *We Have Taken* 73).

The Democratic press's use of this editorial was predictable, and the headlines tell the story: "'Negro Editor Slanders White Women,' . . . 'A Horrid Slander of White Women'; and 'Infamous Attack on White Women'" (Prather, *We Have Taken* 68). It is almost as if this editorial were, in the racist imaginary, the print equivalent of rape itself, as can be seen from a passage from a lengthy article on the events in Wilmington in national magazine, *The Forum:* "Women were assaulted on the streets; and a Negro editor published an editorial defaming the virtue of the poor white women of the South. This fanned the flame of Anglo-Saxon resentment to a white heat." Furthermore, while the paralysis of "business interests" was bad enough, it "did not sting the white blood so savagely as the outspoken contempt of the Negro editor for the white woman's purity" (West 582). Equating Manly's editorial with alleged physical assaults on white women, the Democratic press whipped up a hysteria in the white community, and every day until the election the *Wilmington Messenger* reprinted Felton's response to Manly's editorial: "When the negro Manly attributed the crime of rape to the intimacy between negro men and white women of the South the slanderer should be made to fear a lyncher's rope" (quoted in Gilmore 78). In a climate that, Glenda E. Gilmore writes, had "fully sexualized the home protection campaign" (79), the whites of Wilmington charged that Manly's editorial, "more than anything else, was the catalyst that precipitated the race riot" (Prather, *We Have Taken* 68).

In the days leading up to 10 November, the white supremacy campaign had been so successful in Wilmington that African Americans were frightened away from the polls, and the Democrats won the statewide election. But the Democrats still had a problem: the city's elected Fusion officials had two more years in office. The day after the election, a "White Declaration of

Independence" was issued at a mass meeting and was read to a representative group of "thirty-two prominent African American citizens" (Prather, "We Have Taken" 30). One resolution called for the expulsion of Manly, which, in the superheated racial climate, was to be expected. However, another resolution was quite astonishing in how it openly revealed the motives of the 450 prominent white signatories: "That the negro has demonstrated, by antagonizing our interest in every way, and especially by his ballot, that he is incapable of realizing that his interests are and should be identical with those of the community" (Megivern). This document conjures up "the community" as a (white) solidarity and makes African Americans permanent outsiders to that community. In addition, the "White Declaration of Independence" also recapitulates what happened in the days leading up to the Wilmington events: almost all political and class differences among whites vanished in the face of the threat that African Americans were believed to represent. The Democrats had shifted political differences into racial differences. The representative group of African Americans was given twelve hours to respond to these nonnegotiable demands; the time limit expired, for reasons that remain obscure, with no response. Using that failure as a pretext, some 500 armed, well-organized white men marched into the streets of Wilmington and destroyed Manly's printing press, in the process burning down the building that housed the press. In response to the destruction of Manly's press, African American men assembled throughout the city and the inevitable happened: an exchange of gunfire occurred between a group of African Americans and a group of white vigilantes. After this initial exchange, the vigilantes encountered only sporadic resistance, and when the day was done, the coroner reported that fourteen African Americans had been killed; furthermore, an unknown number of victims had been secretly buried (Prather, "We Have Taken" 35).[3]

While the fighting was still in progress, leaders of the coup d'état went to the city hall and demanded the resignation of the city government. At first, those officials refused, but they soon recognized that the streets were filled with armed men, and, under duress, the mayor, the board of aldermen, and the entire police department resigned and were immediately replaced by Democrats. Having accomplished their political goals, the Democrats turned to the goals that combined political and economic motives. The Secret Nine had a list of prominent Republicans of both races who were to be banished from Wilmington, and the day after the coup those who still remained were escorted by armed guards to the train station, and it was made clear to them that they would be forever unwelcome in the city. After the leadership of the African American community had been removed, the rest of the African American population quickly got the message. Within two years the African American population plummeted, and Wilmington developed a slight white majority (Prather, "We Have Taken," 37–38).

In national terms, the Democrats also realized the importance of representing their point of view to the North, and the Democratic press (which included the vast majority of North Carolina's newspapers) did this very effectively.[4] So effectively did their reporting interpret the events in Wilmington to the nation that "approval, not condemnation, thundered down on the city's vigilantes from white pulpits, editorial pages, and political podiums across the United States" (Tyson and Cecelski 5); this Democratic representation of the events of 10 November "won the day both immediately after the racial killings in Wilmington and in subsequent generations" (Haley 208). For instance, in its reporting, the *New York Times* emphasized that African Americans had been responsible for starting the bloodshed. In a front-page report, the *Times* reporter cited four specific instances of killings, in three of which African Americans were said to have fired first on the vigilantes. Furthermore, the tone of the *Times*'s representation of the coup decidedly favored the revolutionists. The mass resignations the city government in Wilmington were said to have been "in response to public sentiment," and the report asserted that the "entire board was changed legally" ("Nineteen Negroes" 1).

The 26 November issue of *Collier's* national magazine carried a report of the events in Wilmington that was ghostwritten by Charles Francis Bourke for Alfred M. Waddell, one of the central conspirators who became the city's new mayor (Prather, *We Have Taken* 177). Appearing along with Waddell's piece, "The Story of the Wilmington, N.C., Race

Riots," was another article written by Bourke, "The Committee of Twenty-Five," and ten photographs, including one of "Negro Prisoners" being escorted to jail. Both articles offer highly positive evaluations of the Wilmington events, and the one written under Waddell's name has the imprimatur of eyewitness, firsthand testimony. The article published under Bourke's name is the more startling: he claims that the Wilmington "revolution" was a model to be exported throughout the South "in other communities where negro rule is oppressive, and followed by similar revolutions throughout the 'Black Belt' of the South" (5). His reporting was rather bloodthirsty; he wrote of a particular killing: "A 'bad nigger,' running amuck, shot a white man ... and was then given the privilege of running the gantlet for his life up a broad street, where the sand is so deep and yielding it is almost impossible to walk. He was riddled by a pint of bullets, like a pigeon thrown from a plunge trap" (16). In contrast to the article that appeared under Waddell's name, which was quite circumspect about the violence, Bourke's article rather enjoyed representing it; he clearly believed that the killings were entirely justified. He felt it necessary to remind his readers that "a great mass of southern negroes are as utterly ignorant as Hottentots. It is the politician who rouses the slumbering devil in these poor creatures and throws them back to the murderous moods of barbaric Africa" (16).

In addition to the two articles and ten inside photographs, this issue of *Collier's* also featured a cover illustration, "A Scene in the Race Disturbance at Wilmington, N.C." by "Our Special Artist on the Spot," H. Ditzler (see figure 2). Like the article ghostwritten for Waddell, this illustration carried the warrant of eyewitness testimony of the specter of black violence. We know today that no scene occurred during the Wilmington violence like the one Ditzler created; if anything, his depiction shows the reverse of what actually occurred—white vigilantes shooting down African Americans. The whites had almost all the guns, but the illustration foregrounds two African American men, one having fired, one in the act of firing. In the background, another African American with a gun in his hand capers in celebration. Ditzler justifies the actions of the day by representing African American aggression, much in the same way that the conspirators

had used Manly's editorial before the coup/pogrom, by evoking the threat of the black rapist to forge white solidarity.

Along with these representations of the Wilmington events, this issue of *Collier's* contained a number of articles about the results of the Spanish-American War: an article on Puerto Rico, an editorial on "Our Duty in Cuba," a report on the U.S. Navy at the beginning of the war, as well as an illustration of the First Congress of Philippine Insurgents. The article on Cuba contended that the Cubans were not yet ready for self-government and that it was incumbent on the United States to "convince the Cuban people that their true interests lie in a closer relation with the one country upon which their economic dependence is unmistakable" (3). Thus, in an issue that recorded, quite positively, the disenfranchisement of African Americans in North Carolina and advocated the coup/pogrom as a model for the rest of the South, the editorial writers made clear that those "natives" who were forced to join the American commonwealth were also not in the position to exercise any political rights.

Just as revealing is the reporting in the weekly journal *The Independent,* which published an election day editorial, "Peace in North Carolina," that was very perceptive in arguing that the ferment in the state had been about the ballot: "it is not necessary for a negro to take a gun to become dangerous to the peace; a ballot is even worse" ("Peace" 1350). The next issue contained a second, even more trenchant, one-page editorial, the first line of which read, "The outbreak in North Carolina is a crime against the ballot pure and simple [and the] violence inaugurated an illegal city government. . . . In Peru or Nicaragua or Paris we should call this a revolution. It is no less a revolution in North Carolina. We must not think of it as an ordinary outbreak of mob violence. It was a cool, determined, malicious attack on the free government of the State" ("Crime" 1433–34). Based on the analysis by H. Leon Prather Sr. and the other writers included in Timothy B. Tyson and David S. Cecelski's anthology, *Democracy Betrayed,* the *Independent* provided a very accurate reading of the Wilmington events.

In the following week yet another piece on the coup d'état/pogrom appeared in the *Independent,* this one written by the Reverend A. J. M'Kelway, "a leading churchman, humanitarian, and the editor of *The North Carolina Presbyterian*" (Prather, *We Have Taken* 174). This substantial article justified the events in the terms that would become the national consensus. The charge of lawlessness was prominent, but most important was the charge that "white women were insulted on the streets in broad daylight by negro men, and on more than one occasion slapped in the face by negro women on no provocation." He then links these alleged provocations to Manly's editorial: "A negro editor publicly charged to the white women of the South equal blame for that unspeakable crime" of rape, which had, he charged, "resulted in the death of the hapless victim" or in "disgrace worse than death. . . . So the white people began to arm themselves for the protection of their lives and their property and the honor and safety of their wives and daughters" (M'Kelway 1490). M'Kelway had the last word in the *Independent* on the subject of Wilmington; his four pages of detailed analysis outweighs the two editorials in previous weeks (and his article comes with the warrant of native testimony). As Chesnutt said in "The Negro's Franchise" (1901), an article he wrote while at work on

The Marrow of Tradition, "Southerners fill the northern magazines with articles in which they seek to win the sympathy of the North to themselves and alienate it from the Negro" (Essays 166). He also correctly diagnosed the ultimate purpose of articles such as M'Kelway's: "Nothing has seemed more astounding to me than the manner in which the people of the North have passively permitted themselves to be persuaded by the South that the enfranchisement of the freedmen was a colossal blunder" (162). In fact, that was the central thesis of M'Kelway's article, which began by asserting that the "primary cause of the alienation of the two races was the bestowal of unlimited suffrage upon the freedmen . . . in Reconstruction days" (1488).[5]

Ironically, Chesnutt agreed with M'Kelway: the primary cause of the "alienation" *was* whites' refusal to accept the legitimacy of the African American ballot, and the struggle over the African American ballot engaged Chesnutt deeply. Despite his strongly held convictions, he rarely permitted himself public anger, but as Eric Sundquist has pointed out, Chesnutt "took the keenest interest in African American disfranchisement. Perhaps on no other topic was he aroused to such continued passion" (422). The day after the Wilmington coup, Chesnutt wrote to Walter Hines Page and characterized the events as "an outbreak of pure, malignant and altogether indefensible race prejudice, which makes me feel personally humiliated, and ashamed for the country and the State" (Letters 116). Perhaps this stew of feelings—anger, humiliation, and shame—accounts for the fact that when Chesnutt started The Marrow of Tradition two years later, he wrote very quickly, finishing the novel in about eight months (Helen Chesnutt 172). His daughter reports in her biography that Chesnutt went south in February 1901, reading and lecturing, and he visited Wilmington, where he "collected a great deal of material for the new novel. The people there were eager to tell him all the details of the riot" (159). In addition, he got a firsthand report from Dr. Mask, one of the prominent African Americans to whom the "Declaration of White Independence" had been presented (Letters 234 n.2). Chesnutt wrote in 1905 that the subject of the novel "was suggested by a vivid description given me by Dr. Mask . . . of the events of the riot, and a ride which he took across the city during its progress" (Letters 233–34). Given his access to firsthand accounts of the coup/pogrom and his renewed experience of the South, Chesnutt wrote a very different novel from *The House Behind the Cedars,* which is set in the immediate postwar period but studiously ignores the complicated politics of that time. In *The Marrow of Tradition,* Chesnutt presents a historical narrative from the other side, providing an African American account of the Wilmington events. As he said to a reporter from the *Cleveland Press,* "Every phase of the southern white view has been ably presented in fiction, and I thought it only fair that the Negro's side should be given a hearing" ("To Shed").

In writing this historical novel, Chesnutt was creating what one critic has called "his fictional counterhistory" (Finseth 16) and another has called "the counter-memory that revises the official version of history" (Roe 233). As I have written elsewhere, the term *counter-memory* originates with Michel Foucault, but I find George Lipsitz's definition particularly useful: counter-memory is "a way of remembering and forgetting that starts with the local, the immediate, and the personal. Unlike historical narratives that begin with the totality of human existence and then locate specific actions and events within that totality, counter-memory starts with the particular and the specific and then builds outward toward a total story. Counter-memory looks to the past for the hidden histories excluded from dominant narratives" (213). In *The Marrow of Tradition,* Chesnutt has written a counterhistory that resists dominant history and rewrites it in resolutely local terms. Chesnutt's effort in the novel "is counter-writing, part of the extended effort of African-Americans to write themselves rather than being written" (M. Wilson, "Historian" 106). It might at first seem odd to talk about counter-memory and counter-writing in a novel that one critic has termed "aggressively mainstream" (Finseth 9), but Chesnutt not only was writing a hidden history of the events in Wilmington but also was trying to point to certain historical continuities within the African American community as represented by an exchange of positions between two of the twinned characters in the novel, Dr. Miller and Josh Green.

Much critical ink has been spilled in the debate regarding where Chesnutt stands on these events, whether he supports the accommodationist Dr. Miller or the revolutionary Josh Green. Critics of *The House*

Behind the Cedars who have asserted that Chesnutt approves of the behavior of John Warwick (Walden) because he passes successfully make the same kind of argument about Dr. Miller. Miller obviously has more in common with his creator than does the folk character, Josh Green, for both Chesnutt and Miller are part of W. E. B. DuBois's Talented Tenth, the tiny African American professional class at the turn of the twentieth century. Noting the similarities between character and author, Charles Hackenberry, for instance, has written that "Dr. Miller represents Chesnutt's ideal man; Miller is obviously, according to Chesnutt at this stage of his thinking, the model on which members of the black race ought to pattern themselves if they are to ascend to their rightful, equal position before the law and in society" ("Meaning" 195). Hackenberry further asserts that "though Miller is firmly committed to black rights, he, like Chesnutt, is against violence—even in reaction to violence" (196).

From this point of view, Miller is a mouthpiece for Chesnutt. As support for contentions like these, many critics focus on the scene late in the novel where Green and Miller meet, and Green asks Miller to help lead a group of African American men in resisting the marauding white vigilantes. " 'Dr Miller,' cried Green . . . 'we're lookin' fer a leader. De w'ite folks are killin' de niggers, an' we ain' gwine ter stan' up an' be shot down like dogs. We're gwine ter defen' ou' lives an' we ain' gwine ter run away f'm no place where we've got a right ter be; an' woe be ter de w'ite man w'at lays han's on us!' " (281). Miller's response is stark political realism: "We would only be throwing our lives away." Even if Green's group managed to resist for a time, the members would soon be overwhelmed by superior numbers; if they were subsequently captured, they would be sure to hang. "My advice is not heroic, but I think it is wise," continues Miller. "In this riot we are placed as we should be in a war: we have no territory, no base of supplies, no organization, no outside sympathy,—we stand in the position of a race, in a case like this, without money and without friends" (283). If one takes Miller as a mouthpiece for Chesnutt, then he wanted his readers to see Josh's counter-violence as suicidal and counterproductive. Chesnutt knew that in the racist imagination, African American resistance would never be seen as "heroic." Rather, it would be interpreted as a justification for further repression and as evidence of the degeneration of African Americans since the abolition of slavery. As the narrator says after Green and Miller talk, "The qualities which in a white man would win the applause of the world would in a negro be taken as the marks of savagery." Calling "public opinion" "thoroughly diseased," the narrator argues that an African American who died defending his rights would never be admired. In "the white man's eyes, a negro's courage would be mere desperation; his love of liberty, a mere animal dislike of restraint. Every finer human instinct would be interpreted in terms of savagery" (295–96). Thus, in terms of Hackenberry's representative argument, Green's resistance would be doubly condemned as fodder for more racist propaganda, and Chesnutt himself condemned active resistance to white violence. Yet if Chesnutt spoke through Miller and condemned Green's actions, how does one deal with this passage from Chesnutt's 1891 essay, "A Multitude of Counselors," in the *Independent?* "The colored people will instigate no race war," he wrote. "But when they are attacked, they should defend themselves. When the southern Negro reaches that high conception of liberty that would make him rather die than submit to the lash, when he will meet force with force, there will be an end to southern outrages" (82). Sounding very much like Frederick Douglass in his confrontation with Covey, Chesnutt believed that freedom was so precious that one should be ready to die to achieve it or preserve it. It is of course possible that Chesnutt had changed his mind about violence in the years between "A Multitude of Counselors" and *The Marrow of Tradition*, but I see no evidence to support this contention. His passionate commitment to full political rights for African Americans never wavered. In fact, he grew only more insistent on those rights as the political climate for African Americans deteriorated between 1891 and 1901.

So where is Chesnutt in the confrontation between Miller and Green? Is it possible, as some critics have charged, that the author is so ambivalent that he just cannot make up his mind, or is he so enmeshed in his own historical horizon that he is unable to see a way out of the binary structure of accommodation/violence? One way out of that structure might be to look more closely at what Green and Miller say to each other in their several meetings in the novel. For instance, when refusing to lead Green's group,

Miller says, "Dead, I should be a mere lump of carrion. Who remembers even the names of those who have been done to death in the southern States for the past twenty years?" Green's response is highly significant: "I 'members de name er one of 'em . . . an' I 'members de name er de man dat killt 'im an' I s'pec his time is mighty nigh come" (282–83). Here, Green is referring to the killing of his father by the Ku Klux Klan, the subject of the first conversation between him and Miller, early in the novel.

In that scene, Green has come to have Dr. Miller set a broken arm, injured in a fight with one "er dem dagoes off'n a Souf American boat" (109). Miller counsels moderation, saying "You'd better be peaceable and endure a little injustice than run the risk of a sudden and violent death" (110). Green responds that he fully expects to die such a death at the hands of a white man but that the white man will die at the same time. Green asks Miller a crucial question: "Does you 'member de Ku-Klux?" and Miller responds, "Yes, but I was a child at the time, and recollect very little about them. It is a page of history which most people are glad to forget." "Yas, suh," Green answers, "I was a chile too, but wuz right in it, an' so I 'members mo' erbout it'n you does." (110–11). When the Klan killed Green's father, his mother was so traumatized that she never recovered; the children of the town call her "Silly Milly," and she wanders "aimlessly about the street, muttering to herself incoherently" (112). Thus, personal experience of white terror means that Green lives under the injunction to remember, while the more protected Miller remembers "very little." Miller's ideological position is that of historical repression—certain things are best forgotten, the only way to get on in a racist world is to cut oneself off from the past. Therefore, at the beginning of the novel, the positions of the two men are quite clear: twinned in their relation to the past, one says that it is best to forget, the other insists that he cannot forget, a version of the larger racial dynamic in which African Americans could not forget and European Americans were all too ready to forget. But what must be/cannot be forgotten in *The Marrow of Tradition?* The answer is clearly the violence done to Green's family, and although the narrator does not speculate about the reason for the violence, it is fair to assume that the murder of Green's father was part of the Klan's terror campaign waged against Republicans and their African American supporters. This campaign resulted from African Americans having been enfranchised, and Eric Foner has called it a "wave of counterrevolutionary terror" that had no "counterpart . . . in the American experience" (*Reconstruction* 425). Given the trajectory of the novel as it moves into a new era of terrorizing the African American electorate, it is almost as if Chesnutt were saying that Miller is living in a fool's paradise, cut off from the last forty years of African American history.

That history, of course, marks him with its inescapable trauma through the utterly random and poignant death of his son during the coup/pogrom. Green also dies, but his death is quite purposeful: as he tries to defend the African American community, it becomes clear that his group is outgunned and outmanned, and he dies heroically, killing McBane, the white man who had murdered Green's father many years earlier. In the death of Josh Green and in the mass action of taking up arms and self-defense, however, Chesnutt drastically departed from the historical record. He knew that no heroic, collective defense of rights and community had in reality occurred, but he felt it necessary to have a representation of African American agency at the center of his fiction, even though he knew it would be misinterpreted ("Every finer human instinct would be interpreted in terms of savagery" [296]). After the public events of the day are concluded, however, the narrator meditates about their meaning: "The negroes of Wellington [Chesnutt's fictionalized name for Wilmington], with the exception of Josh Green and his party, had not behaved bravely on this critical day in their history; but those who had fought were dead, to the last man; those who had sought safety in flight or concealment were alive to tell the tale" (316). Miller is alive to tell the tale, and as Ian Finseth has observed, "telling the tale, or preserving the history of the event in a way that does justice to the African American perspective, emerges as the more fundamental contribution than the passionate yet futile resistance of the militant Josh Green" (8). I would argue, though, that the trajectory of the novel confirms the importance of both communal memory and resistance. Structurally, at the end of the novel, Miller occupies the position of Josh Green, a repository of memory, a potential teller of the communal tale, which still resonated for the African American inhabitants of Wilmington, North Carolina, more than seventy years later. So instead of an unresolved binary opposition between Green and Miller, there is a process, an exchange, and Green and Miller are constituent elements of Chesnutt's complex double vision—two parts of a whole, necessary components of political discourse for an embattled minority. Chesnutt admired Green's courageous defense of the community as well as Miller's realpolitik assessment of the chances of African American counter-violence, but in becoming someone who can tell the tale of his community through the experience of the death of his son and of his ride across Wellington, Miller moves from seemingly being separated from history to bearing the scars of that history as well as being empowered to tell that story to subsequent generations.

What difference does all of this make to Chesnutt's white audience? If Chesnutt inhabits both subject positions, that of the man who enacts counter-violence and the man who counsels accommodation, how will his audience respond? To the degree to which Miller's ideological position resembles that of Booker T. Washington—an abandonment of overt political struggle—Chesnutt's audience is going to invest in Miller as a character and to excoriate Green, particularly since the violence in Wilmington was reported in the national press as having originated with African Americans. Miller eschews politics, like Washington, and characteristically, as "chief spokesman for black Americans . . . Washington kept silent on the Wilmington controversy" (Prather, *We Have Taken* 158). In fact, the degree to which Miller is acceptable to a white audience is signaled by a conversation that the Big Three (Chesnutt's version of the Secret Nine) have when they are drawing up the list of African Americans and Republican officeholders who are to be expelled from Wellington. In this conversation, Chesnutt foregrounds for his audience one aspect of the Wilmington coup/pogrom that was purposefully obscured in the reporting: that there were important economic as well as political motives at work in deciding who was to be expelled and who was to be allowed to remain. For instance, the African American lawyer is said to be "too mouthy, and has too much business," while the African American real estate agent has been doing so well as to almost drive a white real estate agent into "the poorhouse" (251). When Miller's name is brought up, General Belmont says, "I shouldn't interfere with Miller.... He's a very good sort of a negro, does n't meddle with politics, nor tread on any one else's toes." The lower-class McBane objects, however, because "that sort of nigger ... sets a bad example. ... They make it all the harder to keep the rest of 'em down." Belmont's response is incisive: "a smart nigger without a constituency will no longer be an object of fear" (252). Miller does nothing in the novel to disprove Belmont's assessment, and Chesnutt hoped that his white audience would find Miller's response to the coup and to the death of his only son to be unthreatening and comprehensible. Although Miller does not forgive, he also does not insist on maintaining his rights as a citizen. In other words, through Miller's disavowal of violence and through his pacific response to the Wilmington events, Chesnutt is hoping that his audience would continue to find Miller sympathetic.

In *The Marrow of Tradition*, Chesnutt was in a very complicated ideological position; "he appealed," Jae H. Roe has written, "to the white public, to their humanity and sense of morality; in *The Marrow of Tradition*, however, he thematizes his own disillusionment in the aftermath of the Wilmington Racial Massacre, and the futility of the very project in which he is engaged as a writer" (240). In other words, Chesnutt's white audience was going to see Josh Green only as a threat, a specter of Santo Domingo, a version of Nat Turner; that audience would also perceive the novel's insistence on counter-memory as a rupture in the national move to either forget or romanticize. Chesnutt had begun to realize, in the creation of *The Marrow of Tradition*, that his writing would be ineffectual, and this realization moved him to an unexpected self-referentiality. For instance, when Belmont called Miller "a smart nigger without a constituency," it is easy to see the applicability to Chesnutt himself. Indeed, as Roe has pointed out, Chesnutt writes in the novel that "'the habits and customs of a people were not to be changed in a day, nor by the stroke of a pen,' and later that 'such men are sometimes converted' but only 'in works of fiction' (7, 304). These passages call into question ... the power of writing itself, of the 'high and holy purpose' for which he was supposedly writing this very novel" (238). As Chesnutt worked on this novel (a period that included his trip to the South), his faith in the efficacy of writing began to wane, so that while he felt compelled to record the events from an African American perspective, he also began to wonder whether a counternarrative could ever have the effect he desired on his white audience, which wanted to forget the events he wanted them to remember. Chesnutt began to doubt in *The Marrow of Tradition* whether whites could ever be elevated in his lifetime, whether fiction or writing of any kind could change dominant discourses or people's hearts. To the degree to which he wrote the novel as counter-memory, then, he is much closer to the African American tradition of testimony and tale-telling than he generally receives credit for, but that impulse to preserve the other side of the story brings him into a cultural collision with his white audience.[6] Having read the press reports of the Wilmington events, nearly all of which were positive, his white audience would have been either baffled or enraged at an act that was tantamount to lèse-majesté. In fact, Chesnutt did the same sort of thing here that Manly did in his editorial, assuming that he had the right to enter into discussion in the public sphere with an alternative view of important events, an idea that Chesnutt's fiction challenged. As the narrator represents the Big Three's point of view, he characterizes their attitude toward Manly's editorial: "To meet words with words upon such a subject would be to acknowledge the equality of the negro and his right to discuss or criticise the conduct of white people" (248).

The Chesnutt Papers preserve a review from the *Wilmington (North Carolina) Messenger* that supports my contention that the novel was received in much the same way as Manly's editorial. The review quotes extensively from the *Presbyterian Standard,* which asserted that "the story itself is a tissue of falsehood from end to end. There was material enough in that now historic revolution for a good story on the basis of fact. But the negro's side could not be adequately presented except upon a basis of fiction. . . . [T]he south it seems, has a new kind of liar to deal with, the negro literateur." The *Messenger's* reviewer wrote that this was "the second book in a year that seeks to misrepresent, and pervert the real causes that led to the most remarkable local 'Revolution' that ever occurred perhaps" ("The 'Wellington' Revolution"). So for those on the ground—the whites of Wilmington—Chesnutt was simply a liar, and his ambitious effort to write a historical fiction was nothing more than fiction pure and simple, an account that bore no relation to the actual events.

II

In her review of *The Marrow of Tradition* in the *Atlanta Journal*, Katherine Glover wrote that the novel "is a book that is worthy of being called remarkable because it is on a line that is totally at variance with those on which all that come from his section have been writing." Clearly disoriented, Glover was puzzled by "the general plan of the story itself, which is different" from other novels with which she was familiar, and she proposed an easy solution to the generic problem the novel presented: "Chesnutt should print his picture with his book in order to allow his readers to know whether he is a white man or a negro. . . . If a negro wrote the book his work may in these days be overlooked" (84). For this reviewer, Chesnutt's novel was not "historical" at all; it was nothing more than advocacy fiction and could be "overlooked" because African Americans were always already debarred from the civic realms, their "objectivity" always in question. William Gleason has echoed Glover's sense of the novel's difference from other fictions of its day. "By writing an historical novel—one whose 'history,' moreover, was barely two years old—Chesnutt was attempting something distinctly new" (29). Gleason is not claiming that Chesnutt had discovered a new genre; rather, he is taking the genre of the historical novel and the historical romance in a new direction by adapting it to contemporary events.

In generic terms, Chesnutt's audience had a good deal of experience of historical romance, a form that had become very popular in the years before the publication of *The Marrow of Tradition*. Despite the fact that this literary period is often called the age of realism, Amy Kaplan has noted that "historical romances . . . were the major best-sellers on the earliest lists from 1895–1902, the period of heated national debates about America's imperial role" ("Romancing" 660). For instance, in 1900 half of *Bookman's* top ten best-sellers were historical romances, while in 1901, three of the top ten were historical romances (Mott, *Golden Multitudes*, 213, 214). Although many of these novels were set "long ago and far away," either in invented countries or in the distant past, the interest in the historical romance culminated "in a proliferation of romances about American history, largely revolutionary and colonial, but also including the Civil War and Reconstruction" (Kaplan, "Romancing" 667).

From the beginning, critics tended to interpret this interest in the historical romance in terms of nostalgia and escapism. Howells struck this note in his review, "The New Historical Romances" (1900), inquiring what had happened in "our own case, or the Anglo-Saxon case," that "has brutalized the popular mind and spoiled the popular taste." He implied that "our race, having more reason than ever to be ashamed of itself for its lust of gold and blood, is more than ever anxious to get away from itself, and welcomes the tarradiddles of the historical romancers as a relief from the facts of the odious present" (936). So nostalgia is escapism, "a retreat to a simplified past away from contemporary social strife at home and abroad" (Kaplan, "Romancing" 667). But these novels are also constructing a version of the American past; they turn, in Kaplan's terms, "a potential rupture with tradition into cultural and political continuity, a return to a healthier, more authentic American past" (666). Although Kaplan does not write about any of the Reconstruction novels that fall under the rubric of the historical romance, it is instructive to see how they attempt to bridge what they consider a "potential [historical] rupture" by rewriting the history of the Civil War and Reconstruction.

Two novels, Thomas Nelson Page's *Red Rock: A Chronicle of Reconstruction* (1898) and Thomas Dixon's *The Leopard's Spots* (1902), will serve as examples of how history was rewritten in the historical romance and as examples of what Chesnutt's audience expected from this genre. Both works sold very well and had a large cultural impact. "*Red Rock* was the most significant novel published by a southerner in the 1890s," fifth on the best-seller list in the year of its publication (Bargainnier 44), and it has been called the "clearest and most elaborate fictional description of Reconstruction from the southern point of view" (Gross, *Page* 86). Because of its hysterical advocacy of white supremacy, *The Leopard's Spots* was more controversial than *Red Rock*, but Dixon's novel also was popular, eventually selling "more than one million copies" (Godbold 107). We know that Chesnutt was aware of both Dixon[7] and Page; in a letter to Booker T. Washington written soon after the publication of *The Marrow of Tradition*, Chesnutt wrote that "the writings of [Joel Chandler] Harris and Page and others of that ilk . . . have furnished my chief incentive to write something upon the other side of this very vital question. I know I am on the weaker side in point of popular sympathy, but I am on the stronger side in point of justice and morality" (*Letters* 167). Most critics have seen Chesnutt's linking of Harris and Page as pointing to their performances in dialect plantation fiction. It is interesting, however, that Chesnutt said this a few years after the publication of *Red Rock*, the novel in which Page made the transition from the dialect tale to major historical romance. Chesnutt clearly saw his novel as a response to Page's, as a counter-narrative, a revision of Page's revision of history. *Red Rock* begins in the antebellum period on a note of nostalgia for the "good ole times" of slavery where the plantation of Red Rock is seen as "a sort of feudal domain: the great house on its lofty hill, surrounded by gardens; the broad fields stretching away in every direction, with waving grain or green pastures dotted with sheep and cattle, and all shut in and bounded by the distant woods" (29). This Edenic scene is not disrupted by the presence of slavery, a fact that is reinforced by a slave's disavowal of any desire to be free (41) and by a former slave's indignant refusal, after the war, of any wages for her services. However, what is most interesting about the beginning of this very long novel is the fact that the war itself is not represented. The narrator says that "the part that the men played in the war must be passed over in silence as too large for this history" (49), and the narrative takes up with the return of the defeated soldiers.

The absence of the Civil War from the text is, in Kaplan's terms, the "potential rupture with tradition" that Page tries, heroically, to turn "into cultural and political continuity," a continuity of the tradition of the paternalistic, slave-holding ethic. This is, of course, plantation mythology, but it has been turned to other ends. In the hands of writers such as Page and Harris, the purpose of one of the primary forms of plantation mythology, the dialect story, was, in Chesnutt's words, to "give us the sentimental and devoted negro" (*Letters* 66). By representing old family retainers in their "proper" place, full of deference to their "masters," these writers demonstrated the foolishness of giving African Americans the vote and sentimentalized the ex-slaves as permanent and primitive inferiors. What Page did, though, in *Red Rock* was to turn his attention to the other half of that binary—to the "masters"—working hard to show how, despite their reduced circumstances, they remained the courtly gentlemen that they had been before the war, "exemplars of rectitude and honor" (Bargainnier 47). In addition, these idealized southerners all "desire reconciliation, and so do the honorable men of the North; the obstacles are the carpetbaggers and scalawags who care only for money and power" (Bargainnier 47), men who are "petty . . . without redeeming virtues . . . *not gentlemen*" (50). For instance, Steve Allen, the novel's southern man of action, is centrally involved in the founding of the Klan in his part of the country, but he soon repudiates the Klan and tries to restrain its excesses. The function of the Klan in *Red Rock,* Theodore Gross has written, is "to highlight the noble characteristics of true southerners" (*Page* 92) like Allen, who is the chief antagonist of the subtly named Jonadab Leech, the dastardly, conniving, Machiavellian provost of the Freedmen's Bureau, "a typical carpetbagger of southern fiction" (84). (He and his partner, Hiram Still, are both eventually exposed as criminals, while the southern gentlemen are souls of rectitude.) In representing these southern aristocrats, Page is inventing, as Kaplan put it, a version of "the New White American Man . . . as a tradition [of] an enduringly recoverable past" ("Romancing" 664). Nothing changes these white men—not defeat, not economic ruin, not the loss of their ancestral lands—and they are rewarded in the end: the lands are recovered and all the young folks marry the appropriate partners. And the most important marriage concluded in *Red Rock* is that of Steve Allen and Ruth Welch, a northern woman who has come to have southern sympathies. Of course, their intersectional marriage is meant to represent the healing of the rupture of the Civil War and Reconstruction; her sympathetic understanding of the horrors of Reconstruction is meant to stand in for northern readers, whom Page expected to be just as sympathetic to his account.

The other necessary part of the history of this period is the problem of the former slaves, who inhabit the margins of the text but never become central, as they do in Dixon's work. The struggle for the South is fought over their heads, and they are little more than potentially dangerous pawns in the hands of Leech and Still. However, when the ex-slaves are depicted, they are always potentially disruptive—the African American troops turn into marauders, and on two occasions white women are nearly raped by African Americans. But what is most disruptive is their having the ballot. As Allen says, "We propose to obey the laws, but we do not mean to be governed by negroes, and if you attempt it you will commit a great mistake" (189). When the mistake is committed, Page gives us the standard consensus interpretation of African American rule: when the legislature assembles with a majority of African Americans, they immediately begin to plunder the state, and Leech operates a bar in a committee room, open twenty-four hours a day for eight years, offering "whiskey, champagne, and cigars always free for those who were on his side" (209).

In terms of Page's audience, then, *Red Rock* satisfies the readers' expectation for marriage plots intertwined with the historical events of the novel; satisfies the expectation for "negro incapacity" (quoted in Foner *Reconstruction* xx) both in the ballot and in governance; and most of all satisfies the expectation that southern aristocrats are gentlemen of high honor and morality, long-suffering and patient under the oppression of vicious national policies but manly enough to take the law into their own hands when that oppression threatens the ruin of their section of the South. The critical reception of *Red Rock* was, as one might expect, somewhat mixed; reviewers criticized the problems with the novel (including its inordinate length), but "many of them praised Page for his objectivity and fairness," and while northern reviewers thought the novel overly polemical, "many were sympathetic to the author's views" (94). "Whatever its limitations, however, *Red Rock* achieved its political and literary purpose: [as a contemporary reviewer wrote,] it 'cast a spell strong enough to exorcize Uncle Tom's ghost from all except the darkest, most benighted corners of the land.' The novel was considered by Page's friends and southern sympathizers as the most effective literary refutation of *Uncle Tom's Cabin*" (Gross, *Page* 95).

Dixon's *The Leopard's Spots* also sprang from much the same vexed relationship to Stowe's novel. The impetus to write *The Leopard's Spots* (and two subsequent novels that were part of Dixon's Reconstruction Trilogy, *The Clansman* [1905] and *The Traitor* [1907])[8] also came from *Uncle Tom's Cabin*. Dixon saw one of the innumerable dramatizations of the novel and vowed that he would correct the false story and the "great injustice" it did to the South (Cook 51). Dixon said that his novel "may shock the prejudices of those who have idealized or worshiped the negro as canonized in 'Uncle Tom.' Is it not time they heard the whole truth? They have heard only one side for forty years" (quoted in Bloomfield 392).[9] The connection between Dixon's novels and Stowe's, however, is even more direct; Dixon recycles characters from *Uncle Tom's Cabin*. The son of George Harris plays a minor role in the novel, but the major antagonist of the noble, heroic, honorable southerners in *The Leopard's Spots* is Simon Legree, who, instead of serving in the military during the Civil War, survived "dressed as a German emigrant woman. He wore dresses for two years, did housework, milked the cows and cut wood" (86). A totally improbable feminized villain, Legree is much like the carpetbagger Leech from *Red Rock*. In addition, most of the other elements of the Reconstruction-era historical romance are in place: high-minded southern aristocrats; a nostalgia for slavery; negro incapacity in the legislature;[10] and a long-delayed marriage, but Dixon is more a virulent negrophobe than Page, and *The Leopard's Spots* is hyperbolic in its loathing and revulsion for African Americans. Page tends to suggest the possibility of black violence, while Dixon revels in it, but there is no essential difference between them on the proper place for African Americans—subservient and disenfranchised.[11] There are at least two attempted rapes in the novel and one rape of a little girl, followed by the inevitable lynching. Moreover, Dixon's novel is more overtly ideological than Page's because one of the two main southern characters is a racist ideologue, a Baptist minister who is a transparent spokesman for Dixon.

In historical terms, Dixon brought the novel closer to the present than did Page, and Dixon gave a very quick rendition of the Wilmington coup/pogrom. In his typically hyperbolic version of history, the five hundred white men who went to burn out Manly's press were ambushed by "a mob of a thousand armed Negroes [who] concealed themselves in a hedgerow and fired on them from ambush, killing one man and wounding six" (417). Dixon, however, briefly represented the Spanish-American War, which he saw as a moment of superb national unity. All differences— sectional, religious, and class—were transcended, and "most marvelous of all, this hundred days of war had reunited the Anglo-Saxon race" (412). Samira Kawash has commented that the "Spanish-American War symbolically completed the project of reunification by joining North and South in a specifically national struggle against a common enemy. Similarly, the instigators of the Wilmington riot aimed to restore white supremacy by joining the various factions of white society in Wilmington against the 'external enemy' of blackness" (93). Dixon made explicit the fact that African Americans had no place in the reunited States of America, writing that during the war, African American troops had served well only when they had had white officers; African American troops were, he claimed, "the source of riot and disorder wherever they appeared. . . . [I]t was seen by thoughtful men that the Negro was an impossibility in the new-born unity of national life" (413).

At this moment in history, these three different cultural/historical elements fuse and work in tandem in a nexus of representation of African Americans. The historical romance of Reconstruction makes clear that African Americans were at best utterly incapable of governing and at worst an ever-present threat to white womanhood. The consensus on the Spanish-American War (as reflected in Dixon and in Theodore Roosevelt's account, first published in *Scribner's* in April 1899 [Kaplan, "Black and Blue" 220]) was that African American troops did not fight well and thus had demonstrated once again that they could not be included in the American polity and that the "varied assortment of inferior races" that Americans had acquired in the Spanish-American War, "of course, could not," the *Nation* opined, "be allowed to vote" (quoted in Davenport 353). The consensus on the events in Wilmington was the southern point of view, and the nation supported the disenfranchisement of African Americans. Chesnutt, then, faced an impossible task as he wrote his Wilmington novel. Racist ideologues saw Wilmington as the continuation of the struggle against Reconstruction, and white violence was regarded as a legitimate response to African American political aspirations. Every time, then, that African Americans made gains through the ballot or through economic success, they were accused of terrorizing whites. This terror was, during Reconstruction, seen in the image of the marauding members of the Union Leagues and in Wilmington was seen in the image of Manly's insult to southern womanhood as well as in a host of constructed insults to white pride. So when Chesnutt wrote a novel from an African American perspective about these events, he would be seen, particularly by southern critics as well as by many northerners, as writing a fiction that claimed historicity but had no basis whatsoever in history. Conversely, Chesnutt was convinced of the profound historical truth of the novel, and as a warrant for that historicity he and his publisher, as discussed earlier, connected *The Marrow of Tradition* to *Uncle Tom's Cabin*. In generic terms, as Richard Yarborough has written, "One is struck not that Chesnutt felt obliged to describe *Marrow* in these terms but that he expected this approach to work. The average white reader who approached *Marrow* as a typical plantation tradition tale or as a latter-day *Uncle Tom's Cabin* was in for a serious shock" (245). Yarborough then quotes from a review of the novel by T. Thomas Fortune, who wrote that "it would not be surprising if this book should work some such revolution in public sentiment as 'Uncle Tom's Cabin' wrought" (246). With its meager sales, Chesnutt's novel did not accomplish such a revolution; the change in public sentiment and conviction had already been accomplished and was all on the other side, with novels such as Page's and Dixon's.

III

Although Chesnutt had represented a wide range of white characters in his first two white-life novels, he only gradually moved to depicting a wide range of white "types" in his race fictions. When he turned to the events in Wilmington, his representation of the machinations of the major conspirators meant that he needed to widen considerably his range of white representation, and the novel is replete with white characters—more white characters, in fact, than African American. In this section, I will examine Chesnutt's dilemma as an African-American writer creating white characters for a largely white audience, a dilemma that can be illustrated by the response to *The Marrow of Tradition* by the editor of the *Independent,* a journal in which Chesnutt had published and that had been somewhat sympathetic to African Americans.

In the *Independent's* review, the novel was characterized as "vigorous and vindictive to a remarkable degree" ("Literature" 87), and Chesnutt's publisher wrote to the editor of the *Independent* in protest. In justifying the review, the literary editor, Paul Elmer More, wrote that "Chesnutt had done what he could to humiliate the whites" (quoted in Farnsworth xv). Remarkably, this sentiment has resurfaced in some recent criticism. For instance, in a review of a book on Chesnutt's short fiction, Robert C. Leitz, one of the coeditors of Chesnutt's letters and of his essays and speeches, takes the author to task for underestimating his animus: "Chesnutt's social/racial agenda . . . was often mean-spirited and written with an eye toward getting even with his 'mostly white' readers" (272). Other critics have also castigated Chesnutt for what they consider to be his overreliance on stereotypes—in his depiction of the white-identified African-American characters and in his depiction of almost all of the novel's white characters.

I would argue, though, that in deploying racial stereotypes, Chesnutt is first turning typical practice on its head: readers had come to accept without question the deployment of stereotypes by white writers about racial Others. Chesnutt turns the gaze back onto the white audience and quite deliberately manipulates his white characters as racial stereotypes. In so doing, Chesnutt invented what Stephen Knadler has defined as "a new strategy of disruption: an investigation of the imagined 'white' American" (428). In a very perceptive passage, Knadler goes on to say that Chesnutt intended "to deprive [his white readers] of the privilege of whiteness. Because part of the white man's power lay in his denial of his racial identifications, *The Marrow of Tradition* positioned Anglo-American readers so that they would be compelled to ponder the unnaturalness of their race." Chesnutt was forcing his white readers "to stand in the literary marketplace, as not the makers of history and science, but as objects gazed upon, studied, and assessed by the African-American subject" (429). Chesnutt accomplished this in part by having all of his African-American characters, particularly those who are white-identified, such as Jerry and Mammy Jane, reflect on the white folks' goings-on. Chesnutt used a variety of techniques to insure that his white readers understood that they were the objects of study and speculation on the part of African-American characters. This study can take place in Mammy Jane's ruminations on the Carteret family history that open the novel or in the reflections of her grandson, Jerry, on the strange ways of the Big Three, whom he takes as representatives of the "Angry Saxon race" (90). In employing this technique, Knadler writes, the novel forced its white readers "to see themselves as an Other (and not always an envied one) within the imaginary life of African-American men and women" (435).

In a very revealing passage in a review of Booker T. Washington's *Up from Slavery*, Howells, for one, seemed to suspect the possibility that African Americans might be doing just that—studying and judging white folks. He wrote that "the problem of the colored race may be more complex than we have thought it. What if upon some large scale they should be subtler than we have supposed? What if their amiability should veil a sense of *our* absurdities, and there should be in our polite inferiors the potentiality of something like contempt for us? The notion is awful, but we may be sure they will be too kind, too wise, ever to do more than let us guess at the truth, if it is the truth" ("Exemplary" 196–97). Howells was right, and he and Chesnutt's audience confronted in *The Marrow of Tradition* the "awful" truth of the judgment of a "polite inferior." In taking on the lens of realism and focusing it on his audience, by making his readers the object of the artistic gaze, Chesnutt destabilized them in a way that he had been careful not to do in *The House Behind the Cedars*. By 1901, the reading public was quite familiar with the gaze being turned to America's Others, but those readers were not used to being judged by one of those who belonged to that class of Americans who were written about in local color. In speaking back, Chesnutt takes on the cultural authority of realism, and his judgment of his white characters is seen as a "humiliation" of whites. In Susan Donaldson's terms, Chesnutt's "responsibility, as he saw it . . . was to disrupt the steadiness of the ethnographic gaze under which he himself fell and expose nineteenth-century categories of race for the complicated and compromising fictions they were" (70). The ethnographic gaze was the sort that was constructed at the various world's fairs in this period,[12] and Chesnutt specifically evokes this gaze early in the novel when he conjures up a "celebrated traveler" who had lived "many years . . . in barbarous or savage lands" and who said "that among all varieties of mankind the similarities are vastly more important and fundamental than the differences" (49). From the beginning, Chesnutt signaled that he was consciously inverting cultural common sense. In an era that insisted that racial differences were profound and ineradicable, Chesnutt countered that common humanity was more important than surface differences. In the scene where Chesnutt conjured up the celebrated traveler, he used this gaze to describe two characters, one black (Dr. Miller) and one white (Dr. Burns), who are more similar than different to the ethnographic gaze, but to "the American eye" (49) all of their similarities in training and cultural capital are trumped by the transcendent difference: "the first was white and the second black, or, more correctly speaking, brown" (49).[13] Chesnutt's evocation of a non-American ethnographic gaze has, however, wider application in a novel in which he wanted to reverse that gaze, to turn it on white folks, and to show, allying himself with the tradition of sentimental protest, that our similarities are more important than our differences, that all Americans, within their individual classes, are fundamentally the same. So not only did Chesnutt want to make his white characters the subject of black inquiry, but, by carefully situating his characters historically and generically, he also wanted simultaneously to upset his readers' expectations (by seeing whites from an alternative point of view) and to give them a sense of purchase through some familiar racial "types" (the southern aristocrat, for instance) in a terrain that Chesnutt knew that his readers would find deeply disturbing, the terrain of recent historical events depicted from an African-American point of view. Structurally, he gave his audience three generations of white folks and three of African Americans: the pre–Civil war survivors, a generation that came to its majority during the war, and the subsequent generation. For the white characters, old Delamere is the pre–Civil War survivor; the Big Three—Major Carteret, General Belmont, and McBane—are the generation defined by the war and Reconstruction; and the next generation is represented by Ellis, the city editor on Carteret's newspaper, Tom Delamere,[14] and the Carterets' new baby.

Old Delamere represented for Chesnutt the best of the Old South and is the character designed to give Chesnutt's white audience a sense of generic familiarity. Plantation fiction was replete with characters like Delamere: good paternalists who hold strictly to a code of honor, good masters who attempt to mitigate the severities of chattel slavery. For instance, Delamere has a servant, once his slave, Sandy, and Sandy recounts how, when his father, who apparently lived on another plantation, was about to be "sol' away f'm his wife an' child'en," Delamere "bought him an' dem, an' kep' us all on [his] place tergether" (207). While establishing Delamere as a familiar trope, however, Chesnutt also pushes the logic of the character, of the aristocratic attitude, in such a way that he begins to undermine the stereotype, entitling the chapter in which Sandy tells this story to Delamere, "Two Southern Gentlemen." Sandy has been wrongfully accused of murder and possibly of rape in the commission of burglary, and Delamere has come to try to save his servant from lynching. The chapter is almost an illustration of what Delamere said to Dr. Miller: "I really believe . . . that Sandy has the family honor of the Delameres quite as much at heart as I have" (198–99). In "Two Southern Gentlemen," Sandy is put into a impossible situation: he was discovered with some gold coins that were seen as prima facie evidence of his guilt, since the murdered woman, Polly Ochiltree, was known to have a store of old gold coins. Sandy received the coins from Delamere's grandson, Tom, and Sandy knows that Tom, in blackface,[15] has probably robbed and murdered his aunt, but Sandy refuses to speak, at the risk of his own life, to preserve the family honor, which Tom already has lost. Sandy's performance thus faces two ways. On the one hand, it signifies that African Americans can be educated to the class distinctions of the aristocracy, while on the other it signifies an alternative white position. When he exclaims, "Why, I raised that boy!" (198), Old Delamere signals that he believes Sandy incapable of such a crime because he has been imbued with a sense of morality and honor, something that racist ideologues like Major Carteret refuse to believe that former slaves or their descendants can possess. Such whites believe that Sandy, like Rena, is an imitation—his manners, morality, and honor are little more than a badly applied veneer, a word that is echoed in the reflections of the least racist white man in the novel, Ellis, who comes from a nonslaveholding Quaker family. When Sandy is accused of having robbed and killed Polly Ochiltree, Ellis reflects the racist imaginary: Negroes, he thinks, "were as yet a crude and undeveloped race. . . . No one could tell at what moment the thin veneer of civilization might peel off and reveal the underlying savage" (119). Chesnutt is primarily trying not to disprove this racist myth but to reflect accurately the depth of nonideological racism (like George Tryon's) and to think about the veneer of civilization in general (a point to which I will subsequently return).

By having Carteret assert the belief that morality and honor can be possessed only by white men, Chesnutt establishes the grounds for a critique of these ethical claims. Carteret has just cautioned Polly Ochiltree not to discuss in front of Sandy the money she keeps hidden in a chest in her house, and Delamere objects: "'Sandy is as honest as any man in Wellington.' 'You mean, sir,' replied Carteret, with a smile, 'as honest as any *negro* in Wellington'" (24). From early in the novel, then, Chesnutt distinguishes between old Delamere and Carteret, the latter a symbol of a hardening of racial lines in the post–Civil War period. For Carteret, a negro cannot be a man; racist ideologues see manhood as a constituent element of whiteness. Delamere, in contrast, not only is willing to grant Sandy his manhood but goes even further by asserting that "Sandy is a gentleman in ebony!" (25), whereas Carteret had insisted earlier in the novel that the terms "gentleman" and "white man" "should be synonymous" (73). Even with the most stereotypical of the white characters, Chesnutt was manipulating his white audience, which would tend to take Carteret's position on the issue of manliness. However, Chesnutt was also demonstrating that attitudes like Delamere's were anachronisms in late-nineteenth-century America: the only way that Delamere can save Sandy is by committing perjury, declaring that he was with Sandy at the time of the murder. And the novel records, in Delamere's death, the extinction of the old paternalist ethic.

What replaces that ethic in the next aristocratic generation, represented by Carteret and General Belmont, is ideological racism. Chesnutt used these stereotypical characters—particularly Carteret, who is more fully developed than Belmont—to undermine the plantation tradition. Like his peers in the novels of Page and Dixon, Carteret is a good man in many ways. The narrator states that Carteret "had always tried to be . . . just" (320); he has a finely honed sense of honor, is a loving husband and father investing wisely for his child's future, and is a competent newspaper editor. Like many of his white counterparts, however, he is also a vicious negrophobe, so driven by his hatred that his political machinations begin to erode his private morality, an idea the Chesnutt explored throughout *The Marrow of Tradition*. For instance, the *Cleveland Press* quoted Chesnutt as saying, "I believe that any wrong which a strong race may inflict on a weaker one will react on its own character and civilization. I have tried to make this clear in 'The Marrow of Tradition'" ("To Shed"). In the novel, Chesnutt made his indictment of the public "wrong" of the Wellington events, but in representing the events leading up to the coup/pogrom, Chesnutt used the Manly editorial in particular to show how the fiction of whiteness was manufactured and how that whiteness was employed to create a solidarity that transcended political and class differences. For instance, Manly's editorial was employed tactically: it was set aside until the conspirators felt that time was right to use it to maximum effect as justification for the disenfranchisement campaign and for the overthrow of the Fusion government. In other words, Chesnutt represented these events as highly calculated and well organized, not as a spontaneous overflow of white indignation.

From the point of view of Chesnutt's white audience, all of this would have been disturbing (perhaps unbelievable) enough because it contradicted the consensus view of the events in Wilmington, but Chesnutt went further in his depiction of the civilization of the South. The events of the novel, in its private plots, demonstrate that political immorality begins to leach over into the private realm. For instance, when Delamere comes to Carteret and reveals that Tom has robbed and murdered Polly Ochiltree, Delamere wants Carteret immediately to publish Tom's guilt, but Carteret hesitates because the "white people of the city had raised the issue of their own superior morality, and had themselves made this crime a race question. The success of the impending 'revolution,' for which he and his *confrères* had labored so long, depended in large measure upon the maintenance of their race prestige, which would be injured in the eyes of the world by such a fiasco" (227–28). Carteret realizes that a retraction of the story of Sandy's guilt and the admission of Tom's would have national repercussions by throwing "a cloud of suspicion upon the stories of outrage which had gone up from the South for so many years, and had done so much to win the sympathy of the North and to alienate it from the colored people. The reputation of the race was threatened." Carteret decides that Sandy must not be lynched, but "for the credit of the town, its aristocracy, and the race, the truth of this ghastly story must not see the light,—at least not yet" (228). Tom Delamere leaves town, and there is no indication in the novel that he will be charged with burglary or with murder. More important for Carteret (and for Chesnutt's audience) is the preservation of a fiction: African Americans are always already the criminals, while the white aristocrats are always already innocent, and any inconvenient facts that might tend to contradict that fiction must be suppressed. Their prior innocence and their absolute conviction of their own self-righteousness allows the guilty to go free and allows them in good conscience to overthrow an elected government.

Chesnutt's analysis of the corrosion of the moral standards of the aristocrats goes beyond the suppression of private scandal. Before old Delamere dies, he changes his will, disinheriting Tom Delamere and leaving the bulk of the money to Dr. Miller to endow his new hospital. Carteret and Belmont suppress that will, justifying their actions by claiming that "Mr. Delamere's property belonged of right to the white race, and by the higher law should remain in the possession of white people" (235). The conspirators never define the term "the higher law," but it is used in a number of instances to justify their decisions—for lynching (186), for setting aside the U.S. Constitution (240), and for preserving "the purity and prestige of the white race . . . at any cost" (259). The "higher law" of "race instinct" was commonly invoked, Nell Painter has observed, as a principle that transcended "mere legislation . . . or the Constitution."

"'Race instincts' more powerful than law decreed the protection of Anglo-Saxon civilization by any means necessary, white supremacists argued, and the same imperatives of race made blacks unfit to vote. 'The evil is in the blood of races,' John Temple Graves of Georgia concluded, and 'the disease is in the bones and the marrow and the skin of antagonistic peoples'" (167). For racist ideologues, the differences between the races—fundamental and irradicable—were literally in the blood and the marrow, while for Chesnutt those differences were social constructions—in the marrow of the tradition used to provide justification for the use of terms such as *the higher law*. The higher law was then a transcendent principle that could be used to rationalize any illegal or immoral behavior on the part of white folks; any violence, any action, public or private, could be countenanced by resorting to this explanatory principle.

Most often, in the nineteenth century, as Gregg D. Crane has argued, the term *the higher law* was used to appeal to principles above and beyond laws and the Constitution. For instance, in the debates over slavery before the Civil War, Senator William H. Seward gave a speech in which he "denied 'that the Constitution recognizes property in man'" asserting that "the nation's charter must heed 'a higher law'" (Crane 13). Crane goes on to assert that the "higher law tradition invoked by Seward to read slavery out of the Constitution is complex . . . but the core idea is constant and may be expressed . . . simply: to be legitimate, law must be just" (13). The concept of the higher law clearly gave ammunition to the abolitionists before the war and to men such as Frederick Douglass who continued the struggle against the deprivation of African American rights after the war. Chesnutt has cleverly inverted the use of the "high law tradition": the conspirators invoke the "higher law" of race, not the higher law of abstract justice. If, as Crane argues, "higher law constitutes the ultimate critique and authorization of the American legal system" (19), then it can be hijacked by racist ideologues to overthrow an elected government or the Constitution. In that sense, Chesnutt saw the conspirators as a deadly threat to the civic compact that united Americans.

In examining the nexus between public and private morality in Carteret, Chesnutt was demonstrating that civility and honor were not as deeply ingrained in southern white men as their apologists would have the rest of the country believe. After the coup/pogrom, the narrator reflects that "our boasted civilization is but a thin veneer, which cracks and scales off at the first impact of primal passions" (310). Chesnutt deftly turned the tables here by pointing to the "veneer," a term that he had used in *The House Behind the Cedars* to describe how "blackness" would always (in the view of most Americans) reveal itself. Here, he was not claiming that whites were more prone than any other racial group to violence and the subsequent breakdown of the social compact. What was at stake in the events of Wilmington was "*our* civilization," which was put at risk when racist ideologues inflamed race hatred, and he illustrated how that cultivation of hatred inevitably corrupted the private lives of the white aristocrats. This, of course, was not a tactic designed to endear Chesnutt to his audience or to make the novel more accessible to them. In an era filled with honorable, upright southern aristocrats, an exposure of this sort, the ethnographic gaze reversed, was going to profoundly unsettle his audience.

The third generation of aristocrats in the novel is represented by Tom Delamere, and Chesnutt's exposure here might at first be seen as more conventional. Eric Sundquist's discussion of the function of the character of Tom is definitive, particularly in terms of his blackface disguise and his performance of the cakewalk, and as Sundquist notes, Tom is a figure who echoes "Twain's Tom Driscoll in *Pudd'nhead Wilson,* in both his weak character and his overt role as a racial double" (*To Wake* 431). While the figure of the degenerate aristocrat is rather conventional in African American narratives of this time, white degenerates like these were employed, Sundquist notes, in dialectal relation to the discourse of black degeneracy. By emphasizing "the obvious degeneration of the Old South's aristocratic descendants, particularly Tom Delamere," Chesnutt undermines "the concept of pure blood." This degenerate white aristocrat is an inverse mirror of "the common charge that postbellum blacks and especially mulattoes were a retrogressive or 'degenerate' species, likely without careful regulation by white civilization to revert to the purported savagery of their African ancestors" (408). Tom's degeneracy is, however, more than a stereotypical plot device or a strategic move; Chesnutt seems to be implying that the figure of Tom is the logical outgrowth of a system that justifies everything by recourse to appeals to the "higher law." Growing up in a period when white men justified all their actions by recourse to the higher law of white supremacy, Tom is Chesnutt's illustration of the moral slide inherent in racial ideology.

As Sundquist points out, Tom is feminized throughout the novel (431), but nowhere more so than in his exposure in his club as a gambler. Expelled from the club and owing fifteen hundred dollars in gambling debts, Tom "touched a depth of scoundrelism far beyond anything of which he had as yet deemed himself capable. When a man of good position, of whom much is expected, takes to evil courses, his progress is apt to resemble that of a well-bred woman who has started the downward path" (165). On his way to moral prostitution, Tom conceives a plan to rob his aunt, Polly Ochiltree, and Chesnutt does not represent Tom's deliberations or any of his planning before the robbery, but Tom has started on the downward path of class as well, and he has become a figure close to McBane, the third of the Big Three. McBane's class background is suspect—his father was an overseer—and he is less apt to use circumlocutions than either Carteret or General Belmont. When the three are discussing who is to be expelled from Wellington after the coup, McBane accuses the other two of hypocrisy and justifies whatever actions are deemed necessary: "'This is a white man's country, and a white man's city, and no nigger has any business here when a white man wants him gone.' Carteret frowned darkly at this brutal characterization of their motives. It robbed the enterprise of all its poetry, and put a solemn act of revolution upon the plane of a mere vulgar theft of power" (252–53). Tom has been taught, like McBane, that those who possess power use it; those who have power have the justification to put aside all moral scruples and even ties of affection. Tom (and the neurasthenic Olivia, to a certain extent) are the logical outcomes of American racist ideology—it is not that Olivia is inherently hysterical or that Tom is inherently criminal but rather that their development is the logical outcome of an environment in which, as a result of racial ideology, all "moral standards . . . were hopelessly confused" (271).

After his exposure of Carteret and Tom Delamere, though, Chesnutt has yet another complication of the racial plot in the private realm. During the riot, Carteret's young son comes down with a life-threatening illness. The African American servants have run away; the doctors, except a very young trainee, are unavailable; and the only doctor who can save the boy is Miller, whose own son has been killed by a stray bullet in the course of the riot. Carteret's wife, Olivia, sends him to plead with Miller to come and operate on their son, but Miller refuses, telling him that the death of Carteret's son will balance the scales of justice, that the death of Miller's son is the direct responsibility of Carteret and his campaign against "negro domination." And Carteret's response is a central moment in the novel: "In the agony of his own predicament . . . for a moment the veil of race prejudice was rent in twain, and he saw things as they were, in their correct proportions and relations." Carteret sees Miller's refusal as "pure, elemental justice. . . . He was . . . conscious of a certain involuntary admiration for a man who held in his hands the power of life and death, and could use it, with strict justice, to avenge his own wrongs. In Dr. Miller's place he would have done the same thing" (321). This is, of course, the same rhetorical move as in Tryon's final revelation in *The House Behind the Cedars*. In the face of Rena's death, Tryon could judge his sin against her, and by implication, the sin of prejudice against all African Americans. Here, the veil "rent," Carteret exists, "for a moment" outside of the racialized world in which he has always lived, and he can admire Miller not as an African American but as a man. Even more startling, Carteret can momentarily imagine himself as a black man. As one might expect, many critics have commented on this moment. For example, Michelle Wolkomir has written that Carteret "transcend[s] the boundaries of race and social tradition and [is] able to perceive the other as equally human. Therefore, within Chesnutt's theory on social change, this resolution must be considered optimistic" (255). To classify the ending as optimistic, however, is to miss the profound differences between *The Marrow of Tradition* and the guardedly optimistic *The House Behind the Cedars*. While Tryon can perceive things outside of a racialized matrix, his decisions are based on the concealment of Rena's African American ancestry and are entirely in the private realm. In contrast, Carteret's unracialized vision here is characterized as momentary, and in the face of the violence done to the African

American community, one wonders how quickly the rent veil will be mended. Perhaps, in *The House Behind the Cedars,* Chesnutt still believed in the transformative power of such moments; in *The Marrow of Tradition,* he seemed more skeptical about the durability of conversions or "moral clarification[s]." Not only had Chesnutt revised his early idealism, he had also written a novel that called into doubt fiction's ability to accomplish any social change in the face of deeply entrenched racism. In writing the novel, he was setting out the case, all the time doubting whether that case, in any form, either polemic or fiction, could change hearts or minds.

If there is optimism in the novel, it may exist in the final line. Miller's wife has given him permission to operate on Carteret's son, and as Miller enters the front door of the house (the first African American ever to do so), he hears the voice of the trainee doctor from the top of the stairs: "Come on up, Dr. Miller. . . . There's time enough, but none to spare" (329). Critics have read this as Chesnutt's extremely guarded optimism: if we are to read this statement in terms of national allegory, the patient is seriously ill but still can be saved by major surgery. The problem with a reading that imputes such optimism is that it is contradicted by the events of Wilmington: there were no small victories for the African American community on that day, as Chesnutt knew. Why does a novel that was largely faithful to the historical record[16] end on this most marginal of positive notes? Perhaps Chesnutt's analysis had brought him to too bleak a prospect; perhaps he wanted to continue to believe (despite the logic of his novel) that significant changes could take hold in the white Americans' consciences. Perhaps he sees this as the smallest of incremental changes, but what is the lasting effect of a change coerced by extraordinary circumstances? This question is particularly important because earlier in the novel, when the possibility of Dr. Miller entering his house first arises, Major Carteret thinks, "If the negro's presence were indispensable he would even submit to it" (72). That attitude differs little from that of the northern doctor who came South earlier in the novel to operate on the child: "We have our prejudices at the North, but we do not let them stand in the way of anything that *we* want" (69). Carteret's prejudices do not stand in the way of his desire to save his son's life, so what seems at first optimistic is little more than an acknowledgment of the force of circumstances, but it is also perhaps a sleight of hand on Chesnutt's part, giving his white audience some small hope for reconciliation at the end of the novel.

One way of thinking about the meaning of this highly ambiguous conclusion is to look at the two alternative endings that Chesnutt sketched out in his notebooks. Richard Yarborough has outlined the possibilities that Chesnutt considered: "In the first, Miller saves Carteret's child and is promised safety in return. Chesnutt writes, 'He declines—does not want protection but wants the rights and opportunities of a man'" (242). This alternative ending, which is close to Chesnutt's own personal position, is overtly didactic in its insistence on "rights and opportunities," while the second is more dramatic. "This latter sketch differs from the published novel in that at the end, the Millers leave Wellington in despair, traveling in a Jim Crow car" (242). This ending is, of course, more historically accurate because one of the aims of the Wilmington coup/pogrom was to drive the African American professional class out of the city. So Chesnutt chose a less historically accurate conclusion to the novel because he was not quite yet ready to admit that African Americans were to be deprived of their "rights and opportunities" for the foreseeable future. If Chesnutt wanted a ray of hope at the end, however, it was so small as to not convince his audience or his critics. As Yarborough writes, "If the critic William Dean Howells found the novel as published to be 'bitter, bitter,' one can only guess what his horrified response to *Marrow* would have been had it had one of these alternative closing scenes" (243).

In fact, Howells's responses to the novel allow us to gauge the effect of *The Marrow of Tradition* on a representative white reader (who also happened to be America's preeminent critic) who was sympathetic to African Americans' artistic aspirations. He had publicized the poetry of Paul Laurence Dunbar and written appreciative reviews of Chesnutt's two volumes of short stories and of Washington's *Up from Slavery*. In that review (which was also a review of Chesnutt's biography of Frederick Douglass), Howells wrote that Washington "makes assurance doubly sure that the negro is not going to do anything dynamitic to the structure of society. He is going to take it as he finds it, and make the best of his rather poor chances in it. In his heart there is no bitterness" (196).[17] Howells continues that Washington's example "has been for the Afro-American to forego politics, at least for the present" (197). A few months later, while Howells was reading *The Marrow of Tradition,* he wrote an amazing letter to novelist Henry B. Fuller: "Now and then a good thing escapes into publicity. I have been reading Chesnutt's *The Marrow of Tradition.* You know he is a Negro, though you wouldn't know it from seeing him, and he writes of the black and white situation with an awful bitterness. But he is an artist almost of the first quality; as yet too literary, but promising things hereafter that will scarcely be equalled in our fiction. Good Lord! How such a Negro must hate us. And then think of the Filipinos and the Cubans and Puerto Ricans whom we have added to our happy family. But I am talking treason" (10 November 1901). Joseph R. McElrath Jr. comments that "this insight into Chesnutt's animus, actually focused on Southerners rather than the class of whites represented by Howells and Fuller, was a new one" for Howells, and he was "caught by surprise, even startled, by Chesnutt, whom he had not previously thought of as a man with a chip on his shoulder" ("Howells and Race" 485). Yes, Howells was taken off guard because Chesnutt had violated the compact articulated in Howell's review of Washington's autobiography: Chesnutt had emphasized the issue of disenfranchisement, which Washington wanted to leave alone, and he had judged white people in a way that no African American writer had ever before done in fiction. So we need to take Howells at his word: the *us* does mean Howells and Fuller because, as Chesnutt demonstrated in this novel, he believed that the whole nation was complicit in depriving African Americans of their political rights. But Howells's letter is even more revealing in how it links American imperialism in the wake of the Spanish-American War to Chesnutt's novel, a linkage established in the novel as well. When Dr. Miller is returning to his home in Wellington in a Jim Crow railway car, he reads a newspaper editorial that extols the "inestimable advantages which would follow to certain recently acquired islands by the introduction of American liberty" (57)—the American liberty that Dr. Miller experiences as he rides in a segregated railway car. Howells and Chesnutt see the connection between domestic and international oppression, but Howells suppresses the thought as "treason."

A month later, Howells wrote a review of *The Marrow of Tradition* in which the word *bitter* features prominently. He notes that Chesnutt "stands up for his own people with a courage which has more justice than mercy in it. The book is, in fact, bitter, bitter. There is no reason why it should not be so, if wrong is to be repaid with hate, and yet it would be better if it was not so bitter" ("Psychological" 82). Howells's assessment of Chesnutt's performance here was of a piece with Howells's earlier review of *Up from Slavery;* he would perceive anything short of Washington's political passivity as bitterness because he still expected African Americans to be "polite inferiors" and not to bring unwelcome news to the white reading public. In broader terms, for Howells, "The virtues of realism lay in the close delineation of ethnic stereotypes, not in the attempt to reassess the nature of human beings or to reconfigure white Americans' notions of what constitutes 'civilization'" (Harris 134), exactly the dynamitic reconfiguration that Chesnutt was attempting in *The Marrow of Tradition.* Howells clearly perceived that Chesnutt was taking a position that contested Washington's apolitical stance. While Howells acknowledged that Chesnutt "stands up for his own people with a courage which has more justice than mercy," Howells believed it incumbent on African Americans to show "mercy" to their oppressors, not to rend the veil of whiteness. Seeing that Chesnutt was critiquing American (white) "civilization," Howells recycled the charge, from his letter, that the novel represented a performance that repaid the injury of disenfranchisement and Jim Crow with "hate," a term that continues to baffle me, given the virulent negrophobia of this period. Chesnutt was not saying, as did someone like Thomas Dixon from the opposite ideological position, that all white people were inherently, viciously, inferior and dishonest, as some African Americans had argued in his time.[18] He was obviously angry about the events in Wilmington and the direction of events nationally, but he was nowhere close to being a black Dixon, a reverse racist ideologue. It is almost as if Chesnutt has had to bear the burden of being the first African American writer to represent and critique white folks and whiteness in fiction, and he still remains something of a cultural lightning rod a hundred years later.

Howells, however, was on to something when he wrote about justice in this passage, for the *Cleveland Press* quotes Chesnutt as saying, "I admit that 'The Marrow of Tradition' is the plea of an advocate. I can only hope that it is based on the evidence, and that it will make out a case before an impartial jury" ("To Shed"). Of course, Chesnutt used the word *advocate* in a double sense: one who is making a plea and one who is a lawyer. But given his knowledge of his white audience, his legalistic assumption that they were (or could be) "impartial" is quite curious, especially because he said in the same article that he realized that it is "perhaps as difficult to write without partisanship, upon so strongly controverted a subject, as it is to read without prejudice what has been written." This is the kind of complex double vision that Chesnutt achieved in his determination to write for a white audience from an African American point of view. Despite all evidence to the contrary, Chesnutt still held onto his faith that an audience (and a writer) could be impartial, while the logic of his experience and the experience of writing his fiction told him exactly the opposite.

If one closely reads the end of the novel, it is even less optimistic in its belief in his audience's impartiality. In the concluding chapters, Chesnutt brings together the plots involving Dr. Miller and Major Carteret and the plot involving Miller's wife, Janet, and Carteret's wife, Olivia, and the novel moves into a new register—high race melodrama. These two women are half-sisters, but because of the color line, Olivia has never acknowledged Janet. Olivia sees Janet as a sign of racial shame and is jealous of Janet's healthy seven-year-old boy. Janet, conversely, longs for the impossible: "All her life long she had yearned for a kind word, a nod, a smile, the least thing that imagination might have twisted into a recognition of the tie between them" (65). What Janet wants, however, is just what Olivia can not give. The belief that Janet is the illegitimate child of Olivia's father and a slave shames Olivia; when she realizes that her father had married Janet's mother, she is even more constrained because in the racist imaginary to have married an African American "was to have committed the unpardonable sin" (266). So the half-sisters live parallel lives in the same town until the coup/pogrom. After Dr. Miller refuses Carteret's request to come and operate on his son, Olivia rushes to the Millers' house. When Miller opens the door to her, he is startled to see her similarity to his own wife—"a little older, perhaps, a little fairer of complexion, but with the same form, the same features, marked by the same wild grief. She wore a loose wrapper, which clothed her like the drapery of a statue. Her long dark hair, the counterpart of his wife's, had fallen down, and hung disheveled about her shoulders" (323). This moment of melodrama is, of course, meant to be seen as a moment of sympathy: the "same" grief over a child transcending the logic of race, the effect that Stowe wanted to have on the reader in *Uncle Tom's Cabin*.[19] Chesnutt, however, very quickly moves this moment into forbidden territory as he represents the conversation between Miller and Olivia, and she, under the stress of the moment, is the first to break racial taboo: she laid "her hand upon his arm appealingly,—when he shrank from the contact she still held it there" (324). Earlier in the novel, Olivia's husband, Major Carteret, had refused to shake hands with Jerry, the African American who worked in Carteret's office, and Olivia's small gesture, easily missed, is an acknowledgment of common humanity under the stress of extraordinary circumstances. When Miller remains adamant in his refusal, however, "with a sudden revulsion of feeling, she [threw] herself at his feet,—at the feet of a negro, this proud white woman,—and was clasping his knees wildly" (324). Knadler has written of this moment that "Dr. Miller finds himself the voyeur of naked white womanhood. . . . Although the insistence of the likeness of Olivia to her half-sister Janet reminds the reader of the arbitrariness of racial distinctions, it also presents Olivia as an object of sexual desire, a woman who could be like a 'wife,' whose fallen hair, fit only for her husband's eyes, hangs loosely to the ravager's grasp" (436). At least one reader, the literary editor of the *Independent*, clearly found the events of this chapter deeply disturbing, calling them "utterly revolting" (Farnsworth xv).

Knadler argues that in using a strategy of reversal, Chesnutt was conjuring up sexuality to demonstrate how the mulatto, Miller, can act like a gentleman and not take advantage of Olivia's distress. But Chesnutt must also have known the degree to which he was conjuring up a taboo in a fiction where the issue of sexual desire on the part of the black men for white women was a constituent element of the hysterical campaign leading up to the Wilmington coup/pogrom. Knadler asserts that Miller's dignified restraint is meant as a contrast to the example of Olivia's father, whose self-confessed "weakness" (261) in marrying Janet's mother but in concealing the marriage brought about the split between the half-sisters. But in risking this moment where Olivia touches an African American man and prostrates herself at his feet, Chesnutt was also risking the total alienation of his audience, which "knew" that all mulattoes (like George Harris in *The Leopard's Spots*) desired white women, and readers would see Miller's gentlemanliness as little more than pure fantasy. Since Chesnutt's audience was not impartial, Miller's restraint would have been read either as simple caution (his wife is in the next room) or as a sadistic desire to humiliate this paragon of white womanhood.

After Miller's refusal, he sends Olivia into Janet and tells her to make her plea to his wife, and he says that he will be bound by her decision. Olivia finally tells Janet that they are half-sisters, that their father had legally married Janet's black mother. In her own agony over the death of her son, Janet responds with a strength that one could not have predicted in her character: "I have but one word for you," Janet says, "one last word,—and then I hope never to see your face again! . . . I throw you back your father's name, your father's wealth, your sisterly recognition. I want none of them,—they are bought too dear! . . . But that you may know that a woman may be foully wronged, and yet may have a heart to feel, even for one who had injured her, you may have your child's life, if my husband can save it!" (328–29). In moving the novel into this register, Chesnutt is conjuring up one of the fundamental expectations of race melodrama, and he forces us to ask what cultural work is being done by the melodrama. Susan Gillman has argued that race melodrama "fuses the melodrama of familial love disrupted and restored with the political project of imagining a viable biracial community" (225). By employing melodrama, Chesnutt is working against the grain of the expectations of the genre and of his own belief. Ideally, he would want the family restored, and he would want a "viable biracial community," but the logic of the fiction has brought Janet to a place where she rejects the ideas in which the author believes.

In addition, the African American character shows her innate fineness, her true womanliness, and her sympathy by sending her husband to try to save the child's life, but interestingly, she does not forgive, thus foreclosing any reconciliation. In fact, she is adamant in her renunciation of what she has desired her whole life. Todd McGowan has written of this scene that Miller going to save Carteret's son "is the source of much controversy." Critics charge that "here is Chesnutt's accommodationism in full force, his belief in 'forgiveness of one's enemies' or 'the Christian virtue of charity.'" McGowan argues, however, that this act has a "thoroughly un-Christian dimension. . . . Because it is not reactive, [Janet] Miller's act has no exchange-value, it subverts the circuit of exchange. Miller has given something for nothing, and cannot be repaid" (71). The temptation to read this act as Christian forgiveness begins with Howells's review. He says that Chesnutt gives "the moral victory to the blacks" through Janet's act, and he asserts that neither Chesnutt's "aesthetics" nor his "ethics are false. Those who would question either must allow, at least, that the negroes have had the greater practice in forgiveness" (83). Howells sees Janet as a female Booker T. Washington, proffering mercy to the superior race, but I read the moment in much the way that McGowan does. In her speech, Janet renounces her affiliation with her white family; she moves into a separatism that is the ideological opposite of Chesnutt's notions of amalgamation in the "Future American" series. The cost of racism in the private realm is too high; it has created a chasm that interracial families can never bridge.

As with so much else in this novel, the question of the meaning of the confrontation between Janet and Olivia is vexed, and Samina Najmi has argued that there is a germ of optimism in the relations between Olivia and Janet. Najmi sees in their twinning a "guarded hope of racial harmony" (12), particularly in Olivia's appeal to Janet at the end of the novel. This appeal, Najmi writes, "is to the maternal instinct in his white female audience— that instinct which he, and Stowe before him, believed to be a powerful, life-affirming force, resonating across the color line" (14). Olivia's appeal works: Janet allows her husband to operate on the child, so that the maternal instinct can and does work "across the color line." But Chesnutt no longer saw, as he did in *The House Behind the Cedars,* sentimental cross-racial appeals as the basis for reconciliation, and there is no reason to believe that Janet will recant her repudiation of her white half-sister.[20] So Janet's trenchant refusal to have anything to do with her white relatives has to be balanced against the slightly optimistic final lines of the novel. Even though Howells saw the novel as "bitter, bitter," he could still read Janet's actions in the end as fulfilling what he considered a traditional role for African Americans, while Chesnutt wanted his readers to see her actions as signaling a potential breakdown, a rupture of family continuity, the kind experienced by John Warwick (Walden) in his decision to pass. Even though the half-sisters live in the same town, they will remain separated—by the actions of the plotters of the coup and by Janet's choice, just as John was separated from his mother and as Tryon would have been separated from his family had he married Rena.

In terms of his white audience, then, Chesnutt's complex double vision was at its most productive in *The Marrow of Tradition*, and his desire to have a success was at war with his desire to tell the truth from the other side. That war within him was productive: *The Marrow of Tradition* is his most complicated work of fiction. Chesnutt seems to have had some inkling of what he had accomplished in the novel: he wrote to Booker T. Washington after its publication, "It is by far the best thing I have done, and is a comprehensive study of racial conditions in the South. . . . It is, in a word, our side of the Negro question, in popular form, as you have presented it in the more dignified garb of essay and biography" (*Letters* 159–60). That productive war, however, produced a novel that was too alien for his white audience both in generic and historical terms. He had written his magnum opus, but in so doing he alienated his most influential literary backer, Howells, and lost the audience gained with stories and *The House Behind the Cedars*. In his next novel, *The Colonel's Dream*, Chesnutt would represent the consequences of having lost his audience as well as his faith in fiction's ability to change white folks' hearts and minds.

[6]

The Colonel's Dream

The Eccentric Design of Charles W. Chesnutt's New South Novel

The Negro American consciousness is not a product (as so often seems true of so many other American groups) of a will to historical forgetfulness.

—RALPH ELLISON

In *The Colonel's Dream* (1905), the last novel published in his lifetime, Chesnutt continues to interrogate his desire to "elevate" his white audience by creating a central white character who is a well-meaning liberal on the question of race. Chesnutt diagnoses the contradictions of the most "elevated," the most "ideal" white man he can imagine. A rich northern outsider with family ties to the South and a somewhat sympathetic but critical insight into the life world of southerners is bound to fail as reformer because he, like the South more generally, is incapable of acknowledging the inescapability of the past, how the past has been used to construct a cultural context that consistently undermines any efforts at instrumental reform. So *The Colonel's Dream* is a fiction of contradictory ambitions: it is a novel of economic life that exposes the racist undergirding of the New South ideology at the same time that it doubts the efficacy of fiction to effect instrumental reform. Combined with Chesnutt's willingness to frustrate his readers in terms of genre and plot, the novel is at war with itself, designed (almost intentionally) to baffle and alienate the audience he once claimed he wanted to change. Chesnutt seems to be saying to his white audience that no matter how well meaning and liberal on the question of race, they all inevitably trip themselves up because they are blind to their own racism. When he wrote *The Marrow of Tradition*, though, he still had some lingering faith in his white audience's ability and willingness to be changed intellectually and moved emotionally. By the time of *The Colonel's Dream*, however, he no longer believed change was possible, and while the novel employed many of the same strategies as its predecessor, Chesnutt's deep pessimism made the novel a demonstration of loss of faith in the fairness and impartiality of his white audience.

To deal with the complications of this novel, I have had recourse to the title of Marius Bewley's *The Eccentric Design* (1963), a book that deals with the "classic American novel." Here I am using the term quite differently to describe *The Colonel's Dream*, a novel that I think is self-consciously eccentric in its design and quite unusual in generic terms. To allay his audience, Chesnutt was at first very careful that the novel appeared to be working in familiar territory, that of the recent genre of fiction of economic life (with romantic and melodramatic elements added), but in an almost critically suicidal act, he refused to fulfill many of the expectations his narrative established by thwarting the expectations to which the plot has given rise. So if his complex double vision was productively acute during the writing of *The Marrow of Tradition*, it had become nearly self-destructive in the writing of *The Colonel's Dream*. Even though Chesnutt wrote to Walter Hines Page to assert the continuing desire to have the novel be "widely read" (*Letters* 214), Chesnutt self-destructs as a writer, completely alienating his audience by bringing, as he did in *The Marrow of Tradition*, news that was not only unwelcome but was nearly unbelievable because it so contradicted conventional understandings of the time and did so in a form that was purposely self-defeating.

For instance, in the middle of the novel there is an example that gives his readers a cue about how to read this fiction, a self-reflexive moment that is otherwise almost inexplicable. *The Colonel's Dream* contains only two black characters of any consequence, and one of them, Peter French, is right out of the plantation tradition, seeming to have no life other than his devotion to the family of his former masters. Old Peter tells a story to the young son of Colonel French, and he alludes to Joel Chandler Harris's Uncle Remus stories. Peter begins a story of a talking black cat, and when the boy states that cats cannot talk, Peter responds: "Ain't Miss Grac'ella an' me be'n tellin' you right along 'bout Bre'r Rabbit and Bre'r Fox an de yuther creturs talkin' an' gwine on jes' lak folks?" (146–47). With this allusion, Chesnutt sets up generic expectations that he immediately violates. As Gary Scharnhorst has written, Chesnutt parodies Harris by having Peter tell a story that is so "vapid and pointless" (274) that even the little boy is puzzled by its lack of resolution: "Is that all, Uncle Peter?" he asks (149). While Peter acknowledges that he knows the conclusion to the tale, he is more interested in proving a point ("ter prove dat black cats kin do mo' dan little w'ite boys 'low dey kin" [149]) than he is in telling a story that satisfies his audience's generic expectations. Here, Chesnutt was, I believe, telling readers what to expect from his novel: that every genre he incorporates into the novel will be turned to other ends, and his readers should anticipate being frustrated. The economic plot will be unconventional; the expected intersectional marriage will not come off; and the melodramatic subplot of missing money will also not turn out as expected. It is almost as if Chesnutt's despair about the political and economic situation of African Americans in the South led him in two contrary directions: he wanted to write an exposé of the connections between the lack of economic development and racism, but he ended up doing so in a self-consciously eccentric form that was designed to demonstrate that a significant portion of his audience was unwilling or unable to change.

This notion is, of course, squarely at odds with the passage from Chesnutt's journal in which he articulates his desire for "the elevation of the whites" (139). By the time of *The Colonel's Dream,* Chesnutt had come to doubt white Americans' willingness to be elevated, and he commented ironically on his desire for their elevation by taking on the authority to make a white aristocrat (by birth a southerner but by achievement a northerner) the central figure of his fiction. Only in this last of the three race fictions published in his lifetime does he make a white man the central focus and relegate African Americans to minor roles.[1] Late in his career, Chesnutt speculated that it "might not be a bad idea to create a few white men who not only think they are, but really are fair and unprejudiced in their dealings with colored folk. It might strain the reader's imagination, but it is the privilege of art to depict the ideal" ("No Color Line").[2] Taking Chesnutt at his word, Ernestine Pickens flatly declares that "Colonel French is Chesnutt's ideal reformer" (102), but I believe she has seriously underestimated Chesnutt as an artist. French is ideal to the extent that Chesnutt believes that this is as good as white people get, but Chesnutt is acutely aware of the ways in which French is riddled with contradictions on questions of race, the ways in which he is ultimately undermined by his own unacknowledged and unexamined racist assumptions, and the ways in which he is unconsciously allied with the southerners he seeks to oppose.

Furthermore, by sending his white man South and by representing economic conditions, Chesnutt forces his white audience to consider what they believe it is absolutely necessary for them to forget: the past forty years, a textbook case of Ernest Renan's thesis that "forgetting . . . is a crucial factor in the creation of a nation" (11). As he argued in *The Marrow of Tradition*, the consequences of slavery were still being enacted in the New South, and Chesnutt believed, as Frederick Douglass argued toward the end of his life, that the "people of the South are with few exceptions but slightly improved in their sentiments towards those they once held as slaves" (Douglass, "Introduction" 473). *The Colonel's Dream*, a relatively neglected work in Chesnutt's canon, is a novelistic provocation in which Chesnutt is trying to keep alive an emancipationist vision like Douglass's. The novel is a self-conscious disruption of the national consensus made possible by the nostalgia that saturated southern writers' depictions of the present, a national consensus found in the ideology of the New South in the last few decades of the nineteenth century. To encourage northern investment, New South ideologues argued at the most basic level that the South had no racial problem; the races lived quite happily together, with blacks in the position of proper subservience. These ideologues wanted to assure northern investors of a tractable workforce, not agitated over such issues as disenfranchisement, convict peonage, and lynching. In this national climate, the reception of *The Colonel's Dream* was symptomatic of the unwillingness of the South (and of the United States at large) to listen to critical voices, particularly the critical voice of an African American that threatened to upset the delicate balance of compromise and forgetting on which the New South ideology rested, a compromise sealed from the perspective of white Americans by Booker T. Washington, particularly his Atlanta Compromise speech, given at the Atlanta Cotton States and International Exposition of 1895. Having written this novel, then, Chesnutt realized that the consensus of New South ideology was so powerfully constituted that any critical voice such as his was inevitably marginalized and thereby silenced. In his decision not to write any more novels until the 1920s, Chesnutt realized the impossibility of critical realism from an African American perspective, and he acknowledged the futility of fiction as an agent of social action.[3] In other words, he came to perceive, in a time when southern racial ideology effectively held sway over the whole nation, that fiction could not effect instrumental reform. His white audience was too imbued with racism to be open to change through fiction, and he increasingly came to see that his attempts at realism were received as provocations with no basis whatsoever in historical or social realities.

I

In a letter to his editor, Walter Hines Page, Chesnutt characterized the ambitions of *The Colonel's Dream* as "encyclopedic" and alluded to "Russian novelists of the past generation, who made so clear the condition of a debased peasantry in their own land" (*Letters* 213). The status of the "debased peasantry," like that of the ex-slaves, affected the private lives of the aristocrats and landowners, and because of the ways in which the past inevitably impinged on the present, Chesnutt was interested in demonstrating in the main plot the impossibility of economic development and reform in the New South. New South ideologues, proponents of southern economic development in this period, would have had Americans believe that the South had cast off its past and that the status of the former slaves presented no insuperable regional or national problem. Chesnutt wanted to demonstrate through his protagonist, Colonel Henry French, that the past was inescapable in the New South, that antebellum racism was little different from postbellum racism, and that the South would continue to be a place benighted and underdeveloped because of its inability to forgo the color line.

As a representation of economic conditions, however, *The Colonel's Dream* has received relatively little notice. Chesnutt's decision, for instance, to open the novel with a depiction of the selling of Colonel French's company is important not only because it provides French with the capital that fuels the events of the central plot but also because it indicates the extent of his implication in the practices of late-nineteenth-century American capitalism. "The firm of French and Company," the narrator informs us, "had finally faced the alternative of selling out, at a sacrifice, to the recently organised bagging trust, or of meeting a disastrous competition. . . . Negotiations for a sale, upon terms highly favourable to the firm, had been in progress for several weeks" (4). When the trust buys out French's company, he and his partners will be rich, but the prospects for the employees are not so sanguine: "The clerks were not especially cheerful; the impending change meant for them, at best, a change of masters, and for many of them, the loss of employment" (5). In representing French's selling out, Chesnutt accurately reflects economic developments in the years before the writing of *The Colonel's Dream:* "A merger movement began in 1897 and peaked in 1904, at which point more than 300 trusts existed in the United States with an aggregate capitalization of . . . $7 billion" (Painter 177). French manages to use the monopoly to his own advantage; he is "a victim rather than an accessory" (5) of monopoly. Nor does he believe that he is complicit in the practices of the trust; he does not believe "that competition would be crushed, or that . . . labour must sweat and the public groan in order that a few captains . . . of industry might double their dividends" (5). Instead of being ruined by a monopoly, French bails out at the right time, and Chesnutt signals through his use of this fortunate victim the fundamental difference between his economic fiction and the work of his predecessor in this genre, Frank Norris. Unlike S. Behrman in *The Octopus* (1901), French is no monster of acquisitiveness, and unlike Curtis Jadwin in *The Pit* (1903), French does not become addicted to the narcotic of the market; French is rational and unusually sensitive (he faints when he hears the news that the deal has gone through). In further contrast to the epic quality of Norris's two novels, Chesnutt's is resolutely local in its economic plot, and he wanted it to be seen as closer in generic terms to what Walter Fuller Taylor has called "the romance of economic struggle" or the "romance of business" (111), a genre of novel that "increased to a veritable flood about the turn of the century, a time which significantly coincides with a revival of interest in another kind of romance, the historical" (112).

William L. Andrews has argued that there is a specific predecessor in this genre of New South economic fiction. George Washington Cable's *John March, Southerner* (1894) is, Andrews writes, "the first and only serious fictional study of the New South creed before *The Colonel's Dream*" (*Career* 229).[4] Cable's novel does involve an economic plot: the desire of the central character to develop his family's hundred thousand acres by bringing in settlers and by promoting economic development. Unfortunately, as John Cleman has observed, "the business machinations are difficult to follow and ultimately lack dramatic effect" (148). Even though John March's economic plans fail because of the obscure plots of his southern partners, there is still a happy ending in both the economic and romantic plots through an unbelievable deus ex machina. The heroine remembers an incident from her childhood: "then, naturally and easily, without a jar between true cause and effect, the romantic happened! The memory took form in a dream and the dream became a key to revelation" (501). The point is not to criticize the plot and the fact that this memory resolves the plot in an entirely unbelievable fashion, but rather to point out Cable's investment in and indebtedness to notions of romance in a novel ostensibly about the economic development of the New South. So part of the reason that I do not think that *John March, Southerner* can be thought of as a useful precursor to *The Colonel's Dream* is that Cable's novel is addicted to the conventions of the romance, which take up the latter half of the novel. As the two central characters rhapsodize: "'It's a certain ungeographical South-within-the-South—as portable and intangible as . . . our souls in our bodies.' 'It's sort o' something—social, civic, political, economic [and] romantic! Something that makes . . . [n]o land like Dixie in all the wide world over!'" (327). In *John March*, Cable indulged in a version of southern exceptionalism, and Chesnutt was at pains to deconstruct notions like these in *The Colonel's Dream*, where he was also trying to unmask how those romantic conventions are ultimately implicated in plantation mythology—which was both nostalgic and unreconstructedly racist. From Chesnutt's point of view, this vision of southern exceptionalism tethered the Old and New Souths, and at its heart was a vision of African Americans that had not changed since before the Civil War.[5] I would argue that *John March* could only have been a negative example for Chesnutt, first because its two plots—the economic and the romantic—are unconnected: "the love plot neither grows organically out of nor contributes to the novel's main problems, but it even serves as a positive hindrance to such matters" (Rubin 231). Second, the two plots contradict each other in ideological terms. Cable's romantic love plot is a constituent element of his Old South nostalgia, and that nostalgia, to the degree that it participates in the civil and economic oppression of African Americans, is bound, in Chesnutt's view, to impede fundamentally the New South's ability to progress economically.

Andrews also mentions but rejects Thomas Nelson Page's *Gordon Keith* (1903) as a "serious fictional study of the New South" and as a precursor to *The Colonel's Dream*. Andrews argues that Page's novel is "a reactionary and romanticized portrayal of the New South businessman-aristocrat" (*Career* 233) and that the action of the novel rests on an overly schematic, if not simplistic, clash between northern and southern characters. Wayne Mixon's analysis of the New South complicates Andrews's, and Mixon argues that Page imports the values of the Old South into the New: "He carries as much as he can of the Old into the New South and lets that world stand as an alternative to the grasping North" (41). His main character, Gordon Keith, "personifies what his creator would have the New South be. Honorable, courageous, astute, Gordon functions famously in the New Order as he remembers fondly the Old" (39). Importing the values of the aristocrats from his historical romance, *Red Rock*, into his New South novel, Page saw antebellum values as the answer to all current social and economic questions. In that sense, *Gordon Keith* consciously celebrated the values that Chesnutt wanted to contest in *The Colonel's Dream*. Both white writers wanted the reader to see that little had changed; for Chesnutt that was the fundamental problem that prevented economic and social progress in the New South, while for Page the paternalistic values of the planter class remained as relevant as they had been before the Civil War. For Page, the novel was "an affirmation of the moral superiority of the South's past" (Mixon 39), while for Chesnutt the South's refusal to abjure that past was evidence, as he wrote in "The Disfranchisement of the Negro," of its continuing "barbarism": "What slavery made of the Southern whites is a matter of history. The abolition of slavery gave the South an opportunity to emerge from barbarism. Present conditions indicate that the spirit which dominated slavery still curses the fair section over which that institution spread its blight" (*Essays* 186). For Page, however, the "negro problem" had been solved; in contrast to Cable's *John March, Southerner*, "there is not a single negro character" (Mixon 41) in the very long *Gordon Keith*. A good proponent of the New South, Page has made African Americans disappear.

There is, however, yet another novel written in this period that sheds light on Chesnutt's accomplishment in *The Colonel's Dream*. The little-known *The Bishop of Cottontown* (1906) by John Trotwood Moore is set in a southern cotton mill town. As a novel of instrumental reform, it is most concerned with child labor in the mills, and Moore has a good deal of sympathy for the poor whites working in the mills. Those white children and women are, the narrator says repeatedly, in "slavery." As he represents a child of seven going to work, the narrator says, "thus would she prattle—too young to know that, through the cupidity of white men, in this—the land of freedom and progress—she—this blue-eyed, white-skinned child of the Saxon race, was making the same wages as the Indian sepoy and the Chinese coolie" (90). Although there are almost no African

American characters in the novel except for a saintly mammy completely dedicated to her white family, there is a startling view of white laborers seen through African American eyes: "Never had she seen such white people before, such hollow eyes, with dark, bloodless rings beneath them, sunken cheeks, tanned to the color of oiled hickory, much used. Dazed, listless, they stumbled out past her with relaxed underjaws, and faces gloomy, expressionless. . . . Women, smileless, and so tired and numbed that they had forgotten the strongest instinct of humanity—the romance of sex" (575). Moore offers a solution to the exploitation of women and children in the mills through an unbelievable set of events—the original mill burns down and the main character, the bishop of Cottontown, a sort of pandenominational Protestant, comes into a massive fortune through the discovery of iron and coal on his property, and so he establishes the "Model Cotton Mill" (633), where the employees work moderate hours and where no one is exploited. If the antebellum patriarchal ethos is seen as the solution to the South's economic problems in Page's novel, evangelical Christianity is seen as yet another solution in Moore's work.

All three of these novels are examples of the widespread interest in literatures of the American regions at the turn of the century, and although the interest in local color had begun to wane by 1905, C. Vann Woodward, in his *Origins of the New South*, suggestively links the economic revival in the South in the late nineteenth century with that interest in the local. He thinks of it as a literary revival that was distinctly inferior to its economic counterpart: "For all the shortcomings and the comparative brevity of the revival . . . the southern writers undeniably possessed solid virtues. Among them, however, one will search in vain for a realistic portrayal of their own times. . . . [T]he writers were too preoccupied with the quaint 'types' of the hinterland to notice what was going on in their own parlors" (164). Jules Chamstzky has echoed Woodward's observation, writing that "local color and regionalism . . . became . . . toward the end of the nineteenth century a strategy, largely, for ignoring or minimizing social issues of great significance" (21). Preoccupied with a nostalgic vision of their region, southern writers failed, it is generally agreed, to represent

significant social changes in realistic terms. However, while most southern local colorists were in thrall to "the quaint types of the hinterland,"
that does not mean that their work was not, as Edward Ayers has written,
"riven by conflicting desires and intentions, torn by its authors' own
uncertainties" (340). While from our perspective, these conflicts and
uncertainties are what is most interesting about this writing, from the
perspective of the southern local colorists, their fiction was doing very
different cultural work. Either by preserving a local heritage that was
threatened by a sense of greater national unity or by looking back, nostalgically, to a romanticized antebellum past, they were trying to bridge the
pre–Civil war past by asserting a sense of cultural continuity. Every representation of the "good ole times" worked to justify the status quo in the
South and to legitimate the oppression of African Americans in the present.

Both Woodward and Chamstzky, however, sound rather uneasy; their
analyses seem to have revealed that southern writers evaded realism in
this period. Perhaps that uneasiness has its sources in a nearly conscious
knowledge of repression, an almost conscious history of the kind of forgetting about which Renan wrote. As I have argued in previous chapters,
southerners convinced the rest of the country during the 1890s and
beyond that it was necessary to forget the history of the Reconstruction
and its aftermath; European Americans found it imperative in getting on
with a conception of imperial destiny to forget, in a variation on Eric
Foner's title, the unfinished business of slavery and Reconstruction. To
fashion themselves into twentieth-century Americans, whites had to find
a way to make the problem that African Americans represented disappear.
By a sheer act of will, by continuing to assert that there was no problem
while conjuring up the horror of rape of white women by black "beasts,"
white America created an almost unbearable tension in the national
imaginary, but this tension allowed for an uneasy forgetting, like a dream
disturbingly on the edge of consciousness. If Renan is right that national
unity is predicated on forgetting, then the larger question for Chesnutt
(and other minority writers) is how one changes the discourse that is
predicated on forgetting. If reunion is a product of forgetting and rewriting the past, what hope exists for a writer who wants to remind white

America of the cost of national forgetfulness? In theoretical terms, someone like Chesnutt who insists on the persistence of memory will be seen at
best as a crafter of hyperbolic fabrication or at worst as "an enemy of his
people" (a phrase that is used to describe Colonel French late in the novel),
as a disruptor of the civil peace, as one who wants to tear the nation apart
once again by making it face questions that have been resolved through
the act of forgetting.

To the degree to which Chesnutt insisted on the necessity of historical
memory, on a continuing emancipationist vision, he was upsetting a consensus about the meaning of the Civil War and about the place of African
Americans in a newly reconstituted American polity. In confronting this
will to forgetfulness, Chesnutt was confronting the limits of fiction to
change a discourse and the minds of white people who believed in the
truth of that discourse. Of course, Chesnutt realized better than most of
his contemporaries the cost of reconciliation based on forgetting—the
cost to those who are forgotten as well as the cost to those who insist on
forgetting. Continuing to represent an emancipationist vision, Chesnutt
was fleshing out his observation in his 1903 essay, "The Disfranchisement
of the Negro": "The country stands face to face with the revival of slavery"
(*Essays* 182). Chesnutt echoes Frederick Douglass's analysis in his last
pamphlet, "Why Is The Negro Lynched?" (1894), which stated that "sentiment left by slavery is still with us, and the moral vision of the American
people is still darkened by its presence" (496). Douglass and Chesnutt
stood in complete opposition to the national social and historical consensus that insisted that the history of slavery and reconstruction had been
overcome and well forgotten. As in *The Marrow of Tradition*, Chesnutt
insisted on historical memory, on the connectedness of the southern present with its past. In fact, in this insistence, Chesnutt anticipates Faulkner's
analysis of the paralyzing power of southern nostalgia. Eric Sundquist has
formulated this as a problem that Faulkner "would never fully resolve"
but that became "the implied subject of all of his work." The "estrange-
ment of present from past is absolutely central to the southern experience
and often creates the pressured situation in which the past becomes an
ever more ghostly and gloriously imposing model to the ... extent that ...

it cannot be recaptured, relived, or even clearly remembered" (7). Even more startlingly, Sundquist asserts that when Faulkner began publishing his first novels in the late 1920s (at the same time that Chesnutt was working on his last novel, *The Quarry*), "the 'lost' but feverishly maintained innocence of the South . . . had become nothing less than the entire burden of white identity" (24). In *The Colonel's Dream*, Chesnutt wants to undermine that "white identity" by telling a counterhistory that questions the South's presumed innocence.

If Chesnutt's white audience wants to forget the past through fictions of innocence, he tries to counter that forgetfulness by creating a white main character who is a hybrid: a southerner by birth (although he has been away from the South for a long time), attaining the rank of colonel in the Confederate army by the war's end, but a northerner by accomplishment, succeeding as an industrialist. In other words, Chesnutt created a character who is (like himself) simultaneously an insider and an outsider, whose formative years were spent in the South but whose values are thoroughly northern. By having Colonel French reenter economic life in the South, Chesnutt exposed not only what Andrews has called "the New South's heart of darkness" (*Career* 250) but also the limitations of an "ideal" white man of goodwill who seems relatively unprejudiced and liberal and who seems, at first glance, unimplicated in the oppressions of late-nineteenth-century southern racism.

Chesnutt's attention to the economic effects of French's investment in the town is quite remarkable; the author traces out in resolutely local terms the economic effects of French's private decisions as well as the effects of his public investments. For instance, early in his time back in his hometown, he buys back his family's house from a barber named Nichols, "a keen-eyed mulatto . . . a man of thrift and good sense" (82), and renovates it. After the renovation is complete, French is convinced to throw a housewarming party where the guests are to come dressed in antebellum costume. Although the idea of a costume party might seem innocent enough, Chesnutt is illustrating a blind spot in French. French's nostalgia for the past is deeply problematic. To the degree to which French is in thrall to the myth of an idealized prewar South, he remains an unwitting ally of his ostensible opponent, Fetters, and of those who would continue to disenfranchise African Americans in the present. The narrator generalizes that "like all of Colonel French's enterprises at that happy period of his homecoming, [the housewarming] brought prosperity in its train." In particular, "Old Archie Christmas, the mulatto tailor, sole survivor of a once flourishing craft . . . who had not made a full suit of clothes for years, was able . . . to earn enough to keep himself alive for another twelve months" (97). But Chesnutt is not only interested in representing the direct economic effects of French's money; he also wants to explore the ramifications of that investment in the minds of both the lower and upper classes of Clarendon. For instance, when French buys his old family house, the local newspaper, the *Anglo-Saxon,* has nothing but praise because French's behavior is seen as properly aristocratic, reinforcing traditional racial roles. The *Anglo-Saxon* declares that the "New South . . . was happy to welcome capital and enterprise" (87). While the aristocratic newspaper promulgates the party line of the New South boosters, lower-class whites are already restive: there were "some small souls . . . among the lower whites who were heard to express disgust that so far, only 'niggers' had profited by the colonel's visit" (86).

The tensions created by the lower-class whites and the tension between investment and racism escalate after the colonel decides to build a cotton mill, something that had become in this period "a symbol of the New South, its origins, and its promise of salvation" (Woodward 131). In building his symbol of economic salvation, French employs both blacks and whites under a white foreman, Green, who argues with French over some detail of how the work is to be done: "the colonel, as the master, insisted that certain work should be done in a certain way. Green wished to argue the point. The colonel brought the discussion to a close with a peremptory command. The foreman took offense, declared that he was no nigger to be ordered around, and quit" (90–91). From the point of view of a working-class white southerner, French's insistence on his right to give orders to the men he employs is tantamount to being treated like a "nigger," so white workers instinctively make a connection between chattel slavery and wage slavery. French then compounds his developing problem with the townspeople by hiring a black foreman. The remaining white workers quit, saying. "We don't mind working *with* niggers, but we won't work *under* a nigger," and many in the town "took offense when a Negro was preferred to a white man" (191). Chesnutt demonstrated for his audience poor whites' investment in their whiteness. As Howard Rabinowitz has pointed out, the lives of poor southern whites "were remarkably similar to those of most blacks. They generally could not vote, had little or no schooling, and sought relief in revivalistic religion . . . gambling, hunting, fighting, and drinking" (162–63). The only thing that distinguished them from their poor black neighbors was whiteness, and the colonel's decision to put a black man in a position of power over these whites strikes at the heart of their identity.

The colonel's justification for his decision illuminates his ideology as a capitalist and also points—inadvertently from the colonel's perspective but not from Chesnutt's—to the limits of that ideology. In fact, one of Chesnutt's major accomplishments in this novel was to depict so clearly the stew of contradictions that make up his representative, "ideal" white man. And in representing the contradictions of a racial "liberal," Chesnutt is putting the last nail in the coffin of his career, because even racial liberals like William Dean Howells and George Washington Cable were unable to extricate themselves from the historical horizon of American racism. As the narrator says of one such strand of contradiction, "In principle, the colonel was an ardent democrat; he believed in the rights of man, and extended the doctrine to include all who bore the human form. But in feeling he was an equally pronounced aristocrat" (81). To add to this contradiction, one would also have to say that he is a laissez-faire capitalist of a nineteenth-century stamp as well as a protosocial reformer who believes, like Chesnutt, in the ideology of enlightenment and uplift. These contradictions signal, I would argue, a conceptual gridlock that results in the impossibility of compromise in either French or in the South. For example, in trying to explain his position after his white workers have walked off the job, French says, "These people have got to learn that we live in an industrial age, and success demands of an employer that he utilise the most available labour." The narrator further comments that from French's

point of view, "the right to work and to do one's best work, was fundamental, as was the right to have one's work done by those who could do it
best" (192). French's language here echoes late-nineteenth-century economic and social theorists who argued, economist Gavin Wright has written, "that industrialization and the operation of competitive labor
markets are fundamentally hostile to discrimination and the use of racial
categories. In economics, the basis for this belief is the view that firms will
gain a competitive advantage by using efficiency rather than racialist cri-
teria in hiring and assignment decisions" (177). Despite this theory, cotton
mills in the South remained segregated until well into this century, and
French is complicit in this practice.

After the colonel's ringing endorsement of a capitalist's right to employ
whomever he sees fit, regardless apparently of race, French comments in
passing that when "the mill is completed it will give employment to five
hundred white women and fifty white men" (192). Like the owners of the
mill in a neighboring town, French will employ only white workers, and
African Americans will be excluded from its direct economic benefits, and
neither French nor the narrator point to this assertion as a contradiction
of his capitalist absolutism. Of course, French is acceding to the practice
in mills throughout the South. Ayers has noted that while "the workers in
virtually every other major industry in the South were nearly balanced
between the races, the machine rooms of the cotton mills rapidly became
the preserve of whites only. . . . Black men were permitted to work only at
outside loading and unloading and in the suffocating rooms where they
opened bales for processing. Black women found no work at all" (114).
French's mill was going to be lily-white—no African Americans would be
employed, not even doing the bull work of handling the cotton bales. So
in the racial politics of his planned mill, French goes even further in the
practice of segregation than most mills in the South at the time. But he
does not accept all received notions about cotton mills because what he
sees when he visits that neighboring mill sickens him, "aneaemic young
women [and w]izened children" (114), and a local liveryman puts what he
has seen into perspective: "Talk about nigger slavery—the niggers never
were worked like white women and children are in them mills" (115). The

liveryman also sees an inescapable connection between chattel and wage slavery, but that connection is, of course, an aspect of the nostalgia for the "good ole times" of slavery. Seeing these conditions among white workers, French thinks that the conditions are remediable and that his mill will operate differently. Like the bishop of Cottontown, French will build "a model cotton mill, and run it with decent hours and decent wages, and treat the operatives like human beings with bodies to nourish, minds to develop, and souls to save" (120). If one remembers the clerks in French's New York company, many of whom presumably lost their jobs when he sold it, one has some room to doubt French on this point. So despite his ideology, he unreflectively accedes to the strictures of southern racism, which became naturalized over time; as Wright has observed, industries "increasingly came to see their segregation patterns as . . . dictated . . . by [what they thought were] the observable skills and qualities of black workers" (158).

In terms of his white audience, then, Chesnutt's colonel is, for the most part, well within the American consensus on race, and for the African Americans of his hometown, French is the mildest of reformers. Early in the novel, French thinks of Lincoln and the Emancipation Proclamation in this way: "he would take off his hat to the memory of the immortal statesman, who in freeing one race had emancipated another and struck the shackles from a Nation's mind" (30). As Paul Gaston has pointed out in *The New South Creed*, this is a typical intellectual move among those who celebrated southern industrial development in the last decades of the nineteenth century. For instance, the most prominent New South ideologue, Henry W. Grady, wrote that "the shackles that held [the South] in narrow limitations fell forever when the shackles of the negro slave were broken" (quoted in Gaston 57). In contrast to most of the inhabitants of Clarendon, Colonel French sees the economic benefits of the abolishment of slavery and thinks of himself as freed from the historical consequences of that slavery. In contrast, the narrator states quite explicitly that the "land [of the South] still groaned and travailed" because of the "survival of the spirit of slavery," not only as found in the practice of a convict lease system (one of the subplots of the novel) but as a general impediment to the "uplifting power of industry and enlightenment" (195). Although French thinks of himself as the embodiment of the spirit of rational enlightenment, he is still implicated in the survival of the spirit of slavery through his inability to question the "naturalness" of the place ascribed to African Americans in the post-Reconstruction era.

Like the narrator, the colonel argues to a few of the town's more sympathetic whites that "no State could be freer or greater or more enlightened than the average of its citizenship, and that any restriction of rights that rested upon anything but impartial justice, was bound to re-act, as slavery had done, on the prosperity and progress of the State" (194–95). The crucial word *progress* recurs when French decides "to build a newer and larger cotton mill . . . to shake up this lethargic community; to put its people to work, and to teach them habits of industry, efficiency and thrift." In a more idealistic mode, he thinks this will "be pleasant occupation for his vacation, as well as a true missionary enterprise—a contribution to human progress" (106). French, in his desire to help further progress, is like nineteenth-century missionaries and imperialists: he is a bringer of "enlightenment" to the natives, a connection that helps link southern industrial growth in this period to America's new imperial role in the wake of the Spanish-American War. But the native African Americans have become, in the words of a Presbyterian minister, "hopelessly degraded" (163). The minister goes on to articulate a radical narrative of scientific racism: "there is no place in this nation for the Negro, except under the sod. We will not assimilate, we cannot deport him." French interrupts the minister by asking, "Therefore, O man of God, must we exterminate him?"[6] The minister piously answers that it is "God's will . . . If we but sit passive, and leave their fate to time, they will die away in discouragement and despair. Already disease is sapping their vitals. . . . To a doomed race, ignorance is euthanasia, and knowledge is but pain and sorrow. It is His will that the fittest should survive" (164–65). In his view, any effort to educate African Americans would be tantamount to opposing the "natural" and inevitable course of events that will lead to the extermination of black people in America (and throughout the world). This protogenocidal scenario was, as Chesnutt knew, part of the powerfully sanctioned discourse of racial radicalism. For instance, in 1896 "the superbly respectable American Economic Association" published Frederick L. Hoffman's study, *Race Traits and Tendencies of the American Negro,* which argued that the degeneracy of the black was a result of "a low standard of sexual morality." There could be "no relief . . . either in religion, education, or economic improvement, and he predicted the 'gradual extinction of the race'" (quoted in Williamson, *Crucible* 122). In fact, as John S. Haller has demonstrated, almost all physicians in late-nineteenth-century America subscribed to this extinction theory, and "arguments to the contrary were simply not to be found in the transactions and journals of the medical societies" (68). So while the Presbyterian minister is not as bloodthirsty as Joseph Conrad's Kurtz in his injunction to "exterminate all the brutes" (51), the minister does believe that African Americans are doomed to extinction and that any effort to "enlighten" them is counter to God's will and to the authority of science.

In response to this powerfully sanctioned discourse of degeneracy and ultimate extermination, French (responding like George Tryon) tries to articulate a "moderate" position that acknowledges the right of African Americans to exist in the United States and to share in at least some of the benefits of economic development. In the South, he argues, blacks "constitute the bulk of our labouring class. To teach them to make their labour more effective and therefore more profitable; to increase their needs is to increase our profits in supplying them." He denies being a "lover of the Negro, *as* Negro," and goes on to acknowledge the common history of blacks and whites in the South. "But they are here, through no fault of theirs, as we are. They were born here." He says that whites have given blacks "our language," "our religion," "and our blood—which our laws make a badge of disgrace. Perhaps we could not do them strict justice, without a great sacrifice on our own part. But they are men, and they should have their chance—at least *some* chance" (165). In Colonel French's vision, African Americans will have "some" small chance indeed, and his rhetoric of improvement stops well short of directly including the town's black population. In fact, his economic scheme is a vision of trickle-down economics reconfigured in unacknowledged racist terms. The only improvement in

African Americans' economic status will be the result of minor spillover from the general economic activity engendered by the cotton mill. In contrast to the racial radicals, however, the colonel's position is more inclusive in recognizing historical realities: unlike the minister, who dreams a utopian dream of the disappearance of black people, French acknowledges them as an integral part of the South's collective history, and in his view "progress" over the longer term will result from better access to education for black people. As a first step toward that goal for all the "natives," both black and white, French decides to help build a library for the town, but he belatedly realizes that he will have to build a separate library for the town's black inhabitants. As he is told by his "native" informant, "the white people wouldn't wish to handle the same books touched" by blacks (163).

His next step is to try to improve Clarendon's schools, and his decisions here further illuminate his contradictions and his unconscious racism. At first, French thinks he will build a separate school for the children of his prospective mill hands, but he ultimately decides that to do so would be to continue to draw class distinctions, which he finds invidious. He wants to "avoid drawing of any line that might seem to put these [children of mill hands] in a class apart. There were already lines enough in the town" (155–56), and the first and strongest of these lines, he acknowledges, is the color line. He decides to give money to repair and expand the white academy, but when it comes to the question of a school for blacks, French not only accepts the color line but subtly reinforces it when he tells a meeting of black leaders, "I will give you three dollars for every one you can gather for an industrial school or some similar institution" (161). Chesnutt began his working career as a teacher in black schools, and he knows the considerable sacrifices involved in supporting such schools in the South. The colonel, of course, is at a philanthropic distance from the objects of his charity, a distance that blinds him to his racism. Working-class white children are to be freely included in the community, and he will support the white school without qualification. Black children and their parents, though, are to be excluded and indentured to his charity, something that Chesnutt found objectionable but his audience would have accepted as standard practice in the South.

French's discourse of uplift obviously is very close to that of Booker T. Washington. The colonel says to the town's black leaders, "To make yourselves valuable members of society, you must learn to do well some particular thing, by which you may reasonably expect to earn a comfortable living in your own home, among your neighbors, and save something for old age and the education of your children" (161). As Washington wrote in 1903 in "Industrial Education," an essay published in a collection with Chesnutt's "The Disfranchisement of the Negro," "I believe most earnestly that for years to come the education of the people of my race should be so directed that the greatest proportion of the mental strength of the masses will be brought to bear upon the every-day practical things of life, upon something that is needed to be done, and something which they will be permitted to do in the community in which they reside" (17). For Chesnutt, the example of Colonel French points to the problem inherent in Washington's last phrase and the problem of the integration of African American economic activity into the economic activity of the South's white population. As Washington says later in his essay, "I plead for industrial education and development for the Negro not because I want to cramp him, but because I want to free him. I want to see him enter the all-powerful business and commercial world" (19). As Chesnutt demonstrated in *The Marrow of Tradition*, African Americans who presented successful challenges to whites in "the all-powerful business and commercial world" were targeted for expulsion from Wilmington. However, if middle-class African Americans were always perceived as economic threats, conditions at first glance did not seem to be quite so bleak for industrial workers. As Wright points out, not all of the new southern industries were segregated: the newly developed iron and steel industries were majority African American, as were the tobacco and lumber industries. But Wright also clearly demonstrates that no matter in which industry they were employed, African American workers "could get the going wage in the unskilled market, but there was a virtual upper limit to their progress above that level. . . . In a nutshell, the typical white unskilled worker could expect to move up over time, the typical black could expect to go nowhere" (185). When a black worker "moves up" in *The Colonel's Dream* by being promoted to foreman, the white workers quit, thus insuring that the color line remains in force; they refuse to allow any African American, whether in the business or industrial realms, to rise. To turn Washington's statement on its head, African Americans would be "permitted" to do very little "in the community in which they reside"; they would always be circumscribed by racial ideology.

Racism was so endemic that white people were not only unwilling to give black people access even to economic crumbs but also, in Chesnutt's vision, more than willing to choke off all economic growth if doing so was necessary to preserve the color line. As one white character says toward the end of the novel, "We do not want to buy the prosperity of this town at the price of our principles. The attitude of the white people on the Negro question is fixed and determined for all time, and nothing can ever alter it" (264). In the face of this kind of intransigence, which he sees as deeply irrational, Chesnutt believes that Washington is altogether too optimistic in his hopes that African Americans will be able to "enter the all-powerful business and commercial world." As Chesnutt has already made clear in *The Marrow of Tradition*, racists, under one of the multitude of readily available justifications, will move against any black man who gains a modicum of economic power.

Chesnutt was clearly critical of both Washington and Colonel French because both were accommodationists. Neither was willing to confront directly the racist underpinnings of the New South ideology, and in very important ways, French shared the assumptions of that ideology. His position as reformer and as northern investor is eroded, however, by events in the melodramatic subplots, particularly in his confrontation with Fetters over the convict lease system.

II

Chesnutt comments ironically both on the cultural context and on the main economic plot involving French through a series of sentimental and melodramatic plots, all of which are connected to economic conditions in the South. The colonel's major local antagonist, Fetters, a stereotypical poor white who has made good in the New South, has made his fortune through the convict lease system, a practice of which French becomes aware when Old Peter, a former house slave of the French family, is to be "sold" for vagrancy. The other major melodramatic/economic subplot involves a young man, Ben Dudley, and is adapted from a story that was unpublished in Chesnutt's lifetime, "The Dumb Witness." The contours of the story and the subplot in the novel are much the same and are concerned with the enduring consequences of the Civil War. In the novel, Malcolm Dudley had managed an antebellum plantation for his uncle, and Malcolm had a sexual relationship with one of his uncle's slaves, Viney, "a tall comely young light mulatress, with a dash of Cherokee blood, which gave her straighter, blacker and more glossy hair than most women of mixed race have, and perhaps a somewhat different temperamental endowment" (171). When Malcolm gets engaged to a war widow, Viney breaks out "in a scene of hysterical violence" (171), after which she talks to the widow. The content of the conversation is never revealed, but the widow breaks off the engagement, and in retaliation, Dudley has Viney whipped. It turns out, melodramatically, that Viney has been holding a letter to Malcolm from his uncle that indicates that fifty thousand dollars has been hidden on the plantation, and only Viney knows its location. In shock at her whipping, Viney refuses to speak for the rest of Malcolm's life, driving him insane with the thought of the hidden money, her silence the sign of the money's absence. She does speak, however, on Malcolm's deathbed to reveal that the money was never on the plantation and that Malcolm had been pursuing a phantom. She explicitly states what motivated her silence: "You had me whipped—whipped—whipped—by a poor white dog I had despised and spurned! You had said that you loved me, and you had promised to free me—and yet had me whipped! But I have had my revenge" (273). Paradoxically, her silence enjoins the persistence of memory. Because Malcolm believes the money is hidden on the plantation, he can never forget his order to have Viney whipped and never forget his betrayal of his relationship with her.

In revising "The Dumb Witness," Chesnutt emphasized the sexual involvement of the two main characters and eliminated the recovery of the hidden money, thus creating an irony absent in the story and frustrating his readers' expectations of a happy ending. Both narratives, though, emphasize the grotesque distortion of normal human relations fostered by slavery and its aftermath—Viney remains mute for thirty years, while Malcolm spends all those years monomaniacally digging for buried treasure. Ben Dudley's love interest, Graciella, thinks, in contrast, that the idea of the missing money has "in it the element of romance" (126) and says that the story sounds like something "in a novel" (127). This self-reflexivity on Chesnutt's part signals an awareness of the genre in which he works, but it also stands as a warning to careful readers not to expect a conventional outcome. Malcolm, Ben Dudley, and Graciella are all conventional readers of the narrative of the missing money, all of them in thrall to romance and mystery. Unlike Cable in *John March, Southerner,* Chesnutt refused his readers the satisfactions of expected outcomes, and he resisted in the novel what he indulged in the story—the lure of romance and the melodramatic—so that he could comment ironically on how the past impinges on the present, on the inescapable historical consequences of the slave system.

Chesnutt was also very careful to show the connection between the economic oppression of the convict lease system and black violence in another of the subplots. It is as if this subplot were an effort to shift the ground of the national imaginary, to break the hold of the nexus of rape and lynching. As Chesnutt asked in a 1904 letter, "How can lynching be suppressed?" Part of his answer (one which sounds very much like Colonel French's) is that it can be suppressed "by the fostering of education and the general spread of enlightenment" (*Letters* 217). In the case of this subplot, enlightenment consists of trying to convince his audience that black violence might be a legitimate response to oppression, just as he did with the character of Josh Green in *The Marrow of Tradition.* Although he had a personal motive for his violence, Green was also attempting to defend the black community, but the African American violence in *The Colonel's Dream* is not directly about defending the community; it is solely personal. In Clarendon in the 1890s, black men arrested for minor crimes such as vagrancy are fined, as a justice of the peace claims, "to discourage laziness and to promote industry" (68). But because these men are fined, as French observes, "more money than . . . [they] perhaps ever had at any one time" (67), they are "sold" to local businessmen for a fixed period to work off the fine. The convict lease system, from Chesnutt's perspective (and from French's), reproduces the conditions of slavery in another form; black men are sold to the highest white bidder, and this version of slavery insists as well that resistant black men be broken, like Frederick Douglass was to be broken by Covey.

In the novel, a black man, Bud Johnson, is caught up in this system; refusing to be broken, he runs away from his sentence. When he is recaptured, he is subjected to even higher fines and thus longer periods of bondage. French becomes involved when Miss Laura Tredwell, the southern woman he is engaged to marry, asks him, as a point of honor, to help Johnson. Because of the near absolute power of Fetters, the local financial baron, French cannot be seen to help Johnson, but the colonel becomes passionately interested, as a social reformer, in trying to change the convict lease system. French makes so much trouble that Fetters offers a quid pro quo: Johnson in exchange for French's dropping his efforts to change the system. French refuses, but a young, sympathetic southern lawyer whom the colonel employs reminds him to remember the individual, Bud Johnson: "It's pretty hard on the nigger. They'll kill him before his time's up. If you'll give me a free hand, I'll get him away" (231). French asks to be spared the details, and Johnson escapes.

Thoroughly radicalized by his experience of peonage, Johnson resorts to violence in turn, attempting to murder two white men who were involved in oppressing him. Johnson severely wounds Fetters's son, and French is baffled by this turn of events. Realizing that "with the best of intentions, and hoping to save a life, he had connived at turning a murderer loose on the community" (246), he concludes that the "very standards of right and wrong had been confused by the race issue, and must be set right by the patient appeal to reason and humanity" (247). As part of his project of setting to rights these standards, he reveals to the authorities Johnson's hiding place, which French had learned in confidence from one of Clarendon's black leaders. The results are predictable. Before French can even begin his appeal by explaining what drove Johnson to his retributive violence, the black man is lynched. Again, French asks to be spared the details, but the narrator movingly comments, "A rope, a tree—a puff of smoke, a flash of flame—or a barbaric orgy of fire and blood—what matter which? At the end there was a lump of clay, and a hundred murderers where there had been one before" (277). Quixotically, French tries to bring the lynchers to justice, but the "coroner's jury returned a verdict of suicide, a grim joke which evoked some laughter" (278). Johnson, as the sheriff says, "had declared a vendetta against the white race" (277). In this phrase, I find an echo of the story of Robert Charles, who in 1900 in New Orleans killed seven whites, four of them police officers, and wounded twenty others. A New Orleans paper characterized Charles as "a black fanatic, in revolt against society" (Williamson, *Crucible* 208). His story too was consciously repressed, quickly forgotten.

In trying to ameliorate an injustice, French sets in motion a chain of events in which two white men are seriously wounded and one black man murdered, finding himself increasingly powerless to affect events. When he came to Clarendon, he assumed that his money, his good intentions, and his rationality would give him significant leverage over the town; what he has found, however, is that his money, intentions, and rationality have only exacerbated racial tensions and increased white racism. With the figure of Colonel French and his investment in rationality, Chesnutt was commenting on the loss of his deeply held belief in what Brook Thomas has characterized as "an eighteenth-century vision of a morally principled world in which equitable standards are knowable through reason" (160). In the last engagement with American racism to be published in his lifetime, Chesnutt seems to be fully confronting the ineffectuality of reason in the face of racism and fully taking the measure of the ineffectuality of race fiction based on assumptions of rationality.

The final melodramatic plot, that involving the former house slave, Old Peter, has occasioned some critical commentary because Chesnutt seems to indulge so freely in plantation stereotypes. In this subplot, however, I would argue that Chesnutt questions the interlinking of plantation mythology with New South ideology through his use of the stereotypical retainer figure. When the colonel returns to Clarendon, practically the first person he meets is Old Peter, who is tending the French family grave-yard, and he functions as "the guardian of the old memories and tradi-tions" (Gaston 182). Both French and Old Peter indulge in the nostalgia of plantation mythology and lament the past. As Old Peter says, "'Deed dem wuz good ole times" (26), a direct allusion to Page's "Marse Chan," but Chesnutt also makes clear that the New South has made no economic place for the likes of Peter, who has been exploited and then disabled in the postwar period. Old Peter exhibits all the characteristics of a man who laments the lost past, not because, as the narrator makes clear, he is innately or "naturally" subservient but because "Clarendon was a great place for looking back, perhaps because there was so little in the town to which to look forward" (38).

Although Old Peter is much more stereotypical than his literary pred-ecessor, Uncle Julius McAdoo of the *Conjure Woman* stories, French is aware of the need to fend off the romantic vision of slavery popularized through plantation mythology. French resistingly thinks, "How easy the conclusion that the slave's lot had been the more fortunate! ... Had Peter remained a slave, then the colonel would have remained a master, which was only another form of slavery. The colonel had been emancipated by the same token that had made Peter free" (29).[7] But French is less emanci-pated than he imagines; ultimately, he cannot think beyond the received cultural script. He can envision no roles for himself and Old Peter beyond the stereotypical ones: the generous ex-master and the grateful ex-slave. Here Chesnutt demonstrates the totalizing power of plantation mytho-logy: just as Old Peter was the colonel's "boy Peter ... who took care of me when I was no bigger than Phil" (25), the former slave becomes the guardian of the colonel's son, Phil, and the turning point for Colonel French's vision of reform comes out of the intersection of the economic plot and this particular sentimental plot. So devoted is Peter that he gives his life in attempting, futilely it turns out, to rescue French's son from an accident. Melodramatically, Phil and Old Peter die together, but before he dies, Phil extracts a promise from his father that the boy and Old Peter will be buried side by side. French feels honor bound to carry out this promise, and in the face of community opposition buries them both in the family plot in a segregated cemetery.

The community's response to the outrage of burying a black in a white graveyard is swift, decisive, and macabre. French finds the coffin on his piazza, with the following declaration attached:

> *Kurnell French:* Take notis. Berry yore ole nigger somewhar else. He can't stay in Oak Semitury. The majority of the white people of this town, who dident tend yore nigger funarl, woant have him there. Niggers by there selves, white peepul by there selves, and them that lives in our town must bide by our rules. By order of
>
> CUMITTY

He left the coffin on the porch throughout the day, but he received no sympathy from anyone in the town. "If there were those who reprobated the action they remained silent. The mob spirit . . . dominated the town, and no one dared speak against it" (281–82). This "mob spirit," however, has been carefully nurtured by "the foreman of Fetters's convict farm" (271) and fueled by free drinks in the local barroom. Chesnutt wants the reader to understand that this is no spontaneous overflowing of communal outrage. The outrage exists, of course, particularly among the lower-class whites, but Fetters whips up that outrage to defeat Colonel French. So even this macabre event is represented as highly calculated. Like the pogrom/riot in *The Marrow of Tradition,* race hatred is used strategically to further ambitious southerners' economic aims.

When the colonel returned to Clarendon, there was a split between the aristocrats and the lower-class whites, and French believed that while one could begin to use reason with the aristocrats, there was no talking to the lower-class whites. For instance, when Bud Johnson is lynched, French can think that only the "riffraff" (277) rather than the aristocrats were involved, but by the time of the desecration of Old Peter's grave, there is a virtual communal unanimity, and none of the aristocrats even privately condemns the mob's actions.[8] The absence of aristocratic condemnation is even more striking when one recalls the actions of Major Carteret in *The Marrow of Tradition.* When the repression his paper has instigated turns into pitched racial battle, Carteret at least attempts to restrain the mob. In *The Colonel's Dream,* "no one dare[s] speak against" the racial radicalism that extends even to the dead. After these events, French quickly decides to wash the dust of the town from his feet and flees, leaving his cotton mill unfinished. What Chesnutt did, then, with these events, was to take his white audience, through the vehicle of his well-intentioned central character, to the point where southern racism became intolerable. It is almost as if Chesnutt felt the necessity to create an event so outrageous, so Grand Guignol, that he hoped his audience would follow French in his righteous rage and rejection of the South.

This intersection of the economic and the sentimental/economic plots has puzzled critics. Andrews, for instance, has written, "The nagging question at the end of *The Colonel's Dream* is why the desecration of Uncle Peter's grave should destroy the Colonel's will to struggle against the injustice he now has seen in its most extreme form" (*Career* 251). This desecration, I would argue, graphically embodies for French (and for Chesnutt) the limits of instrumental notions of social reform. Pickens has observed that "French's problem is that he believes that white citizens are rational, moral, and capable of being uplifted and enlightened by philanthropy and a strong economic and educational program" (116). French discovers that white southerners are incapable of being elevated; furthermore, Chesnutt illustrates in this novel how notions of instrumental reform will inevitably be steamrolled by the irrational forces unleashed by racial radicalism. In the face of a powerful discourse of degeneracy and bestiality, even seemingly rational decisions such as economic investment and economic improvement become inflected with and infected by the irrational and atavistic fears of white people. After the exhumation of Peter's coffin, French says, "To mar the living—it is the history of life—but to make war upon the dead!" (*Dream* 283). To mar the living, whether in the battles of the Civil War or in the cotton mills is, indeed, the "history of life," in French's view, but to mar the dead is also the logic of a system of extreme oppression—to mar the dead in incomprehensible acts of mutilation after lynchings and to mar the dead by consigning them forever to a place in the national imaginary where they oscillate between being children and beasts, a place where they never are, in Chesnutt's terms, granted the right to be men.

The colonel had previously argued that he had been emancipated from the past, from the consequences of slavery, and here he sees that both blacks and whites are locked into a historically tragic embrace. In the desecration of Peter's grave, Chesnutt represented the general impossibility of emancipation from the past, and he came close to Marx's observation that the past "weighs like a nightmare on the brain of the living" (quoted in Foner, *Nothing* 37). In fact, this is a novel of disunion, a recognition of continued sectional antagonism. Neither poor nor upper-class whites, in Chesnutt's vision, are willing to relinquish the ideology of racism, and as Colonel French has perceptively argued, the restriction of rights is bound to impact southern prosperity. In addition, the burden of the past also accounts for Laura Tredwell breaking off her engagement to French; he tries to convince her to leave with him, but she is resolute in her determination to remain, while he cannot wait to escape: "I go tonight—not one hour longer than I must, will I remain in this town" (285). Laura realized, well before French, that she was an aspect of his nostalgia, "a part of the old and happy past" (284), and when his plans for economic uplift and moral regeneration founder, she realizes that he will have to reevaluate his nostalgia. She was for him "the embodiment of an ideal" (284); with the ideal shattered, she cannot accompany him back into the metropolitan world to which he has become accustomed. This is a highly conscious refusal, on Chesnutt's part, of the "standard device" of the "intersectional marriage" as a "symbol of national reconciliation" (Gaston 181). Chesnutt's refusal of this device flew in the face of the national consensus; he believed that racism was so deeply entrenched in the South that national reconciliation was impossible. In Chesnutt's bleak vision, a reconciliation based on the deprivation of the rights of African Americans condemned the South to continuing moral, economic, and cultural impoverishment—conclusions that contradicted everything his white audience believed it knew to be true.

III

French's flight signals more, I would argue, than his abandonment of this investment and the failure of his scheme of social reform. One needs to read this failure of French's along with Chesnutt's 1903 essay, "The Disfranchisement of the Negro," where he chronicles how African Americans had been systematically deprived of the vote and where he concludes that full voting rights "will be, after all, largely a white man's conflict, fought out in the forum of public conscience" (*Essays* 193). In this novel, Chesnutt saw with full clarity the fatuousness of the hope he expressed, as a younger man, for "the elevation of the whites" (*Journals* 139). His economic plot showed that whites had a greater investment in racism than in industrial development; he disagreed with Washington's program of education in the industrial arts; and he saw no way that African Americans would be able to regain, in his immediate future, the right to vote. I believe that at this moment he abandoned his abiding faith in what Richard Brodhead has termed "the novel as agent of social change" (Chesnutt, *Journals* 50 n.1).

If Chesnutt had any doubts about the efficacy of his novel, he had only to read the southern reviews, which were uniformly critical. For instance, the anonymous reviewer for the *Knoxville Sentinel* accused Chesnutt of deep prejudice against "southern laws and customs" and advised Chesnutt to "remember the advantage given the black man by southern whites, not the least of which was educating and civilizing them away from the savages from which they sprang" (Metcalf 63). One can hardly imagine a response more clearly designed to illustrate the failure of the novel as an agent of social change. In response to his representation of conditions in the South, Chesnutt was told that he was not properly grateful for the enslavement and exploitation of his African ancestors. Another review began by characterizing Chesnutt as "a man whose blood and rearing have made him alien in knowledge and sympathy to the people he would educate." For this reviewer, Chesnutt has clearly "overstep[ped]" himself, moved out of a traditional subservient role, and Chesnutt is advised "to make his stories the simple tales his heart moves him to write" (rev. of *The Colonel's Dream*). The only subject position that African Americans could assume as writers was as tellers of "simple" dialect stories conforming to plantation mythology; this reviewer saw Chesnutt as violating his "simple" nature in attempting to write a novel of the economic life. The *Nashville Banner* wrote that the novel was "grossly libelous as to southern conditions in general"; "The millions of white and black people who live together between the Chesapeake Bay and the Rio Grand preserve a remarkable amity. The entire section is prospering, as statistics can be produced in abundance to prove" ("Some New Books"). As with Manly's editorial, Chesnutt was again seen as a provocateur, "a new kind of liar . . . the negro littateur" ("The 'Wellington' Revolution"), who violated the national compact of silence. This review went on, though, to assert that the "negro problem would likely be no problem, if it were possible to stop its discussion, and it is greatly aggravated by being made material for novels" ("Some New Books"). This reviewer wanted the "problem" that African Americans represented to disappear. In this view, Chesnutt was not a realist, fearlessly confronting major southern social problems; rather, he was "an enemy of his people." By stirring up trouble, Chesnutt was seen to be retarding investment in the South and making life more difficult for all southerners, black and white.

Despite these angry and patronizing reviews, Chesnutt made a very odd comment about them in a letter: "A curious but interesting fact is that perhaps the most appreciative reviews have come from the South. They disagree with my conclusions, they deprecate the publication of the book, but they treat it with respect and do not deny its correctness as a picture of widespread conditions" (*Letters* 233). Given my reading of the novel and its reception, I can only see this as an aspect of Chesnutt's complex double vision pushed to the point of near blindness—as a refusal to acknowledge the chasm between his conflicted intentions and the novel's reception. These reviewers clearly perceived Chesnutt's novel as a provocation that broke part of the compact on which the New South ideology rested—that the press was "to create a friendly atmosphere by playing down social conflict and radical movements" (Gaston 73). If, as Chesnutt wrote in a 1904 letter, he classified himself as a member of the "more radical school" on the issue of "the rights of the Negro in the South" (*Letters* 208), then that very radicalism fundamentally contradicted his desire to emulate Stowe's and Tourgée's popular success in writing race fiction. Chesnutt wrote in another letter to his cousin, John P. Green, "I think you understand how difficult it is to write race problem books so that white people will read them,—and it is white people they are primarily aimed at. . . . If I could propose a remedy for existing evils that would cure them over night, I would be a great man" (*Letters* 156). This letter, written a year before the publication of *The Marrow of Tradition,* exhibits an attitude that Chesnutt will come to deconstruct in *The Colonel's Dream.* In 1901, Chesnutt could still sustain a marginal but still utopian faith in the efficacy of fiction as agent of social change. In that faith, I would argue, he was misreading the culture that he diagnosed so accurately in other ways. What Chesnutt saw, through the writing of *The Colonel's Dream,* was the failure of any possibility of instrumental reform and the fading of his utopian hopes for race fiction. The long-term reception of the novel confirmed this conviction. Almost ten years after the publication of *The Colonel's Dream,* Chesnutt commented in another letter on its almost negligible effect on debate in the public sphere: the novel was out of print, he had no copies of his own, and the book "was not a pronounced success" (*Exemplary Citizen* 118).

The contradictory ambitions embedded in the novel are emphasized by the coda to *The Colonel's Dream.* Several years after the main events of the novel, French meets the only developed black character, Henry Taylor, who had taught in the black school in Clarendon and had informed Colonel French where Bud Johnson was to be found. As a result of Taylor's act of good citizenship, he is ostracized from his community, having become, he says, "an enemy of my race," the same phrase used to describe French when French buries Old Peter in the white graveyard (271). The meeting on the train, however, serves to underline only the asymmetry between these two outcasts. Although French has lost his son, he has remarried and is traveling in luxury to the West to investigate a new investment opportunity; Taylor is now a railroad porter, expelled from his hometown. In sorrowfully surveying the events in Clarendon,

Taylor says to French, "You was the only white man that ever treated me quite like a man—and our folks just like people." In his private reflections, however, Taylor thinks that "his people will never get very far along in the world without the good will of the white people, but he is still wondering how they will secure it. For he regards Colonel French as an extremely fortunate accident" (293). Chesnutt's answer seemed to be that it was impossible to secure the goodwill of white people and that the accidental missionary philanthropy of men such as French could do nothing to change conditions in the South; indeed, their philanthropy ironically reinforced racist ideology.

In addition, the contradictory ambitions are further emphasized by the ambivalence of the last two paragraphs of the novel. On the one hand, Chesnutt seemed to want to believe that social conditions in the South were improving for African Americans. Part of him thought that the racial climate in the South was slowly, almost imperceptibly, improving: convict peonage had been abolished; "here and there a brave judge has condemned the infamy of the chain gang and convict lease systems" (293); and men of both the North and the South had banded together to promote the "cause of popular education" (294). In these "great social changes," Chesnutt discerned a "changed attitude of mind" in which "lies the hope of the future, the hope of the Republic" (294). Remarkably, though, when he turned to Clarendon in the final paragraph of the novel, he saw only further stagnation and decay—"leaner pigs and lazier loafers" is how he summed it up—but in the last sentences of the novel he swerved again, reaching for a utopian vision of the future, a visionary hope his novel has shown cannot be sustained. The narrator acknowledges, once again, the conditions that have been diagnosed in the novel: "White men go their way, and black men theirs, and these ways grow wider apart, and no one knows the outcome." He then invokes a contradictory, utopian hope for change, invokes those who "hope" and "pray, that this condition will pass, that some day our whole land will be truly free, and the strong will cheerfully help to bear the burdens of the weak, and Justice, the seed, and Peace, the flower, of liberty, will prevail throughout all our borders" (294). Again, Chesnutt vividly illustrated his own ambivalence. Despite the undeniable social fact that whites and blacks were increasingly divided into two nations and that "no one knows the outcome," he was still possessed by the hope that in a utopian future he could not imagine, peace and liberty would triumph.

At the beginning of the twentieth century, then, the first major African American writer of fiction confronted the limits of political action, social reform, and fiction, and he wrote no more novels for more than fifteen years. His novelistic silence from 1905 until the 1920s has everything to do with the recognition of those limits, and rather than being dismissed as he was for writing *The Colonel's Dream*, he subsequently put his public efforts into direct social action, both locally and nationally. As Chesnutt became aware of the limits of critical realism as social protest, perhaps he fully realized the force of a comment he had recorded in his journal almost twenty-five years earlier, when he was twenty-three. An African American acquaintance told him of a conversation with a white man about Chesnutt, and Chesnutt's friend reported that the white man concluded the conversation by saying that whatever Chesnutt's attainments, whatever his culture and learning, "He's a nigger; and with me a nigger is a nigger, and nothing in the world can make him anything but a nigger" (161). In the end, one might see Chesnutt's move from dialect tales to his disillusionment in *The Colonel's Dream* as his rejection of the compromise typified by Booker T. Washington: increasingly, during Chesnutt's short career, he refused to conform to the stereotype of the black writer, a stereotype that he saw only helped buttress the complicated intertwinings of plantation mythology and New South ideology. Chesnutt's critical realism (and his hyperbolic melodrama) in *The Colonel's Dream* was a recognition that early-twentieth-century U.S. culture offered African American writers no place where they could be anything but "niggers" in the eyes of the white reading public.

[7]

Paul Marchand, F.M.C.

The Strange Alchemy of Race

When Charles W. Chesnutt returned to novel writing fifteen years after *The Colonel's Dream* was published, he had given up on the potential elevation of his white audience. The ambivalence that he expressed in the final paragraphs of *The Colonel's Dream* had vanished and had been replaced by a thorough despair at the lack of African American improvement that had occurred in his lifetime. Perhaps his only concession to his potential audience is the setting of the novel in antebellum New Orleans. Representing conditions there before the Civil War, he moved directly into George Washington Cable's imaginative terrain, (and this is his only generic accommodation of this audience), but did so in a way that signaled how far his convictions about race in the United States had shifted. Despite what Arnold Rampersad has termed the arthritic conventions of local color and melodrama (3), *Paul Marchand, F.M.C.* is by far Chesnutt's most pessimistic novel. There is not a single positive white character in the novel. At the end of the tale, the central character, Paul Marchand, and his family emigrate to France, and the descendants of his "white" family, the Beaurepases, are committed racists in the 1920s.

Paul Marchand, F.M.C., the penultimate of Chesnutt's six manuscript novels, was written in 1921, after Chesnutt had returned to full-time work in his court stenography business and had seemingly given up the writing of novels. Chesnutt tried unsuccessfully to interest Houghton Mifflin,

Harcourt Brace, and Alfred Knopf in *Paul Marchand* (Andrews, *Career* 265), and after their rejections, he put the novel aside, never to return to it. No doubt the editors at these publishers saw this novel as little more than an anachronism, an imitation of Cable's New Orleans writings, particularly *Old Creole Days* (1879) and *The Grandissimes* (1880). Like the editors at Small, Maynard, and Company, who in 1919 had rejected a volume of Chesnutt's dialect stories entitled *Aunt Hagar's Children,* the editors who read *Paul Marchand, F.M.C.* probably thought that Chesnutt had chosen to work in an "outdated genre" (Andrews *Career* 264), one that had not been current for almost a quarter of a century. For these reasons, William L. Andrews has characterized Chesnutt's writing in this period as "increasingly retrospective" (*Career* 264).

This "retrospective" move on Chesnutt's part not only returned him to the genre of local color, which he had explored in one of his first two volumes of short stories, *The Conjure Woman* (1899), but also imaginatively reconnected him to Cable, Chesnutt's first literary contact and mentor. A few years earlier, in his last novel, *Lovers of Louisiana* (1918), Cable had returned to the issues that had engaged him during the period of his polemical writing on race, but the setting of the novel is contemporary New Orleans. Cable's central character, Philip Castleton, is polemically antiracist, and his position on race has alienated his community and presents endless complications to his marriage to the Creole woman with whom he is in love. Both Castleton and an outsider, a Scotchman, insist that the race question still needs to be solved, as in this excerpt from a discussion between the two about the major African American character in the novel: "'Our old south could give him no worthy, no American freedom, nor the North give him an American freedom over the New South's head, and the New South crowds him half-way down again to his old slavery and—' 'And points wi' pride,' ... put in the Scot" (41). In Cable's view, no changes for the better had occurred in terms of the civil rights of African Americans, but they are, as in *John March, Southerner,* largely absent from the novel. African Americans are, rather, the essential background against which Cable staged Castleton's dilemma of white manhood, and there seems not to be a great deal of distance between Castleton and Cable on the issue of African American rights.

Like Cable, Castleton is a voice crying in the wilderness, and the only way that Cable could signal any optimism in the novel was through the romantic plot. By having Castleton and the Creole woman marry, he reconfigured the national reconciliation plot into a sectional reconciliation between two southern positions—the archconservative and the mildly liberal. Although he believes in political rights for African Americans, Castleton remains a white supremacist. Lest he become a totally alienated enemy of his race, Castleton signals the limits of his liberalism: "his one great care had been to make clear that, whatever his convictions, his supreme sympathies and solicitudes were for his own race" (108); furthermore, just as much as any Creole, he believes in "safeguarding racial purity" (124). In the wake of World War I, Cable returned to the imaginative terrain of New Orleans, and his ideological position had changed little in more than thirty years. Like Chesnutt, he still believed in civil rights for African Americans, while his spokesman, Castleton, remains committed to the social separation of the races. So while Cable writes about the contemporary South, Chesnutt chooses, tactically, to represent antebellum New Orleans and to conduct an experiment there in racial heredity and environment.

I

Almost nothing of the context out of which this novel grew is known except for a few hints from Helen Chesnutt's book. Living in Cleveland, Ohio, Charles Chesnutt knew that the color line was inescapable in literature and that it ran "everywhere so far as the United States is concerned" (*Letters* 171). Although this was a deep and long-term conviction, Chesnutt, his daughter recorded, was surprised when he unwittingly crossed that line. In 1917, he had been on vacation with his family, touring the Gettysburg battlefield. The Chesnutts subsequently went to have a meal in the Gettysburg Inn and were about to be ejected from the restaurant when they all began speaking French, apparently convincing the manager and the hostess that they were foreigners rather than African Americans. Helen Chesnutt claims that the family was "very much shocked for they had not had this particular kind of experience before" (274). Nevertheless, Chesnutt certainly knew the all-encompassing quality of the color line, and he also was bitterly aware of white Americans' general lack of sympathy and understanding. Chesnutt also realized in the aftermath of World War I that racial conditions had deteriorated. Not only were returning African American servicemen attacked in the South, but antiblack sentiment had escalated. The number of lynchings had begun to rise again—from thirty-six in 1917 to sixty in 1918 to seventy-six in 1919, "including ten veterans, some still in uniform" (Painter 365), and 1919 in Chicago there "was the closest thing to a race war that anyone could remember" (364). The ferocity of this postwar racial anger can be gauged by the incident that set off the racial violence in Chicago: "a black boy swimming off a Lake Michigan beach drifted across an imaginary color line. Whites on the beach stoned him to death as a white policeman looked on impassively. Blacks mobbed the policeman, and the worst riot of a grim season began" (364). Events like these must have fed Chesnutt's pessimism. After all, he had moved North to escape this kind of virulent racism, and while he had no illusions about the national extent of racism, he must, with his aversion to violence, have been deeply shocked by the events of 1919. Despite the work of W. E. B. DuBois and the National Association for the Advancement of Colored People (in which Chesnutt was involved from its founding), few white Americans in the 1920s would have admitted, as Chesnutt argued in 1893, that "the present [racial] situation is all wrong." In his pessimism, Chesnutt was participating in a moment of "African American cultural grief" that "became especially graphic in all forms of black cultural production during the first two decades of the twentieth century" (Tate 15).

Chesnutt's daughter, though, was critical of what she perceived to be her father's post–World War I optimism. Her parents, she wrote, thought that "conditions seemed to be improving," but to the Chesnutt children it appeared that "the recognition of the Negro as a human being was rapidly disappearing from American thought" (281). If Charles Chesnutt told his family in conversation that he had grown to be more optimistic, the novel that he wrote demonstrates that he had in reality given in the to the "bitterness" with which William Dean Howells had charged Chesnutt twenty years earlier. Apparently, post–World War I conditions were so bad that he chose in *Paul Marchand* to step outside the realities of contemporary America by writing about New Orleans in the first quarter of the nineteenth century. But Chesnutt's choice of a central character—a man who supposes for most of the novel that he has mixed racial ancestry—returned the author to the liminality he explored in *Mandy Oxendine* and *The House Behind the Cedars*. In fact, one might argue that Chesnutt was taking up again the kind of figure he created in John Warwick (Walden)—a supposedly mixed-race man who was not abashed or apologetic about his ancestry, but, as I observed in my discussion of *The House Behind the Cedars*, John disappeared into the white world and from the latter part of the novel. With *Paul Marchand*, Chesnutt brought the dilemma of a supposedly mixed-race man center stage, more than ever before, and Marchand is to be seen as a revision of Cable's Honoré Grandissime F.M.C., a character in *The Grandissimes*. In choosing to revise the figure of someone we take to be a mulatto in antebellum New Orleans and to make him more honorable than his white peers, Chesnutt shed new imaginative light on his decision as a young man not to pass and "to own his color," in Howells's phrase ("Chesnutt's Stories" 701).

In rejecting his whiteness at the end of the novel, Marchand, like Chesnutt, can be seen as a "voluntary Negro" (quoted in Hackenberry, Introduction xxiv), and both decide to stay loyal to their upbringing and family. This choice is the obverse of that made by John Warwick (Walden) in *The House Behind the Cedars* and could also be seen as an exorcism of Chesnutt's decision not to pass. In passing, Warwick (Walden) remakes himself, but that remaking involves a painful renunciation of family, and while Warwick (Walden) is willing to pay that price to become white, Marchand is not. Significantly, though, Warwick (Walden)'s family consists of his mother and sister, while Marchand would have to renounce his wife and bastardize his children were he to become white. For Marchand, given the history of slavery and the history of octoroon women in New Orleans, family continuity becomes of paramount importance.

That emphasis on family connects Marchand to another of Chesnutt's post-1905 characters, Tom Taylor, the central figure of the 1912 short story

"The Doll." Confronted by the white man who has killed Taylor's father, Taylor, a barber, has the opportunity to slit the murderer's throat but resists the temptation to preserve his family: "His own father had died in defense of his daughter; he must live to protect his own" (*Short Fiction* 412). This emphasis on family continuity also helps to account for how Chesnutt in *Paul Marchand* revised the conclusion to Twain's 1894 novel, *Pudd'nhead Wilson*. In that novel, to keep her infant son from being sold, the white slave, Roxy, switches her baby with the master's (both are blue-eyed and blonde), and so the nominally "black" child grows up as the white master, while the "white" child grows up as a slave. At the end of the novel, when the children are grown, the deception is discovered, and they are switched back. The nominally black character who has been brought up white becomes part of the estate that was once his, and "the creditors sold him down the river" (115). Conversely, the "white" character, Tom, because of his upbringing, is permanently unsuited for life as a white man, and Twain goes into painful detail in describing the effects of his transformation: "He could neither read nor write, and his speech was the basest dialect of the negro quarter. His gait, his attitudes, his gestures, his bearing, his laugh—all were vulgar and uncouth; his manners were the manners of a slave.... The poor fellow could not endure the terrors of the white man's parlor, and felt at home nowhere but in the kitchen" (114). Because of his upbringing, he clearly will never be able to take possession of his whiteness.

In *Paul Marchand*, Chesnutt concurred with Twain on the issue of environment. One's upbringing and one's socialization are irreversible, but Chesnutt lacked Twain's ambivalence about heredity, which is dramatized in *Pudd'nhead Wilson* in the narrative of the "black" child brought up as the master's son. He turns out, of course, to be weak and vicious, a combination that his slave mother, Roxy, blames on his black blood: "It's de nigger in you, dat's what it is. Thirty-one part o' you is white, en on'y one part nigger, en dat po' little one part is yo' *soul*" (70). Despite his interest in environment as an explanatory principle, Twain participates in the American consensus on race mixing: Tom is evidence of how race mixing leads inevitably to degeneration. By the 1920s, Chesnutt has long since rejected the discourses of blood and degeneration, and he constructs a character who does not, when he believes himself to be of mixed-race parentage, bewail his "fate" or curse "the drop of black blood that 'taints' [his] otherwise pure blood" (*Letters* 66) as do the mixed-race characters of Albion Tourgée. Instead, when Marchand rejects his white patrimony, he says, "My cousin Henri once said . . . that blood without breeding cannot make a gentleman. It may be said with equal truth that the race consciousness which is the strongest of the Creole characteristics, is not a matter of blood alone, but in large part the product of education and environment; it is social rather than personal." He concludes that one cannot "change easily his whole outlook upon life, nor can one trained as a quadroon become over night a—Beaurepas"—that is, a white man (138).

In choosing to have Marchand remain faithful to his upbringing instead of his "blood," Chesnutt is turning on its head one of the tropes of nineteenth-century race fiction, in which "white" characters discover, much to their horror, that they are actually "black." In *Paul Marchand, F.M.C.,* a "black" man discovers much to his horror that he is "white." And in one of the few humorous passages in all of Chesnutt's writing, Paul's wife, Julie, tells their children about his change in status: "'My poor children. . . . We have met with a great misfortune—a terrible calamity! . . . Prepare yourselves, my angels, for terrible news. . . . Your papa is—white!' Loud was the weeping, as Julie gathered her chickens under her wings. Their papa had hated white people" (89). Of course, Julie realizes that his whiteness means that they are no longer legally married, but in the eyes of his children he has turned, by the strange alchemy of race, into the very thing he hates.

Marchand's decision, however, to renounce his biological whiteness and the advantages that come with it in favor of his upbringing and his family is made possible by his wealth, which has come from his wife, and by his decision to leave the United States. As Andrews has pointed out, Marchand's move to France recalls the conclusion to Howells's 1892 novel, *An Imperative Duty* (266), but in that novella the main characters live out their lives with an awareness of a "secret" to be hidden. Although physically outside of the United States, they have internalized American race prejudice. Marchand, in contrast, rejects the basis of American racism, and like Chesnutt's contemporary, painter Henry O. Tanner, emigrates to France, where he will have nothing to hide and where his children will become full French citizens, one of them, ironically, returning to New Orleans as a French military observer during the Civil War.

II

In the scene where he relinquishes his whiteness and his leadership of one of the first families of New Orleans, Marchand says somewhat mysteriously to his cousins, "I must confess, gentlemen, that my father's experiment has proved a failure." In what sense might Pierre Beaurepas's treatment of his son be considered an "experiment"? The knowledge of Paul's birth was concealed because his parents married secretly after the supposed death of her first husband; that husband returned, only to die two days after his reappearance. Pregnant with Pierre's child, she retired to a remote plantation where Paul was born, but because of her sensitivity to scandal and her sense of propriety, she was never willing to acknowledge him as her son, and after her death, in respect of her wishes, Pierre never reveals to Paul who his parents are. However, as the family lawyer says in revealing this story, Paul "was always amply provided for, was carefully educated, and is prepared at every point to take up the responsibilities which have been so suddenly thrust upon him." More ominously, the lawyer continues: "If there have arisen seeming obstacles to this, growing out the misconception of his race, they are not such as the law, in its wise and humane provision, cannot and does not correct" (79). Pierre's concealment of Paul's parentage and education could be seen as an exploration of the effects of heredity and environment, like Twain's *Pudd'nhead Wilson,* but Marchand's use of the word *experiment* points to how Chesnutt has characterized Pierre and to the possibility that what began out of necessity became, in Pierre's mind, something entirely different— an experiment, but one with unexpected results.

Early in the novel, Pierre Beaurepas is described as an eighteenth-century rationalist: in his library is a reproduction of Houdon's statue of Voltaire, and Pierre is said to be a "disciple of Rousseau and Voltaire, cynical in his attitude toward life" (26) Seated in his library, Pierre is discovered reading one of the few books named in *Paul Marchand*: "In his hand he held a copy of *Émile*, autographed by the great Jean Jacques himself" (26). *Émile* is Rousseau's extended treatise on education, in which he argues that education is a deformation of the natural man. "Good social institutions are those best fitted to make a man unnatural" (8), he writes, and he further argues that eighteenth century educational practice is like "an intolerable slavery" (50). In contrast, Rousseau proposes a theory of educational benign neglect, in which the natural will be cultivated, an educational philosophy that would result in a balance between desire and ability. Rousseau's "fundamental maxim" is "[t]hat man is truly free who desires what he is able to perform, and does what he desires" (56).

Pierre Beaurepas's reading of *Émile* is a sign by Chesnutt that the novel is in some way about the consequences of education, about a "cynical" educational experiment set in a system of racial oppression. This experiment, however, involves not only Paul Marchand but also Pierre's five nephews. Knowing that his health is failing, Pierre uses an old trusted family slave, Zabet, to set them all up; he interrogates each about his financial circumstances and knows that all lie to him. Pierre is subjecting his nephews to a final test, and all except Philippe are found wanting. Late in the novel, though, there is yet another surprise about Pierre's experiment with his nephews. In going through his father's papers, Marchand discovers a letter to Pierre from the mother of the nephews, a letter in which she refers to her youngest child as "*la petite*," the feminine form of "the little one" (92). Marchand threatens Zabet, who brought the nephews from Haiti to New Orleans, and she reveals that the little girl died during the voyage, and Zabet substituted her own grandson, the son of Pierre's brother and a slave woman. Pierre, then, knows from the time that the five nephews arrive in New Orleans as children that one of them is not white, but he chooses to bring up that child as a white man. When Marchand asks Zabet the name of the child and she whispers it in his ear, the "sinister look" on his face which "might very well have masked the joy of anticipated revenge, gave place . . . to an expression very like disappointment" (96).

The only possible reason for him to experience disappointment at this juncture is because the mixed-race nephew is the only decent one, the only one not to insult Marchand—that the racial ringer is Philippe.

Now what is Chesnutt up to here? He has reproduced, in the special circumstances of Cable's New Orleans, with its quadroon class, the basic plot of Twain's *Pudd'nhead Wilson*: a "white" man brought up black, a "black" man brought up white. In both parts of the plot, though, Chesnutt revises Twain. At the end of Twain's novel, when the truth of ancestry is discovered, places are traded, and each character returns to his "proper" place in the American racist imaginary. But the conclusion of Twain's novel is bitter because upbringing—environment—has made each man unsuited for the place he is forced to occupy. The man brought up white is totally unsuited to be a slave, while the man brought up black is completely incapable of being a master. For Chesnutt, on the other hand, the "black" man brought up white turns out to be the most decent and humane of all the nephews, unlike Twain's character, who has been betrayed, his mother claims, by his black "blood." One is left wondering, then, how to account for Philippe's difference. All the nephews were treated the same—"sent to good schools" and each "upon reaching his majority, was given sufficient money to set himself up in the business of his choice" (28). Despite this scrupulously equal treatment, the pure "white" nephews turn out badly: one brother is about to lose his house; the second has embezzled funds from his firm; the third is the head of a business about to go bankrupt; the fourth owes "more debts than he could ever hope to pay out of his income" (29) Like his half-brothers, Philippe "had been bred a gentleman, had been educated, clothed and nurtured as a gentleman, and expected by his own exertions to be able to live as a gentleman" (40–41). Unlike them, though, "he had no expensive vices—he was neither drunkard, nor gambler, nor roué" (41). The only way the novel gives us to account for the differences among these men who received the same educations and who were given the same opportunities is race—that somehow Philippe is a finer character *because* of the mixture of races he represents.

What Chesnutt did here was to recast imaginatively an idea at which he had hinted twenty years earlier in his series of articles, "The Future

American." In the first of them, he ridiculed a current "popular theory" that claimed that the "harmonious fusion of the various European elements which now make up our heterogeneous population" would result in a kind of racial "perfection." Somehow, Chesnutt wrote, all of the "undesirable traits" would be eliminated, and the new American would be "as perfect as everything else American" (*Essays* 121). In the conclusion to the final article, Chesnutt returned to the idea of improvement, but he applied it to racial amalgamation: "The white race is still susceptible of some improvement; and if, in time, the more objectionable Negro traits are eliminated, and his better qualities correspondingly developed, his part in the future American race may well be an important and valuable one" (*Essays* 135). The racial amalgamation that results in Philippe Beaurepas makes him a finer man than any of his half-brothers, but it does not make him in any way a paragon. Although he is decent, honorable, and the first to welcome Paul to the family, he is ultimately not a very "good business man," and under his stewardship "the family fortune . . . sadly dwindled" (144). Years later, Philippe entertains Paul's French son in New Orleans, and Philippe is "one of the first of the reconstructed rebels" (143). More importantly, as a result of his knowledge that he or one of his brothers is "black," he is the only one of the nephews who becomes "more tolerant of those of darker blood" (144) (when Paul offers to tell them which brother is of mixed race ancestry, they choose, out of fear, to remain ignorant).

If one side of Pierre Beaurepas's experiment proved that the white Beaurepas brothers were evidence of white degeneration, and while their half-brother is evidence of a successful racial fusion, the results of the other part of the experiment, the education of a white man as a quadroon, are more complicated and more ambivalent. Confirmed racists, like the cousins, would say in the case of Paul Marchand that environment and training will overrule biological whiteness: "He has been bred a quadroon, and blood without breeding is not enough to make a gentleman. . . . He has been trained to subordination, to submission. How could he resent an insult?" (85). When Marchand challenges them for insults given when he was believed to be a quadroon, they switch to the opposite discourse—that of blood—to explain his behavior. His sense of honor "was a proof . . . of his purity of race. No quadroon could have taken such a course, it was foreign to the quadroon nature" (102). In the racist imaginary, blood always trumps environment. However, none of them can conceive that their uncle's experiment demonstrates something altogether different—that education in large measure determines "nature," that education can make a gentleman but cannot make a white man. In this regard, a crucial difference between Marchand and his cousins is that he is brought up in New Orleans but educated in Paris, "where he had spent several happy years, finding, in the free atmosphere of student life in the French capital, the opportunity to expand in mind and spirit. There was no color line in France, nor ever has been, and in that country men of color even at that epoch had occasionally distinguished themselves in war, in art, in letters and in politics" (14). In fact, while in France, Marchand had been "an ardent Republican and had accepted and proclaimed the radical doctrine of *The Rights of Man* as applying to all men, with no reservations" (84). Having lived outside of American racial categories, Marchand is in some ways more French than American. However, as Dean McWilliams has observed, Marchand "regards himself as the equal of his white peers. As the novel progresses, he proves his moral superiority to them, growing in self-understanding and in identification with oppressed blacks" (Introduction to *Paul Marchand* xiii). Despite this identification, Marchand helps to save his father's friend, Don José Morales, and his daughter from an attack by two slaves who had escaped from jail. Marchand understands what drove them to their retributive violence, and at the end of the novel, before handing over the estate to Philippe, he frees all of its slaves. Even more of an advocate of the rights of man at the end of the novel than at the beginning, Marchand chafes at living under a system that had deprived him of legal rights and even of the right to his own honor. So the education that his father provided has made Marchand a hybrid, someone who can understand the lives of whites, quadroons, and slaves, whereas the education of the cousins enables them to understand nothing but their own narrow experience.

Even though his cultural hybridity gives him a wide range of sympathy and understanding, it does not blunt Marchand's sense of abiding outrage. What is most upsetting for him in finding out that he is biologically white is that he has become what he hates, and his children decry the knowledge of his whiteness because "they had . . . heard their father swear a great French oath, that if all the white people of New Orleans had but one neck, and he could hold it in his hands, he would strike it through at a single blow, or wring it like a pullet's" (90). Refusing to become white, Marchand argues for the paramount importance not only of upbringing but also of education, because if he has been brought up as quadroon, he has been educated as a Frenchman, and if, as Rousseau argues, happiness consists of a sense of proportion between "our desires and our powers" (52), then the only place where he can experience that sense is France. Only outside the system of America's binary racial categorization and oppression can Marchand, in Rousseau's sense, be truly free. But is it possible to argue that, in emigrating to France, he is inevitably becoming that thing he hates, which is a white man? We need to remember, though, that only in the United States are he and his children seen as "white" or "black." As the concluding paragraphs of the novel make clear, they all escape the trap of whiteness by becoming French.

III

Although Andrews calls Chesnutt's writing in this period "retrospective," Chesnutt uses New Orleans as a plausible setting for his startling experiment in upbringing and education. But the novel is also a simultaneous homage to and critique of Cable, with whom Chesnutt had been imaginatively engaged through most of his writing career. Chesnutt initially had been drawn to Cable during the late 1890s because Cable's was almost the only white voice raised in protest against the post-Reconstruction treatment of African Americans (and in the second decade of this century Chesnutt may well have also seen the collapse of Cable's career as mirroring that of Chesnutt).[1] In a series of essays written from 1885 to 1888, Cable argued that race prejudice is "caste" prejudice, "not the embodiment of a modern European idea, but the resuscitation of an ancient Asiatic one" (*Negro Question* 135). At the beginning of his career, "caste" gave Chesnutt a way to conceptualize race as a social construct,[2] but he also saw, from the beginning, how Cable, like Colonel French, was still implicated in the same racism he was attempting to critique. For instance, in the essays, Cable accepted that blacks were "an inferior race" (*Negro Question* 126) (although he did question the permanence of that inferiority), and he asserted that the importation of Africans into America "grafted into the citizenship of one of the most intelligent nations in the world six millions of people from one of the most debased nations on the globe" (*Negro Question* 52). In Cable's fiction, the result of this presumed debasement is the "melancholy Honoré Grandissime, F.M.C." who, out of a paralysis of will—his presumed heritage as a man of mixed race—eventually commits suicide.

In *Paul Marchand, F.M.C.* Chesnutt's reengagement with Cable is strategic; Chesnutt needs New Orleans because it is the only place in the antebellum period with a recognized legal class of persons, the quadroons, between whites and blacks, a class in which Chesnutt lived in and wrote for much of his career (and Louisiana is one of the two "liberal" states on issues of race in the period when the novel is set). However, in the twenty years between the appearance of Dr. Miller in *The Marrow of Tradition* and *Paul Marchand*, Chesnutt's use of male mixed-race characters became less nuanced, and in the later novel he creates what I think of as a paragon figure, the kind found in earlier novels such as Sutton Griggs's *The Hindered Hand* (1905) and J. McHenry Jones's *Hearts of Gold* (1896). Through their high degree of education, their sophistication, and their wealth of cultural capital, these paragon figures functioned as counterarguments to notions of the "natural" inferiority of blacks. Employing this representative figure, Chesnutt betrayed a nineteenth-century rather than a twentieth-century attitude about African American cultural progress as a sign of innate equality, the sign of the representative man. This attitude can be seen in Howells's, review of Chesnutt's short stories, which lists Chesnutt among other African American exemplars: Frederick Douglass, Booker T. Washington, Paul Laurence Dunbar, and Henry O. Tanner ("Chesnutt's Stories" 701). The cultural function of the all-knowingness and hypercorrectness of the paragon figure in Griggs, Jones, and Chesnutt acted as a counterstereotype for a culture that largely believed that mixed-race figures could "*imitate* or parody but not . . . own the property of whiteness" (Sundquist 249). Marchand's largely French education accounts for his qualities as a paragon, but there is a certain aura of irreality about him, particularly when it is revealed that he is one of the best fencers in New Orleans, and when in what is supposed to be a pro forma duel he wounds, with supreme ease, three of his cousins.

As a paragon, Marchand would have been deeply problematic for an audience in the 1920s because of the discourse of blood, which Chesnutt had only partially rejected but which his audience had not. By my count, Chesnutt uses the term *blood* in its metaphysical, fetishistic[3] sense more than thirty times in the novel. For instance, when Marchand is in jail for having attended the quadroon ball and for having fought with his cousins, who were attempting to abduct his sister-in-law, the narrator says, "Whether it was the fiery spirit of some adventurous European ancestor, or the blood of some African chief who had exercised the power of life and death before being broken to the hoe, or whether the free air of revolutionary France had wrought upon him—whatever the reason, he had chafed more than most under the restrictions of his caste" (60). Even though Chesnutt's last option was the one in which he believed—education—he still felt compelled to include the other two options. Of course, he was trying to balance the possible reasons for Marchand's difference from his peers, and Chesnutt equated the "fiery" European spirit with the "blood of some African chief." But every time he invoked blood, he was calling on an explanatory principle that undercut, with his potential audience, the position that he wanted to maintain. His audience would have seen Marchand's sense of honor as a product of the "purity" of his blood, whereas four of the five nephews cut the other way: their pure white "blood" did not seem to have prevented their degeneracy, and even Philippe seemed to have been "tainted" by his white blood.

The only way out of the trap of American racism that Chesnutt could envision in this novel was emigration, an option (like passing) that he rejected early in his life. In 1887, Judge Williamson, with whom Chesnutt had been reading law, offered to loan Chesnutt the money to enable him to emigrate to Europe. Chesnutt refused, his daughter concluded, because he was "an idealist. . . . He felt that success in his own country against terrific odds would be worth more than success in a foreign country" (Helen Chesnutt 41). In *Paul Marchand,* Chesnutt's idealism was in abeyance, and in the 1920s, the liminality that Marchand found so burdensome had become less of a problem in African American thought because the "mulatto elite," rather than seeing themselves as set apart—between black and white—had begun to identity with the black masses (Williamson, *New People* 112). Although Marchand identifies culturally with his upbringing as a man who believed that his ancestry was racially mixed, he has no loyalty to any group beyond his immediate family. Like Chesnutt, Marchand at one point "dreamed . . . that he might . . . preach the doctrine of human equality; not offensively, but persuasively, appealing to men's reason and their sense of justice. He soon learned that this was impracticable, if not impossible" (129). Like Chesnutt and Colonel French, Marchand learns that racism is not amenable to reason, and his emigration is a rejection of the underlying assumptions of that racism. Andrews, however, calls this rejection "an exercise in wish-fulfillment. . . . Chesnutt finally realized in fantasy what would never be actualized in his own lifetime— the liberation of the mixed-blood from the social and psychological prison of racially defined identity" (*Career* 266). Although the novel may have some aspects of wish fulfillment, those aspects are more than offset by Chesnutt's pessimism, bitterness, and anger. To the degree to which *Paul Marchand* touches on racial realities in the 1920s, it is a rejection of what Chesnutt had tried to achieve throughout his earlier novel-writing career. He seems to be telling his audience that the United States is intolerable for an educated African American man, and Chesnutt has given up any hope of elevating his white audience. Had the novel been published in the early 1920s one wonders whether its potential audience would have been able to see past the old-fashioned conventions of local color to its bitter disillusionment and to the rather sophisticated playing out of variations on the question of heredity and environment?

In arguing that Chesnutt has collapsed into the fantasy of liberation from racial oppression, Andrews underestimates the cultural force of the offer that Marchand refuses. Biologically white, he rejects the privileges and opportunities of his whiteness, a choice, as I pointed out earlier, that was seen as close to insanity: "No white person of sound mind would ever claim to be a negro" (*House* 153). Of sound mind, Marchand chooses to identify with his upbringing and to nurture his family and to give them the best opportunities that life can offer, something that Chesnutt clearly did for his own children. In having Marchand make this choice, Chesnutt argued more forcefully than perhaps anywhere else in his writing that race is little more than a social construction. In *Paul Marchand* he identified this particularly American racialized thinking as a "legal fiction," and by this "habit of thought that was to last for generations to come, a man was black for all social purposes, so long as he acknowledged or was known to carry in his veins a drop of black blood" (131). Twenty years earlier, in "The Future American" articles, Chesnutt had called race a "social fiction" (*Essays* 134), and Chesnutt has Marchand rewrite the social and legal script through the extreme step of emigration.

Our identities are not, Chesnutt would argue, an essence, nor are they a product of "blood," but of experience, and although Paul Marchand believes that the only way he can stay true to his experience is by leaving the United States, he is, in his counteremigration, being a good American— moving to where his family can have the greatest opportunity, a utopian space outside of American racism. In the end, then, Chesnutt seemed to have taken his lifelong struggle against racism in another and more theoretical direction. Through most of his writing career, Chesnutt straddled three centuries: an eighteenth-century rationalist in his intellectual convictions; a late-nineteenth-century realist who relied heavily on nineteenth-century sentimental strategies; and an early twentieth century social constructionist who anticipated views which gained currency much later in the century. In *Paul Marchand, F.M.C.* Chesnutt struggled artistically with these convictions and his artistic predilection, and he was, ultimately, unable to resolve them. But on some level, Chesnutt must have known that they were unresolvable, and he lived out most of his life torn between two positions: the conviction that the race problem had reached an impasse and the utopian belief that there was a way out of the impasse. The only way out in *Paul Marchand* was emigration, and Chesnutt made clear in the final paragraph of the novel how dire the situation was by chronicling the deeds of the descendants of the degenerate Beaurepas nephews: they fought in the Civil War; they were in forefront of the Ku Klux Klan; and a "grandson of Henri Beaurepas not long since introduced an amendment to the criminal code, making marriage a felony between a white person and a person of colored blood to the thirty-second degree inclusive" (144). In the hardening of racial lines after World War I, Chesnutt's response was again an eccentric design: an arthritically old-fashioned novel in which he argued that race is a social construction and in which he finally achieved the full measure of bitterness with which Howells had charged Chesnutt twenty years earlier.

[8]

The Quarry

"No White Person of Sound Mind Would Ever Claim to Be a Negro"

When Charles W. Chesnutt began writing his final novel, *The Quarry,* in 1927, he made a major alteration in the orientation of his novel-writing career. Unexpectedly, he shifted from the pessimism of *Paul Marchand* to a quiet optimism; even more remarkably, he acknowledged, for the first time in his career, African American writers and an African American audience, in effect turning away from the white audience he had addressed in the rest of his novels. In 1928, he submitted *The Quarry* to Knopf and subsequently to Houghton Mifflin, but both declined to publish the book (McWilliams, Introduction to *The Quarry* x). In the novel, Chesnutt employs essentially the same plot he used in *Paul Marchand, F.M.C.* Through a series of coincidences, a child whose parents are European American is raised as an African American. Chesnutt complicates that plot ideologically, however, by transposing it from antebellum New Orleans into the 1920s and the Harlem Renaissance. His central character, Donald Glover, can pass as white, and Chesnutt gives him several opportunities to do so before he learns of his biological parents' racial background, but he, like Paul Marchand, refuses to do so. In generic terms, the novel is a passing narrative turned inside out—a white man unknowingly becomes black—and as a result, African American experience is at the core of the novel in a way that it has never been before in Chesnutt's work. Chesnutt wrote, in other words, a kind of bildungsroman of the race philosopher as a young man in which the narrative traces out how Donald becomes an African American. For Chesnutt believed, more strongly than ever before, that race was not a given or an essence but rather a product of history, environment, and experience. In *Paul Marchand, F.M.C.*, in contrast, Chesnutt was less concerned with directly representing how Paul becomes who he is; the author focused on Paul's present experience—how he experiences his life as a quadroon and his change of caste and of status. Because of his French education, Marchand thinks of himself as unraced, as neither black nor white, while in *The Quarry*, Chesnutt was more interested than he had been in any novel since *Mandy Oxendine* in what it was like to be an African American—albeit an exceptional one both in terms of appearance and accomplishment.

Unlike any of Chesnutt's other novels, *The Quarry* was based on an incident in the author's personal experience. According to his daughter, a white man named Blank showed up at Chesnutt's door asking for advice. He and his wife had adopted a child, whom they deeply loved, but the child at two years old had begun to show unmistakable signs of a mixed-race ancestry. Because Mr. Blank and his wife had concealed the fact that the baby had been adopted, the neighbors had begun to whisper that the Blanks were also black" (Helen Chesnutt 286). Heartbroken at the idea of giving up the child, Mr. Blank and his wife asked Chesnutt to help them find an African American family to raise the boy. Mr. Blank explained, "We really love him dearly, but if we keep him the price will be too high for us to pay. We are not heroes or martyrs, but plain ordinary people who must live in a world that is intolerant and inhuman" (287). Chesnutt saw the child and concluded that "he obviously had some dark blood. It might have been Italian or Syrian or Negro, but the chances were that it was a strain of Negro blood" (286). Chesnutt apparently agreed to try to help the Blanks place the child with an African American family, concluding that "it is too much to expect any white American to assume voluntarily the burdens he will have to carry if he becomes involved in the race problem" (287), a sad acknowledgment from a man whose hope it had been to elevate those same whites.

Using this incident as the basis of his novel (Helen Chesnutt 297), Chesnutt made the baby's appearance less obviously "black" and complicated the narrative by having Donald discover, late in the novel, that he is not black but white. Donald Glover rejects his biological whiteness in favor of his upbringing but, unlike Paul Marchand, is engaged in the struggle against American racism, which gives him the intellectual grounding for his affective connection to his adoptive mother's people. However, the novel is much more than a "novel of passing turned on its head by recounting the story of a white man who decides to be colored" (McWilliams, "Harlem Renaissance" 598). Donald Glover learns of his "true" parentage only in the last two chapters of the novel; the rest of *The Quarry* is taken up with Donald's growth and intellectual maturity. Focusing on those aspects of the experience of child born at the beginning of the twentieth century, Chesnutt took on the period of the transition between the waning of Booker T. Washington's influence and the rise of the Harlem Renaissance and, for the first time in fiction, attempted to position himself among competing African American voices and subject positions. For a writer in his seventh decade, his shift to a concern with African American developments was quite remarkable, and he was, as a result, less concerned with whiteness than in any of his other novels. In fact, one could argue that in this novel he reversed the cultural script of many American novels, and whiteness becomes the background against which Glover stages his drama of racial self-definition. Finally, Chesnutt was also less concerned with the enduring consequences of the past than he had been in his previous work. It is as if Chesnutt had been, quite unexpectedly, partially liberated by living into the Harlem Renaissance, and he could turn his attention from the effects of the past to present possibilities embodied in an African American intellectual. Chesnutt's final word as a writer of fiction is then perhaps more positive than any of his other novels, but whatever optimism is expressed in the novel is guarded and typically eccentric in the form of its expression.

I

As we have seen in the preceding chapters, throughout his career as a writer of fiction, Chesnutt was engaged with an array of white writers, such as Mark Twain, George Washington Cable, Thomas Dixon, and Thomas Nelson Page. In Chesnutt's speeches and essays, he seemed unaware of other African American writers of fiction, and late in his life, in his 1928 speech accepting the Spingarn Medal from the National Association for the Advancement of Colored People, he claimed that when he began to write, "the Negro was inarticulate" and that he had been "the first man in the United States who shared his blood, to write serious fiction about the Negro" (*Essays* 514). In another of his retrospective pieces, "Post Bellum— Pre-Harlem" (1931) he asserts that when he "first broke into print seriously, no American colored writer had ever secured critical recognition expect Paul Laurence Dunbar, who had won his laurels as a poet" (*Essays* 544). Of course, Chesnutt is right in his second claim, but the first claim seems odd, particularly in light of the writings of Frances Ellen Watkins Harper, Pauline Hopkins, and Sutton Griggs. If he knew their fictions (and his *Essays and Speeches* do not contain a single reference to them and none of their books are found in what remains of his library), perhaps he thought them not serious enough, employing as they did overly sentimental and melodramatic strategies, or perhaps he found their fictions insufficiently realistic.

In the period when he was writing *The Quarry,* Chesnutt began for the first time in his life to read novels by African Americans, and he was imaginatively engaged with the first generation of Harlem Renaissance writers, both black and white. Two sources exist that allow us to measure that engagement—the Harlem Renaissance books in his library and one of his last major speeches, "The Negro in Present Day Fiction," delivered to the Dunbar Forum at Oberlin College in 1929. Of the Harlem Renaissance novels that appeared before 1928, Chesnutt's library contained Jessie Fauset's *There Is Confusion* (1928) and Carl Van Vechten's *Nigger Heaven* (1926), a Harlem Renaissance novel by a white writer that became a touchstone in the developing ideological positions among Harlem Renaissance writers. In "The Negro in Present Day Fiction," Chesnutt surveyed much recent writing that represented African American experience, including works by African American writers (Claude McKay's *Home to Harlem* [1928] and Wallace Thurman's *The Blacker the Berry* [1929]) and by white writers (Van Vechten's *Nigger Heaven* and Thomas Stribling's *Birthright* [1922]).

Taking the long view in "The Negro in Present Day Fiction," Chesnutt sketched out the developments in African American writing since the turn of the century. Noting the disappearance of such figures as the Uncle Tom, the mammy, and the "colored person who fawns on white folks" (*Essays* 521), Chesnutt also observed that the "beautiful octroon" had been replaced by college-educated African American women who took advantage of their light complexions either to pass strategically or to pass over completely into the white world. The "types" used in the past, he argued, had been replaced by others that were in their own way just as controversial, and Chesnutt lamented the absence of any "outstanding noble male character in any of the Negro novels, written by white or colored writers. The male characters are either weaklings, like the principal male character in *Nigger Heaven* or in *Birthright,* or addicted to degrading vices, such as gambling, lechery, drunkenness, [or] the use of narcotics." He noted that the "returned soldier in *Home to Harlem* is by no means an admirable character" (*Essays* 523) and that some of the "male characters are steeped in baseness, some of which is so vile as to be merely hinted at. But the very nadir of vileness is reached in a novel by a colored writer. W. Thurman, . . . *The Blacker the Berry*" (524). In these pronouncements, Chesnutt clearly allied himself with W. E. B. DuBois, who "feared that one negative image—that of the carefree plantation darky fostered by white writers—was in danger of being replaced by a more glamorous but no less dangerous stereotype—that of the pleasure-seeking jazz hound" (McWilliams, "Harlem Renaissance" 593). DuBois and Chesnutt also faced class issues in these new fictions in the 1920s: the two men were disturbed by the exposure of the black urban underclass, with which both felt very little sympathy. Proper Victorian gentlemen, DuBois and Chesnutt felt that art should be elevating, and although Chesnutt never attained the level of near-hysteria that DuBois did in his review of Van Vechten's *Nigger Heaven,*[1] Chesnutt was clearly trying to create a subject position for himself as a writer that would allow for an idealizing elevation but would not leave realism behind.

An example of Chesnutt's effort to carve out a comfortable subject position for himself as a fiction writer can be seen in his response to the seven questions posed in 1926 by the editors of *The Crisis* in its symposium, on *The Negro in Art: How Shall He Be Portrayed?* A wide range of white and black writers responded; Chesnutt's was the final response. He began by sounding very much like the same writer he had been twenty-five years earlier, insisting on the freedom of artists of whatever race to write about whatever they chose: "We want no color line in literature" (*Essays* 491), he asserted. He also went on to point out that African American writers still labored under the burden (even during the Harlem Renaissance) of being representative. "The colored writer," he argued, "has not yet passed the point of thinking of himself first as a Negro, burdened with the responsibility of defending and uplifting his race" (492). By extension, then, Chesnutt believed that artists should be completely unfettered and that African American artists should have the freedom to write about whatever range of experience they chose, a right that Chesnutt certainly had claimed earlier in his career. But then his responses to the questions posed by the editors were evidence for the flattening out of Chesnutt's complex double vision. He speculated, for instance, that "effective" characters for African American writers might be a Negro oil millionaire, or a Pullman porter–detective, or a "Negro visionary who would change the world over night and bridge the gap between the races in a decade" (*Essays* 493). As in *Paul Marchand*, Chesnutt still feels the lure of the paragon figure that functions as counterevidence to notions of the "natural" inferiority of African Americans. For Chesnutt (and for DuBois throughout this period), African American cultural progress becomes a sign of innate equality, the sign of the representative man. This use of the paragon figure, though, pits him against the Harlem Renaissance writers, who are, in some sense, more fully committed realists and less interested in the burdens of being representative than is Chesnutt late in his life.

An example of the attitude against which Chesnutt is defining himself can be found in Langston Hughes's 1926 article "The Negro Artist and the Racial Mountain," where Hughes articulates a kind of artistic credo for his generation: "We younger Negro artists who create now intend to express our individual dark-skinned selves without fear or shame. If white people are pleased we are glad. If they are not, it doesn't matter. . . . If colored people are pleased we are glad. If they are not, their displeasure doesn't matter either." And Hughes concludes, "We stand on top of the mountain, free within our selves" (168). Hughes is celebrating here the lifting of the burden under which Chesnutt labored for almost his whole writing career: the awareness of his white audience. Hughes identifies whiteness as a fundamental problem for the African American artist: "this is the mountain standing in the way of any true Negro art in America—this urge within the race toward whiteness, the desire to pour racial individuality into the mold of American standardization, and to be as little negro and as much American as possible" (166). From the perspective of Hughes's generation, one could argue that, despite his intellectual convictions and his commitment to African Americans, Chesnutt was caught in the trap of white "American standardization" throughout his writing career. As he said when accepting the Spingarn Medal, he tried to write of African Americans "not primarily as a Negro writing about Negroes, but as a human being writing about other human beings" (*Essays* 514). Hughes would probably assert that this is a fundamental mistake, that art can only be created from within the experience and assumptions of "our individual dark-skinned selves." One could also argue that in choosing the position of "a human being writing about other human beings," Chesnutt is adopting necessarily a white perspective. The universal Enlightenment subject has always been constructed as white, and Chesnutt had construed his audience as white throughout most of his career. But by 1928, Chesnutt knew that he was writing for a dual audience, that significant numbers of African Americans were book-buyers.

Instead of freeing him from the burden of being a representative of his race, that knowledge seemed to have made him, at least in terms of his paragon figures, even more conservative, as if his artistic burden had been increased. He seemed to feel the need to reaffirm his solidly middle-class values for both audiences and in so doing fell into the trap that was articulated by James Weldon Johnson in his essay, "The Dilemma of the Negro Author" (1928). When an African American writer chooses to write exclusively for a black audience, Johnson claims, "he runs afoul of the taboos of black America. He has no more absolute freedom to speak as he pleases addressing black America than he has in addressing white America. There are certain phases of life that he dare not touch, certain subjects that he dare not critically discuss, certain manners of treatment that he dare not use—except at the risk of rousing bitter resentment" (480). Having alienated his white audience a quarter of a century earlier, Chesnutt did not wish to alienate his potential African American audience so thus chose instead to focus on the most positive aspects of black life—improvement, uplift, and education. As a result, he created a curiously lifeless central character in *The Quarry*'s Donald Glover, as the editors at Knopf and Houghton Mifflin noticed. In responding to the editor at Knopf, Chesnutt acknowledged the "'priggishness' of the hero" (Helen Chesnutt 307), while the editor at Houghton Mifflin wrote that "the book had 'rather the color of a thesis novel'" (McWilliams, Introduction to *The Quarry* x). By the time that Chesnutt came to write his last novel, then, his vision was less complex and hardly double, and the tension between idealization and realism had been flattened out. Nevertheless, despite the absence of this tension in the novel, Chesnutt was attempting something new in *The Quarry*. He tried to account for the growth and maturation of an African American man in the early twentieth century under a set of social and historical conditions very different from those he explored in *Mandy Oxendine* and *The House Behind the Cedars*. In addition, he continued his exploration of the fictitiousness of the idea of race, replacing it with something very closely allied to race pride, a concept that he had rejected quite vigorously in his 1905 speech, "Race Prejudice: Its Causes and Cures." In arguing against what he termed "a new doctrine—that of Race Integrity," Chesnutt asked, "But of what should we be proud? Of any inherent superiority? We deny it in others, proclaiming the equality of man" (231–32). Fifteen years later, he still rejected the idea of "inherent" superiority, having replaced it with pride in family and pride in the accomplishments of one's social group.

II

The most obvious way to think about Chesnutt's ambitions in *The Quarry* is to connect it immediately to *Paul Marchand, F.M.C.* as I did earlier in this chapter; for most of the novel, however, readers do not know of that connection. Only in retrospect do we know for certain that Donald Glover's parents are European Americans and that he has no African American ancestry. In other words, while *The Quarry* is a reverse-passing novel, Chesnutt reveals that motive only in the last two chapters. He is trying, in the rest of the novel, to come to terms with the realities of early-twentieth century America for African Americans. Those realities, as I argued of *Paul Marchand,* had driven Chesnutt into an increasing pessimism about the racial situation in America, but Dean McWilliams argues that *The Quarry* is the only one of Chesnutt's novels "to conclude optimistically" ("Harlem Renaissance" 602). If that is the case, the few years between the writing of *Paul Marchand* and *The Quarry* made for a significant revision of Chesnutt's thinking about the racial situation in the United States. He shifted from a rejection of America and American racism in Paul's emigration to France to Donald's embrace of his American experience as a "black" man as seen in his several refusals to pass as white (and in his refusal to marry a foreigner and move to England) and his final refusal to acknowledge his biological whiteness.

As a way of exploring the question of the novel's optimism, I will look at a character who is a kind of double for Chesnutt, Senator James L. Brown, "the leading colored citizen of Cleveland" (*Quarry* 33). The white Mr. Seaton approaches Brown for advice after the neighbors have begun to talk about Donald's appearance (one of them says he "looks almost like a little coon" [17]) just as Blank had approached Chesnutt. Like Chesnutt, Brown agrees to help the Seatons find an African American family willing to raise young Donald, but in contrast to Helen Chesnutt's account, Brown is willing to confront Seaton about his behavior: "Why couldn't you bring him up in your own family?" Brown asks. "I should like to see a white man, by God, who had the courage to bring up a colored child!" He then talks about the history of slavery and how the masters "used their own blood to enhance the marketability of their mulatto sons and daughters—they were social cannibals, devouring and battening upon their own flesh" (37). Seaton makes the standard white response: neither he nor Brown have had anything "personally" to do with slavery, and Seaton refuses to see the connection between his behavior and the behavior of the slaveholders who sold their children. As the Seatons are leaving the Browns' house, Mrs. Seaton asks Brown's adult daughter whether her father had not been "a little hard on us?" (40). The daughter's response is very telling: "He's the kindest man in the world . . . but this awful race problem has embittered him. He used to be an optimist, and believed in the best of all possible worlds, but of late years he has become pessimistic and cynical" (41). Chesnutt was never naive enough to believe in "the best of all possible worlds," but he retained his optimism at the turn of the century despite the worsening situation for African Americans. By the time of the writing of *Paul Marchand, F.M.C.*, however, like Senator Brown, a man of Chesnutt's generation, Chesnutt had become embittered.

Donald Glover, a member of a younger generation, can participate in, as McWilliams says, "the spirit of a unique and very brief moment in the history of black America," and this seeming improvement in racial conditions results in the "book's optimistic tone" (Introduction to *The Quarry* xi). The novel concludes at the height of the Harlem Renaissance, a period during which Chesnutt prospered. "He had succeeded in business, his children had completed studies at prestigious universities, and he had been honored by both the white and black communities" (McWilliams, "Harlem Renaissance" 603). As evidence to support his contention about the book's optimism, McWilliams points to a conversation between Brown and Seaton at the end of the novel, when Seaton has discovered that Donald is really white. Brown argues that "things are looking up a little for the colored people. Their education for the past two generations, limited though it has been, is raising the level of culture. Negro wealth is increasing." He believes that "the color line is weakening in spots" and that "all colored people may not always be social pariahs. And men of real parts like Donald and some of the younger men may find it in the future no great hardship to be classed with that race. It may even work to their advantage for a considerable time to come" (264–65). After quoting this passage, McWilliams concludes that the "change in Senator Brown's attitude mirrors Chesnutt's own shift from the discouraged pessimism which caused him to interrupt his literary career to the guarded optimism voiced in his last novel" ("Harlem Renaissance" 603–04). Their positions, however, are more complicated than McWilliams allows, because later in the same conversation, Brown's tone shifts when he thinks about conditions in the South and throughout the world: "The enfranchisement of the Negro in the South has been only a joke. At this very moment the white race everywhere has its iron heel on the neck of the darker world, and shows no intention of lifting it. I see no ultimate future for the Negro in the Western world except in his gradual absorption by the white race" (265–66). Brown's conclusion mirrors that of Chesnutt in his "Future American" series—amalgamation is the only answer to the race problem, the only way to erase racial hierarchy, but whereas Chesnutt offered amalgamation as a utopian solution, Brown chooses it out of political and social despair.

I must admit that I find Brown's position here contradictory. At one point in the conversation, he seems to be optimistic, arguing that significant changes have taken place (in the North only?) and that those changes may even be an "advantage" to African Americans. A few moments later, when he turns to the situation in the South (and the rest of the world), he seems completely pessimistic, arguing that the only solution to the race problem is the disappearance of African Americans. The question here is whether Brown's confusion mirrors Chesnutt's or whether Chesnutt is attempting to establish some distance from Brown. McWilliams says that Chesnutt was always identified with the " 'assimilationist' position" (Introduction to *The Quarry* xi) that the race problem would not disappear until the concept of race disappeared and that the only way to eliminate the concept was through a blurring of racial types. If Chesnutt is still arguing for assimilation through Senator Brown, then how do we understand Donald's refusal to become white—not only at the end of the novel, when he discovers his "true" ancestry, but on the four previous occasions when he has the opportunity to pass yet resolutely declines to do so.

The confusion is seemingly even greater when one takes into consideration McWilliams's insightful analysis of the relation between *The Quarry* and James Weldon Johnson's *The Autobiography of an Ex-Colored Man* (1912). In addition to pointing to similarities in plot, McWilliams argues that Chesnutt is reversing the pessimism of the last line of Johnson's novel, when the central character says that he feels "small and selfish. I am an ordinarily successful white man who has made a little money." Conversely, his African American peers "are men who are making history and a race. I, too, might have taken part in a work so glorious. . . . I cannot repress the thought that, after all, I have chosen the lesser part, that I have sold my birthright for a mess of pottage" (156). The pessimism expressed by Johnson's character is mirrored, as Werner Sollors has pointed out, in the pessimism at the end of Abraham Cahan's *The Rise of David Levinsky* (1917). Levinsky has succeeded in the business world but feels bereft and culturally unmoored. Sollors argues that the ex-colored man and Levinsky are ironic "antithetical construction[s]" (171), that they lead lives diametrically opposite of those of their authors. In *The Quarry*, though, there is no antithetical irony; Glover is an idealization of Charles W. Chesnutt. The last line of *The Quarry* is given to Mr. Seaton, who comes to see Donald after his marriage and says, "I'm not at all sure that you didn't make the wise choice" (286). The term "wise choice" must be seen in relation to the phrase "mess of pottage," which, as McWilliams points out, is used in *The Quarry* by Donald's Jewish friend when he expresses "profound contempt for those of his people who . . . denied their race—sold their birthright, as he put it, for a mess of pottage" (136–37). Of course, like Esau, the ex-colored man, David Levinsky, and Donald's Jewish friend can sell their birthright, but Donald has no birthright to sell—or, rather, he has already sold his birthright as a genetically white man in his decision to remain African American. Unlike the narrator of Johnson's novel, Donald has chosen his life among those who are to make "history and a race."

McWilliams tries to assert that there is no quandary here, no contradiction between the position of Johnson's narrator passing as white and Chesnutt's Donald Glover passing as black. McWilliams claims that in *The Quarry*, "Assimilation . . . does not mean blacks becoming white as much as it does whites becoming black. . . . Whites must be persuaded to enter the black world, morally and spiritually, to see the black condition from the inside" ("Harlem Renaissance" 601). McWilliams's understanding of assimilation in this passage is a cultural one and is very close to the strategies of women sentimental writers such as Harriet Beecher Stowe, strategies employed by Chesnutt and a range of antiracist writers throughout the nineteenth century. In other words, assimilation, as McWilliams articulates it, is the attempt to understand the Other's experience from the Other's point of view, much as Chesnutt was asking his readers to do in *The House Behind the Cedars* and *The Marrow of Tradition*. However, when Chesnutt wrote about assimilation a quarter of a century earlier in the "Future American" series, his understanding of that process was radically different: it meant a literal and physical amalgamation of racial differences into a homogeneous racial whole that would essentially erase race as a concept, a position, McWilliams notes, also held by the anthropologist Franz Boas, who figures in *The Quarry* as Franz Boaz, one of Donald's graduate school professors. The locus classicus of Boas's assimilationist phase was articulated in his 1910 essay, "The Real Race Problem," published in the first issue of *The Crisis*. Like Chesnutt in 1900, Boas argues that "the inexorable conditions of our life will gradually make toward the disappearance of the most distinctive type of Negro, which will . . . tend to alleviate the acuteness of race feeling" (25). However, by 1928, Boas has noticed a shift in the African American community; he notes that there are fewer "mating[s]" between whites and blacks. "The effect of this selective process . . . will be the passing of many of the lightest men out of the Negro community. . . . For the remainder it must inevitably lead to a darkening of the whole colored population, for the daughters of each generation . . . will be darker than their mothers." He concludes that this process will lead to a heightening of the differences between the two races (*Anthropology* 77–78). Boas's belief in the possibility of racial amalgamation had disappeared by the late 1920s, just as Chesnutt's belief in that solution had begun to erode in the face of the intransigence of white Americans and in the face of the resurgence of African American cultural work in the Harlem Renaissance.

If *The Quarry* is, in some ways, about reverse assimilation, as McWilliams posits, then we have to consider Donald's extremely atypical experience as a black man. Obviously, since he is biologically white, he is more than able to pass as white, and his only direct experience of racism is one with a reverse twist. While he is attending Athena University, outside of "the thriving metropolis of what was claimed to be the most progressive of the southern states" (104), Donald and the African American woman student with whom he is walking are arrested. When asked why, the arresting officer says, "disorderly conduct . . . an offense against the peace and dignity of the state, against an ordinance of the city, and against the unwritten law of the South" (111). In other words, one of Donald's few experiences of racism occurs when he is mistaken for a white man publicly consorting with an African American woman.[2]

To observe this is not, however, to try to cast doubt on Donald's commitment to his "race." He has imbibed his adoptive mother's values, those of uplift and leadership. From the moment that she takes Donald from the Seatons, Mrs. Glover begins to prepare Donald for his role: "when you grow up and become the leader of our people, we'll prove to the white folks that we're just as good as they are" (56). Obviously, her notion of leadership is grounded in the nineteenth century. Donald is to be a "representative" man in the tradition of Frederick Douglass and Booker T. Washington, a sign for his people and to white folks of the equality of African Americans. His mother is, the narrator says, an "ardent 'race' woman. . . . [S]he believed in the Negro" (62). She had faith in the existence of lost African civilizations, and she kept herself current in all the debates about African Americans in her time. More to the point, Mrs. Glover "believed that the Negro had a future, and a worthy one. She anticipated the scientists of our day in maintaining that there is no essential intellectual difference in races, any apparent variation being merely a matter of development; that the backwardness of the Negro was due to his historical environment" (63). Like Chesnutt, Mrs. Glover is an environmentalist; she rejects racial essentialism and heredity as explanations for any perceived racial differences. As an environmentalist, she dreams of changed social circumstances and a time when African Americans would be "adequately and personally represented in lawmaking bodies, in the courts, and in all branches of the public service. She dreamed of the day when they should produce great healers, lawyers, writers, artists, thinkers—great men in every walk of life," and when she took over the care of Donald, "she transferred her dreams to him" (63). So her dream and Donald's dream are a combination of race pride and a desire for intellectual accomplishment.

But a curious thing happens to Donald as he matures. He is fully committed to his mother's vision of his potential leadership and to his people, but his cultural values, as McWilliams has pointed out, are decidedly Euro-American. "Donald, the aspiring black leader, is culturally white. He has studied black culture thoroughly, but he frequently seems indifferent to it. . . . He discourses on Eugene O'Neill's plays . . . but he does not refer directly to a single contemporary black writer" ("Harlem Renaissance" 599). Donald goes beyond mere "indifference" to African American culture, however; when the narrator describes Donald's musical tastes, the passage is very revealing: "His taste was for the better class of music"—that is, opera and romantic composers. When he would speak about "the achievements of his people, he would, of course, mention jazz music and the Negro spirituals as creations of theirs. But in his heart, or rather in his mind, which always took precedence . . . these forms of musical expression were essentially primitive—a survival of the tom-tom, the war chant, and moaning of the slave coffle" (135–36). The word that leaps out of this passage is the highly charged "primitive." Despite (or because of?) his higher education, and despite having studied with Franz Boaz, Donald still believes in a connection between race and culture, something that Boas took pains to deny in *Anthropology and Modern Life,* which appeared in 1928, the same year in which Chesnutt finished *The Quarry.* Boas insisted on the "independence of race and culture" (62), writing that "it does not matter from which point of view we consider culture, its forms are not dependent upon race" (60). When culture and race are divorced, then one cannot characterize the cultural productions of any race as "advanced" or "primitive." But Donald (and Chesnutt?) still inhabits the assumptions of the nineteenth century: he can see little value in African American vernacular culture, which does not constitute cultural production on a high enough level to suit him. And although McWilliams says that other black writers of this period—DuBois, Locke, and Cullen—were "also criticized for their Eurocentrism" (599), it does nothing to lessen the paradox of Chesnutt's race leader, who is at best indifferent, if not ashamed, of the cultural accomplishments of his people.[3]

If Donald is, as McWilliams claims, "culturally white," and if he has had almost no direct experience of racism, where does his allegiance to his race originate? When Seaton reveals to Donald that his birth parents are European American, he reflects on why he is not going to become a white man: "Circumstances had made him one of a certain group. He had been reared as one of them. He had been taught to see things as they saw them, he had shared their joys, their griefs, their hopes and their fears—in fact, he had become psychologically and spiritually one of them. He could no more see them with the eyes of the white man of the street than he could make himself over." If he were to attempt to make himself over it would be "at the sacrifice of love and loyalty and the whole setup of his life. . . . Manhood and self-respect were more important than race" (277–78). In his mother's terms, environment is all; it has determined who he is in the core of his being, and to pass as white, he would have to give up his fundamental sense of his self, much as John Warwick (Walden) was forced to do in *The House Behind the Cedars*. "Racial identity," McWilliams observes, is for Donald "independent of genetics and legal categories; it is [an] affinity developed through shared social experience" ("Harlem Renaissance" 597). In other words, Donald's sense of racial identity is based in family, particularly in his mother's dreams for him. If he were to become white, he would have to separate himself from his parents and their racial dreams, as Rena Walden had to separate herself from her mother in *The House Behind the Cedars*. Any acknowledgment of his biological whiteness would be a betrayal of his psychological blackness as well as a betrayal of his relationship with his mother.

By giving Donald repeated opportunities to pass into the white world, Chesnutt was conducting, like Pierre Beaurepas, an experiment in education and environment. Early in the novel, Dr. Freeman, the superintendent of the Infants Ward where Donald had been adopted, tells Seaton of what is believed to be Donald's degenerate, mixed-race ancestry. Freeman speculates, "From a scientific standpoint, I should like to see the boy brought up as white. It would be a psychological experiment of rare interest, and, if he turned out well, might shake some prevalent theories and prejudices" (23). In this novel of reversals, the experiment is carried out, and it does seemingly validate the theory that environment is more important than heredity. Of course, this is determined not by bringing up a black child as a white one

but by bringing up a white child as black. But then, because of his investment in the paragon figure, Chesnutt complicated this script by making
Donald a product of excellent heredity as well. When Donald's biological
parentage is discovered, he is found to come from two distinguished families: on his mother's side, he is descended from impoverished Sicilian nobility, while on his father's side, he is descended from a first family of New
England that can trace its ancestry back to the *Mayflower.* So the novel
overdetermines Donald: are we to see that his commitment to his mother's
people comes from environment but his intellectual brilliance comes
from his white heredity? Or was Chesnutt trying to find a way out of the
binary structure of either/or and move to a more nuanced and/but? In
Anthropology and Modern Life, Boas took this position when he wrote, "I do
not believe . . . that the mental activities of man are entirely due to his individual experience and that what is called character or ability is due to outer
conditions, not organic structure. . . . [W]e must admit that the organic
differences are liable to be overlaid and overshadowed by environmental
influences" (49). Chesnutt faced the problem of the protean quality of racist
discourse, however: as soon as he admitted the possibility of good heredity,
he opened the possibility for bad heredity, for degeneration, and terms such
as *heredity* and *degeneration* remained racially inflected during the 1920s. As
soon as Chesnutt admitted the discourse of blood as a metaphor for heredity, he gave his potential contemporary audience a way of interpreting
Donald that cut against the grain of his argument. Many white readers
would have seen Donald as a brilliant success because of his fantastic heredity. In the end, I would argue that Chesnutt's insistence on the paragon
figure and his endowing of that figure with a birthright of American intellectual aristocracy and European nobility undermines his ability to demonstrate that Donald's intellectual success is connected to his environment.

III

In generic terms, it is easier to define what Chesnutt is not trying to do
in *The Quarry* than what he is. The novel is not an exploration of black

middle-class life, like Jessie Fauset's *There Is Confusion,* which was in Chesnutt's library, nor is it an exploration of the life of the black under-class, like Thurman's *The Blacker the Berry. The Quarry* is a survey, using one of Chesnutt's paragon figures, of the range of possible subject positions for African Americans (and their leaders) in the 1920s, and as such it is filled with recognizable historical figures—Marcus Garvey, W. E. B. DuBois, and Booker T. Washington—so in a surprising sense, Chesnutt is attempting in *The Quarry* what Ralph Ellison later accomplished in *Invisible Man* with its central character's progression through various leaders in the African American community. The narrator of *The Quarry* introduces the first two figures when discussing Mrs. Glover's beliefs. Neither man is mentioned by name, but Washington is characterized as "the opportunist" who "preached patience and forbearance and the importance of winning, by whatever temporary compromise or concession might seem necessary or expedient, the friendship and good will of the white people" (65–66). DuBois is characterized as an "idealist" and "crusader" who "buckled on his armor, grasped his sword and set out to slay with the weapons of knowledge and reason and ridicule and sarcasm the flaming dragon of race prejudice" (66). Mrs. Glover is a proponent of the latter position, as is Donald. At Athena University, he studies with Dr. Lebrun, the DuBois figure in the novel, and Donald seconded Lebrun's "protests against racial intolerance of every kind, and his demand for equality for the Negro—not one kind of equality or another, but *equality,* which, he maintained, as soon as it was limited or confined, became something less than equality" (106). This was very much Chesnutt's personal position and the fundamental ground of his disagreement with Washington. Despite that disagreement, he takes Donald into more personal and direct contact with Dr. Jefferson, the Washington figure in the novel. Since his mother believes that he "should study every phase of Negro life" (188), he goes to work for Dr. Jefferson as an editor and proof-reader of his writing and as a kind of front man who can pass as white. To fulfill these duties, Dr. Jefferson sends Donald to England to discuss "a plan for introducing industrial education" in one of the British West African colonies (204). Intellectually, unlike Dr. Lebrun, Donald has little interest in Africa, and when he is planning his second book, he decides not to take an internationalist tack, in part because "his mother, to whom the book was to be to be in part payment of his debt to her, was not so internationally minded as Dr. Lebrun. . . . [S]he was interested in Africa merely as the mother country of her race, and . . . the welfare of one negro in the United States meant more to her than that of a hundred Bantus or Croos or Kaffirs in Africa" (238).[4] While in England, Donald receives the opportunity to travel to Africa, but he declines. For similar reasons, he is not attracted to the Marcus Garvey figure in the novel, who is referred to as "the President of the African Empire" and the head of the "Universal Negro Progress Association" (153). Donald finds the president's dream of a return to Africa "the wildest of fantasies" (168) and is disturbed by the President's "abuse of the mulattoes" (167). As an intellectual, Donald has no interest in Africa or in the international situation as well as no interest in industrial education and the compromises forced on a figure such as Dr. Jefferson, but Donald needs the experience of their positions to help him define his own.

Unlike Paul Marchand, who one might think of as a failed intellectual, Donald Glover is a portrait of the engaged African American intellectual in the sense discussed by Ross Posnock: "The black creative intellectual at the turn of the century emerged as social type by resisting the lure of the prevailing ideology of the authentic" ("How It Feels" 324), and writers like Griggs, DuBois, and Chesnutt "emancipated themselves from the imprisoning rhetoric of authenticity, with its inevitable racializing of culture" (341). Donald Glover, like DuBois, wants to "deracialize culture" ("How It Feels" 325 n.5) and refuses to valorize folk culture as "authentic" or to think that he is somehow less psychologically black because of his investment in European American cultural capital. However, his refusal of the concept of authenticity does not mean that he is intellectually disengaged from the race question. For instance, he discovers, in his first book, "a simple, clear, rational and humane solution" to the race problem in the United States (178).[5] Even though he is, like Chesnutt, something of an idealist, Donald also possesses Chesnutt's later realism, knowing that any "solution" would mean the "scraping of many cherished taboos" by white folks and that the solution is impracticable under current conditions in the 1920s, when the "cleavage between white and colored had gone so far in the country that there seemed no place anywhere for them to meet in friendly intercourse" (179). After the publication of his book in which he details his "solution" to the race problem, however, Donald "was inclined to believe that white people, generally speaking, did not want to get rid of the race problem, that they found it less irksome and more profitable to label it insoluble and let it ride, than to make any genuine effort to settle it" (178–79). Chesnutt has created a dilemma for his character. Having endowed him with the ability to resolve, intellectually, the race problem, Chesnutt also gives Donald the wisdom to know that white folks prefer deadlock, prefer the racial status quo. Anything but that status quo would mean that white Americans would need to examine their history, their attitudes, and their behavior, something that is traumatic, even in our time. Donald, however, is not embittered or paralyzed by that knowledge: he will keep his nose to the grindstone and work to improve conditions for African Americans. So Chesnutt's paragon figure is tempered with a good seasoning of cynicism about the same white America he is continually asked to join throughout the novel.

At the end of the novel, Mr. Seaton comes to see Donald one last time, and Seaton remarks to Donald, "Your wife is a beautiful and charming woman and the boy is the image of you at his age" (286). So Chesnutt concludes his career as a writer of novels with yet another mixed-race son, like the unnamed son of John Warwick (Walden) in *The House Behind the Cedars*. In that novel, though, Chesnutt smuggled the son past the reader's consciousness and enacted how one could become white. Here, in Chesnutt's final novel, there is a reverse amalgamation: rather than blackness disappearing into whiteness, white disappears into black. It may well be, despite all his hesitations, that by the end of his life, Chesnutt, in his own eccentric way, had come close to an idea that he had rejected earlier in his career, that of race pride. But not race pride as reverse essentialism or as a fiction of lost African glories, but pride of family and a way of seeing the world. Like Charles Chesnutt, Donald Glover becomes a "voluntary negro," and he will devote his life to the betterment of his family and his adoptive race. In a way, Donald Glover is a highly idealized version of Charles W. Chesnutt as the successful crusader against racial injustice. As I mentioned in the previous chapter, Helen Chesnutt wrote that her father refused to emigrate because he was "an idealist. . . . He felt that success in his own country against terrific odds would be worth more than success in a foreign country" (41). In *The Quarry*, Chesnutt rewards Donald with family life and with a successful career as an antiracist intellectual. An idealist to the end, Chesnutt believed that the race problem could be solved, but he also knew from bitter experience that there was no will in the country—either through legal measures or through assimilation—to address that problem. His final word on the issue of race, then, is as contradictory as ever, but in his last novel, he turned toward a new audience, African American readers, as he mapped out a constellation of subject positions on art and race. Although he could not completely reject his internalized white audience, as had Hughes, Chesnutt was nevertheless more concerned with black experience and less concerned with any potential white audience than he had ever been in his career.

Postscript

When he was seventy-one, three years before his death, Charles W. Chesnutt completed his ninth novel, *The Quarry*. From his late adolescence until his old age, Chesnutt possessed striking literary ambitions. Even when his career seemed to have come to an end in 1905 with the failure of *The Colonel's Dream*, he persisted, writing at least four more books (*Paul Marchand, F.M.C.; The Quarry*; and two works that are no longer extant: a book of short stories entitled *Aunt Hagar's Children* and a book of children's stories). This middle-class autodidact, as his journals demonstrate, worked very hard to acquire cultural capital, and as Richard Brodhead has noted, Chesnutt is an example of a post–Civil War development among African Americans—the growth of what has been variously "labeled the black intelligentsia, the black bourgeoisie, or the black professional class" (Introduction 15). As a self-identified African American who happened to live far from the centers of literary power in Boston and New York and as an autodidact, Chesnutt's exposure to what we think of today as the high literary culture of his time was spotty at best. He read almost no African American writers of fiction, and his reading of other contemporary novelists apparently was somewhat eccentric. From the evidence of his library and from the references in his essays and speeches, one can reconstruct at least a part of Chesnutt's reading, and the absences are striking: there are no references to Hawthorne, Crane, Dreiser, Norris, Chopin, or Wharton, no references to British writers such as Austen, Eliot, and Conrad (although he had apparently read Dickens, Thackeray, and

Hardy). Chesnutt did read, however selectively, novels dealing with race in America: his library included well-known writers such as Cable and Tourgée as well as less prominent books by Dixon (*The Clansman*), Dunbar (two of his white-life novels), and Howells (*An Imperative Duty*) and the pseudonymously published *Appointed: An American Novel* (McElrath, "Chesnutt's Library"). Like other autodidacts, Chesnutt acquired the cultural capital he felt he needed, and he thought that he had found in his exemplars—Stowe, Tourgée, and to a lesser extent Cable—an approach to writing novels that would allow him to change the discourse as he believed that Stowe had done.

The problem that he faced, however, was that the discourse was mutating during his lifetime. The discourse of race that had begun as a scientific effort in the eighteenth century to classify all the various peoples in the world on the basis of their physical characteristics had been transformed by Chesnutt's time into the metaphysical. In other words, the existence of mixed-race people—*white negro* was the term Chesnutt used—could make blackness invisible, transform blackness from a visible to an invisible sign. At the turn of the century, African Americans who passed as white were figures of cultural anxiety because of their invisible blackness, while Chesnutt in his life asserted that invisible blackness as a point of familial and ethnic pride. Further compounding Chesnutt's difficulties in trying to change the discourse was the fact that, as F. James Davis has pointed out, the one-drop rule is "unique"; it is "found in the United States and not in any other nation in the world" (13). This hegemonic discourse was protean; it could transform antiracist arguments into support for racism. While this process was at work, the issue of race retreated, as Jane Smiley has written, into the realm of the private (67). Seeing these factors at work and realizing that he could not change the discourse through fiction, Chesnutt gave up novel writing for fifteen years and turned his attention to direct work in the public sphere, particularly with the nascent National Association for the Advancement of Colored People. He wrote in "The Disfranchisement of the Negro" that the Negro "must do his part, as lies within his power and opportunity" to help attain his full measure of rights, but he also realized that "it will be . . . largely a white man's conflict, fought in the forum of public conscience" (*Essays* 193). And that "public conscience" had to be translated, in Chesnutt's view, into law. As he said to Washington, there was "no expectation of justice" from white folks "unless it is founded on law" (*Letters* 182). Chesnutt was prescient in his analysis: laws changed only when the public conscience became activated by the civil rights movement in the late 1950s and by televised images of racial oppression.

If Chesnutt realized the impossibility of changing the racial discourse through fiction, he also experienced the impossibility of making a living as a writer of race fictions. All of his books, with the exception of *The Conjure Woman*, had disappointing sales, and he could not support his family on the meager earnings from his writing. So despite his ambitions, he renounced full-time writing, returning to his legal stenography firm. Of course, other major writers in the period also had slim earnings. Henry James, for instance, reported making less than six hundred pounds total on *The Ambassadors* and *The Wings of the Dove* (Pierpont 71), but Chesnutt's commitment to his family and to their upward mobility (all of his children attended college) meant that he was unable to continue to be a full-time writer of fiction. Like his characters Tom Taylor from "The Doll" and Paul Marchand, Chesnutt's first allegiance was to his family; his first commitment was to seeing that they did well in the world.[1]

Because of his commitment to his family and to maintaining an upper-middle-class standard of living and because of his limited output, there has always been a sense of unfulfilled expectations in his career. Nevertheless, Chesnutt was a teller of the communal tale. Like Dr. Miller in *The Marrow of Tradition*, Chesnutt was the teller of the tale of the African American community, but he was also the teller of the tale of and to the European American community. Throughout his writing career, he turned the ethnographic gaze back at whites and represented white experience and the ways it impinged on blacks. In that sense, Chesnutt's enduring accomplishment was his ability to reverse the forms of the dominant culture, to turn them back on white people and to represent them from an unwonted point of view. Chesnutt, then, is like other minority writers in the twentieth century in whose work imperialists and missionaries are seen from the other side, in the sometimes unflattering gaze of the oppressed and formerly oppressed.

Writing as a member of an oppressed minority who took an unraced subject position as a writer, Chesnutt critiqued whiteness, representing not only the ways in which white folks acted as oppressors but also the ways in which their oppression inevitably rebounded into and degraded the quality their private lives. Chesnutt believed that he was perfectly positioned, as a liminal person, betwixt and between, to represent white experience. Those representations of whiteness can be nearly as uncomfortable, for some readers, in our time as they were in his, but his ability to unsettle, both in literary and in racial terms, makes him appear more complicated and more rewarding than he has at any time during the past one hundred years.

Notes

Introduction

1. I am not claiming, of course, that Chesnutt was the first African American to write novels. Both Douglass and Brown wrote fiction in addition to their better-known autobiographies. But they did not conceive of themselves primarily as artists, as writers of fiction. However, Chesnutt's generation included a number of African American writers of fiction, among them Pauline Hopkins, Frances Ellen Watkins Harper, and Sutton Griggs. These writers wrote primarily for an African American audience: Hopkins published serialized novels in the *Colored American Magazine* and *Contending Forces* (1900) with the Colored Co-Operative Publishing Company; Griggs published by subscription; and Harper published *Iola Leroy* (1893) with Garrigues Brothers. In contrast, Chesnutt published his first two novels with Houghton, Mifflin, the premier turn-of-the-century publisher.

2. A good deal of work has been done and continues to be done on Chesnutt's adaptation of local color in short stories. Because so much criticism traces out Chesnutt's complicated uses of the plantation tale, I decided to focus in this study exclusively on his novels and on his use of the various genres of novel that he adapted to manipulate and change his audience.

3. The passage in "Marse Chan" continues: "Niggers didn' hed nothin' 't all to do—je' hed to 'ten' to de feedin' an' clean' de hosses, an' doin' what de master tell 'em to do; an' when dey wuz sick, dey had things sont 'em out de house, an' de same doctor came to see 'em whar 'ten' to de white folks when dey was po'ly. Dyar warn' no trouble nor nothing' " (13). The cultural authority of a African American speaker is lent to this depiction of the antebellum South as a paradise of racial relations. As hard as it is to believe today, white Americans apparently believed that the plantation school accurately represented slavery. While the "image of the loyal slave may be one of the most hackneyed clichés in American history, . . . no understanding of the place of race in Civil War memory is possible without confronting its ubiquitous uses in turn-of-the-century culture" (Blight 284).

4. Three of the six manuscript novels have been published at the time of this writing: *Mandy Oxendine, Paul Marchand,* and *The Quarry*. The three white-life novels—*A Business Career, The Rainbow Chasers,* and *Evelyn's Husband*—still remain only in manuscript form.

5. This genre in which African Americans study white experience has received almost no critical attention. As David Roediger has written, "The serious 'white-life novel' has left very little impact on American literary criticism. Even its most spectacular successes, such as James Baldwin's *Giovanni's Room* or Zora Neale Hurston's *Seraph on the Suwanee,* are little read. Less artistically successful works, such as Richard Wright's pulpy and revealing account of loss and violence in the white middle class in *Savage Holiday,* vanish with hardly a trace" (Introduction 8).

6. This phrase come from Marius Bewley's *The Eccentric Design* (1963), which focuses on the "classic American novel" by writers such as Cooper, Hawthorne, Melville, and James.

7. While rereading Chesnutt's biography of Douglass, I was struck by several phrases in the preface to that text: Chesnutt wrote that Douglass's life "appealed to his imagination and his heart" and of having a "profound and in some degree a personal sympathy with every step of Douglass's upward career" (ix). Chesnutt clearly identified with Douglass and worked to preserve Douglass's uncompromising vision during this era of national forgetfulness.

8. According to Ellison, being black in the United States "imposes the uneasy burden and occasional joy of a complex double vision, a fluid, ambivalent response to men and events which represents, at it finest, a profoundly civilized adjustment to the cost of being human in this modern world" (131–32). In an earlier draft, I used Ian Finseth's phrase, "literary schizophrenia" (17, n.1), but as the reviewer of my manuscript pointed out, this term pathologizes a subject position that is very productive for Chesnutt. I also prefer Ellison's formulation rather than DuBois's more famous articulation of "double consciousness" because Chesnutt would probably have disagreed with DuBois when he wrote in 1897 that "one ever feels his two-ness—an American, a Negro; two souls, two thoughts, two unreconciled strivings; two warring ideals in one dark body" (194). Chesnutt would not have seen a contradiction between being a Negro and an American; he insisted that African Americans should have the same rights as any other citizens of the United States. The doubleness in Chesnutt's vision is a result of thinking about how to affect his white audience emotionally and how to change its mind rationally while doing so from an African American point of view and while doing justice not only to African American experience but also to African American views of white people and white experience.

Chapter 1

1. I have lifted this phrase from Barrett and Roediger's essay, "Inbetween Peoples: Race, Nationality, and the 'New Immigrant' Working Class." Although they use the term to

describe the process by which immigrants, who inhabited a space between white and black, became white, I find it also a useful term to describe how Chesnutt tends to think of mixed-race people.

2. Of course, Chesnutt had a personal motive here as well, since he belonged to the class that he is describing, but I am less interested in how Chesnutt positioned himself in his life than I am in the subject positions he created in his writing.

3. These dates are important for my discussion of *The House Behind the Cedars*. For reasons that will become clear, the novel must be assumed to be set before 1879, when the 1831 ruling was still in place.

4. Frederick J. Hoffman's *The Race Traits and Tendencies of the American Negro* (1896) was used in this period "to convince most white insurance companies that they should deny coverage to all Negroes on the grounds that the membership in the race by itself constituted an unacceptable actuarial risk" (Fredrickson 249–50).

5. We have recently seen this strand of thinking developed among critical whiteness studies theorists. As Peter Kolchin has observed in his overview of whiteness studies: "The British sociologist Paul Gilroy suggests that it is time to abolish 'race' itself, . . . and the historian Mia Bay, raising the question of 'anti-racist racism,' suggests that 'the concept of race is virtually inseparable from the idea of a hierarchy among the races'" (169).

Chapter 2

1. Andrews quotes a few phrases from the letter. The relevant portion of the letter reads, "I doubt that 'Evelyn's Husband' will do your reputation much good. It might be published to fair advantage, perhaps; but we are convinced that in leaving your earlier work . . . you have made a literary misstep. This sounds rather harsh, I am afraid. I don't want you to think for a minute that we are not appreciative of the many excellent and charmingly written passages . . . particularly your narrative and running comment, which is so vastly better than your dialogue. Though we are returning this, I shall be decidedly interested to hear of the progress of the novel you sketched to me, centering about an Octroon" (Bynner). Bynner clearly thought that Chesnutt should have been writing exclusively race fiction; nothing is known about the "Octroon" novel mentioned here.

2. The first novel in this genre is Amelia E. Johnson's *Clarence and Corinne; or, God's Way* (1890) (Fikes 105) published by the American Baptist Publication Society.

3. There was, of course, no racial symmetry in this period. White writers considered themselves untrammeled by any racial constraints. Joel Chandler Harris, Thomas Nelson Page, and a plethora of other white authors wrote in the voice of black men. Critics also had no problems with the midwestern Dunbar representing the experiences of rural southern black folk in his plantation tales because those performances were seen as simple and uncomplicated. When African Americans wrote exclusively about white-life,

however, they were transgressing (as the epigraph to this chapter points out) and attempting to represent a complex reality that most white Americans believed blacks could not understand because of the fact of race.

4. This conceptualization of popular fiction is more dynamic than Jauss's formulation. Here, audience and genre are in a reciprocal relationship with each other.

5. Chesnutt, for instance, never decided on the name of the central male character. At some places his name is indicated by a blank space (Mr. ———), while in others he is either Mr. Quilliams or occasionally Mr. Bramble. (Since he seems to be called Quilliams more often than the other two options, I will use that name here). When Chesnutt abandoned the novel—probably when *The House Behind the Cedars* was accepted for publication—he was in the process of recasting the concluding chapters and had not fully worked out the implications of that revision. There are also a few places in the manuscript where Chesnutt wrote notes to himself about changes he wanted to make, but those notes were never recast into description or dialogue. The novel is heavily rewritten in Chesnutt's hand throughout the manuscript.

6. The manuscript of *The Rainbow Chasers* is so chaotic that even Chesnutt's page numbering of the manuscript is incorrect. I have renumbered the pages throughout.

Chapter 3

1. We know that Chesnutt read this essay of Tourgée's (with its reference to Chesnutt's "curious realism" [408]) because the Chesnutt Papers contain a letter from Tourgée to Chesnutt dated 8 December 1888 in which Tourgée says, "Of course, it was to you that I referred. I did not dare make the reference more explicit lest it should do you an injury." Tourgée goes on to say, in an extraordinary passage, that he thinks "that the climacteric of American literature will be negroloid in character—I do not mean in form—the dialect is a mere fleeting incident, but in style of thought, intensity of color, fervency of passion, and grandeur of aspiration. . . . Literature . . . will win his earliest, perhaps his brightest laurels." This exchange with Tourgée must have convinced Chesnutt that the ambitions for representing African American life that he had expressed in his journal were definitely worth pursuing.

2. To explain her sexual desirability, Dean McWilliams posits something he calls "the white unconscious," which is "aroused . . . by the merest suspicion" of black blood (*Fictions* 132). I think that this idea contradicts what Chesnutt is trying to accomplish in *Mandy Oxendine*. He has given Mandy none of the typical markers that were thought to reveal hidden racial ancestry. If the white men nevertheless know, that undermines Chesnutt's conviction that race is nothing more than a social and legal fiction. If they can scent her African ancestry, race is always already inescapable.

3. In an interesting moment when Utley is trying to make Mandy believe that he is not going to marry his intended, he calls her "that dark, ugly, cold-blooded creature" (72). One expects that term *cold-blooded,* but *dark* seems to me almost racially inflected. In contrast to Mandy's "nut-brown hair," Utley's fiancée's hair is "abundant [and] black" (63).

4. This is not the same process as McWilliams's "white unconscious" (*Fictions* 132). I am not talking about the characters in the novel but the cultural common sense of the audience, which "knew" that mixed-race women were more highly sexualized than their white counterparts.

5. Brodhead cites a study of black professionals in North Carolina in 1890: less than "0.5 percent of the black population[held] professional positions," and 95 percent of those were either teachers or ministers (Introduction 15 n.15).

Chapter 4

1. Chesnutt published some nine sketches in *Puck* between 1887 and 1891, with only three of them involving African American characters. Two of these sketches accede to cultural stereotypes. However, "A Roman Antique" seems to be a sly satire of plantation school stories, with a two-thousand-year-old black man reminiscing about being a slave of Julius Caesar's and saving Caesar during the war in Gaul. Chesnutt parodied the plantation school in the last words of the old black man: "Ah but dem wuz good ole times!" (*Short Fiction* 76), a direct allusion to Thomas Nelson Page's "Marse Chan," published in 1887.

2. The Chesnutt Papers at Fisk University include scrapbooks of the reviews of his novels. I find the reviews—particularly the unfavorable ones—a valuable resource. Janet Malcolm has remarked that "negative contemporary criticism of a masterpiece can be helpful to later critics, acting as a kind of radar that picks up the ping of the work's originality. The 'mistakes' and 'excesses' that early critics complain of are often precisely the innovations that have given the work its power" (16). I am not claiming that *The House Behind the Cedars* is a masterpiece, but I do believe in the explanatory power of negative reviews.

3. In a canceled passage, he was even more explicit: "I suspect that my way of looking at these things is 'amorphous' not in the sense of being unnatural but unusual. There are a great many intelligent people who consider the [mulatto] class to which Rena and Wain belong as unnatural" (*Letters* 67 n.4).

4. In his essay, "Why Charles W. Chesnutt Is Not a Realist," Joseph R. McElrath Jr. has drummed Chesnutt out of the realist corps, noting in particular that in the passage just quoted, Chesnutt goes on to say that if he wanders from the path of realism, he will depict life "as I think it ought to be" (146). McElrath sees that Chesnutt's violations of the ideology of realism make him a lesser artist, uncommitted to the rigors of Howellsian realism.

In this book, I am less interested in whether Chesnutt was a realist than in exploring Chesnutt's multiple contradictions as writer and his position as an African American writing for a largely white audience, a dilemma and an opportunity for Chesnutt.

5. The only other novel of the period that I know of that uses something like this device of dual sympathy is the anonymously published *Towards the Gulf* (1887). But as Fick and Gold point out, this novel employs "strategies" whereby "the 'tragedy' of the 'tragic mulatto' is transferred from the black woman to the southern man's dilemmas of identity" (29). In other words, this pro-southern novel employs the tragic mulatta plot to make the dilemma of white identity the tale's focus. Much as Toni Morrison argues in *Playing in the Dark,* the African American character is only incidental to the dilemma of the white protagonist. Chesnutt balanced the dilemmas of both characters, the white man and the black woman.

6. The figure of Wain poses a potential problem for Chesnutt because the character would tend to confirm the audience's preconceptions about mulattoes. Chesnutt did not fully resolve this problem in *The House Behind the Cedars.*

7. In *White Supremacy and Negro Subordination* (1868), J. H. van Evrie opined that race mixing was a kind of "original sin" and that "the children it produces" would be punished "to the third and fourth generation for the sins of the fathers" (quoted in Sundquist, *Faulkner* 110).

8. This phrase is from Howells's review of Booker T. Washington's *Up from Slavery* (1901) in which Howells praised Washington: "In his heart there is no bitterness" (196). Howells commended the patience and calm of men such as Washington and Chesnutt because "it enables them to use reason and the nimbler weapons of irony and saves them from bitterness" (195).

9. I am using this somewhat awkward nomenclature to signal his dual identity, to emphasize the fact that his decision to pass as white has erased his family name, Walden.

10. I use this term to emphasize that fact that Tryon's assumptions were typical for the period. Racism was rational, warranted by the discourses of history, religion, and science. Chesnutt's positions and his argument for amalgamation were seen as deeply irrational, as attempts to overturn the natural order of things.

11. Interestingly, all of the central male characters yield to this "sentimental weakness": Judge Straight when he lets young Warwick study law; Warwick when he returns home; and Tryon several times throughout the latter part of the novel. In every case, these men regret their "indulgence," almost as if they had all been trained to distrust any sentiment. After such indulgence, they feel guilty and faintly feminized, except in the case of Tryon's final shift to sentiment.

12. When the central white male character of *Towards the Gulf* discovers that his wife is part black, there is this interchange between husband and wife: "'Are you ill? Oh, John, what can it be?' 'Nothing,' he answered, slowly and hoarsely, looking at her with the

expression of one who sees beyond material things into the region of horrible mystery, and then with a shiver he turned away from her" (197). The "horrible mystery" is the infectious quality of black blood, which means a reversion to type. Within the racist imaginary, no matter how a mixed-race character is brought up, he or she will inevitably reveal the lurking black ancestor.

13. An example of this kind of scientific superstition can be seen in the antebellum work of physician John Van Evrie in his popular *Negroes and Negro "Slavery"* (1853). He argues that "the Negro's incapacity to speak the white man's language proves his God-given political disability. . . . Language is so deeply rooted in racial identity that the Africans of Haiti, Van Evrie predicts, will inevitably and spontaneously relapse 'into their native African tongue'" (Crane 51).

14. On this point I disagree with SallyAnn H. Ferguson, who has written, "According to High Gloster, at this point in the novel George seeks Rena for a mistress. . . . Although his racial bigotry earlier prevented him from marrying her because she was black, George's flaming aristocratic lust does not put him above desiring to take her to bed" (50). I see no textual evidence to support this contention.

15. Chesnutt did not want to resort to expatriation as a solution to the problem the novel poses. He would have seen expatriation as an evasion of a particularly American problem that needed to be solved on American soil. He would also have seen expatriation as a tacit acknowledgment that African Americans were not full citizens, entitled to all of the civil rights that European Americans enjoyed, including the right to marry the person of one's choice.

16. Richard Watson Gilder, who was so negative about "Rena Walden," was also a poet, and at the time of the World's Columbian Exposition, Gilder published a poem, "The White City," in which he connects the exposition to the world of ancient Greece:

> Her white-winged soul sinks on the New World's breast.
> Ah happy West—
> Greece flowers anew, and all her temples soar.

He constructs a tradition in which the Greeks were white and the United States is the fruition of that whiteness. Rena's identification with Greece can be seen then, as a confounding, for Chesnutt's audience, of racial mythology.

17. This description is atypical. Not only is Frank intelligent and imaginative, but he is also literate (he writes Rena's mother's letters for her). He is, however, typical in his worship of Rena from afar. It is as if Chesnutt had transferred the idea of fidelity to one's master from slavery times to Frank's fidelity to Rena and her family. In his fidelity, was Frank a kind of sop to Chesnutt's audience? Having asked so much of them in terms of the trajectory of Tryon's experience, did Chesnutt feel it necessary to hold onto

an element of stereotypicality to ground the narrative in contemporary racial common sense? In other words, Chesnutt knew how difficult it would be to get his readers to accept the fluidity of whiteness as a concept. He could risk departing from the typical only so much with the character of Frank. Of course, his depiction of Frank was complicated by Chesnutt's distance from lower-class African American life.

18. In *Mandy Oxendine,* the male triad consists of a degenerate aristocrat, a white preacher, and a mixed-race man. In that novel, the only possible suitor was the mixed-race man. In *The House Behind the Cedars,* the only impossible suitor is the mixed-race man.

Chapter 5

1. It has been claimed that the events in Wilmington were "the only known instance of a coup d'etat in American history" ("1898 Education")

2. Several of the ads placed by Houghton Mifflin connect *The Marrow of Tradition* to *Uncle Tom's Cabin.* In the most elaborate of these ads, the publisher posits the South as a "stage." Stowe and Tourgée's novels are earlier acts in the national drama, and Chesnutt's novel is characterized as the next act, "a novel that will recall at many points its great precursor 'Uncle Tom's Cabin'" (*The Marrow,* Advertisement). One of the novel's characters, Delamere, the old aristocrat, says to Dr. Miller, "It is a great problem . . . the future of your race. . . . It is a serial story which we are all reading, and which grows in vital interest with each successive installment" (51).

3. Prather also says that "oral traditions" recount a much higher number of victims. Some contemporary accounts registered "hundreds" of killings ("We Have Taken" 35).

4. Of the papers in North Carolina, 20 were Republican, 36 were Populist, and 145 were Democratic (Honey 171).

5. M'Kelway returned to the national press a little over a month later in the *Outlook* with an editorial, "North Carolina Revolution Justified." In this article, he connects the events in Wilmington with the Spanish-American War: "The truth is that a great deal more was accomplished than was intended at the outset—just as the United States finds itself to-day with results achieved which it did not contemplate at the beginning of the war with Spain" (quoted in Wegener 12). Prather notes that ministers and journalists were the first to justify the events in Wilmington (*We Have Taken* 174).

6. Joseph R. McElrath Jr. notes that in this novel Chesnutt had "strayed radically from the course he had set in 1880 toward the goal of seducing, rather than browbeating, the white American readership into a more benign attitude toward the African American" ("Howells and Race" 475). First, critics have a tendency to hold Chesnutt to the pronouncements he made in his early twenties, as if his ideas never changed. Second, I disagree that Chesnutt is "browbeating" his audience. His decision to write a historical

novel based on recent events forced him to confront the complete success of the disenfranchisement campaign in Wilmington and throughout the South, and he was caught in a terrible contradiction between his faith in efficacy of fiction to change people's hearts and his despair at the hardening of racial issues. And if one compares his performance in this novel to Dixon's in *The Leopard's Spots*, which was published a year later, Chesnutt is the model of restraint.

7. Chesnutt had read *The Leopard's Spots* by May 1902 and hoped that Dixon's views were "extreme" and represented "a very small proportion of Southern people" (Helen Chesnutt 181).

8. *The Clansman* sold more than a million copies within a few month of its release (Williamson, *Crucible* 174). Its vision of the history of Reconstruction and of black men as rapists received a longer lease on life when D. W. Griffith adapted the novel for his film, *Birth of a Nation* (1915).

9. On one hand, Dixon felt that representations of the South and of African Americans had been entirely one-sided for forty years. On the other, Chesnutt felt that the African American point of view had hardly been presented at all. Historically, of course, Chesnutt was right, but it is a gauge of the degree of American racism and the hysteria about the position of African Americans in the polity that Dixon could feel so beleaguered in a period that saw the almost complete disenfranchisement of African Americans.

10. In Dixon as well as in Page, the legislature sets up a round-the-clock free bar for its members. In addition, Dixon writes that "in a suite of rooms in the Capitol they established a brothel. From the galleries a swarm of courtesans daily smiled on their favourites on the floor" (117).

11. Bloomfield has claimed that "Dixon was no isolated crank, but a representative spokesman for his time" (396). Dixon is representative to the degree to which he takes the racial discourse of this period to its logical conclusion. Although many nonideological American racists may have been troubled by the hyperbolic quality of his representations of history and of African Americans (as such readers would have been by the character of Dr. Green in *The House Behind the Cedars*), they would not have dissented from his underlying assumptions.

12. See the discussion of racial ideology and the world's fair at the turn of the century in M. Wilson, "Advent."

13. The scientific gaze here has to note this important difference: Miller's skin color is "brown"; the word *black* evokes a social construction.

14. In one of the subplots, Ellis and Tom are rivals for the hand of Carteret's niece, Clara. When Delamere's degeneracy is revealed and he is expelled from his club and leaves town, the honorable Ellis's way is clear with Clara. To the degree to which he is a nonideological racist, the suggestion of a marriage between the two is a positive one in the world of the novel. Conversely, even in a novel as unconventional as *The Marrow of*

Tradition, Chesnutt could not eschew romance, a plot element of which he would be more critical in his next published novel, *The Colonel's Dream.*

15. In 1894, Frederick Douglass observed, "A white man has but to blacken his face and commit a crime to have some Negro lynched in his stead" ("Why" 494). It would be interesting to know what currency this idea received in the African American community at the time.

16. The major change that Chesnutt makes in the Wilmington events is to move them from the day after the election to before the election, thereby emphasizing the degree to which they were about electoral intimidation.

17. Howell's use of the strange word "dynamitic" in this passage is quite revealing in light of the controversy over the word *dynamite* in Howells's serialized version of *The Rise of Silas Lapham* (1885). The word was so heavily fraught that the publishers stopped the presses to contact Howells and ask him to reconsider his use of the word even in an ironic way. Richard Watson Gilder (the same critic who savaged an early draft of Chesnutt's *The House Behind the Cedars*) wrote to Howells that "it is the very word, *dynamite,* that is now so dangerous for any of us to use, except in condemnation" (339). Howells's use of the word in the context of his review of Washington's work makes clear the degree to which the critic worried about retaliation by African Americans for the years of injustice they had endured.

18. Mia Bay has written about this strand in African American thinking. During the 1890s, she claims, "discussions of whites as brutal and aggressive Anglo-Saxons were commonplace in black thought" (102), and a number of African American writers held up "both lynching and American imperialism as evidence of Anglo-Saxon barbarism" (103). Although Chesnutt seems close to this strand of thought, he is much too complicated a thinker to get caught in the trap of mirroring claims to barbarism.

19. Lest one think that strategies of melodramatic sympathy are confined to the mid–nineteenth century, consider this passage from a letter by Angelina Weld Grimké written at the beginning of the twentieth century. She asked whether women had "a vulnerable point and if so what was it? I believed it to be motherhood. Certainly all the noblest, finest, most sacred things in their lives converge about this. If anything can make all women sisters underneath their skins, it is motherhood. If, then, I could make the white women of this country see, feel, understand, just what their prejudice and the prejudice of their father, brother, husband, sons were having on the souls of the colored mothers everywhere . . . a great power to affect public opinion would be set free and the battle would be half won" (quoted in Tate 219).

20. Najmi also argues that *The Marrow of Tradition* "addresses white *women* especially" (15). Chesnutt knew that most book buyers were women, but I do not think that he conceived of his audience in gendered terms. He is too interested in public counterhistory, and as I argued earlier, he is acknowledging the limits of sentimental protest in this final scene.

To acknowledge that women share maternal instincts that can be invoked cross-culturally in moments of crisis does nothing to cancel out the history that enmeshes Janet and Olivia (and as we know from Stowe's example, maternal solidarity is also possible while maintaining the essential inferiority of African Americans).

Chapter 6

1. After having written *Evelyn's Husband*, with its cast of white characters, Chesnutt was able, in *The Colonel's Dream*, to focus almost exclusively on white experience in a race fiction.

2. The text from which I quote here, "No Color Line in Literature," is an alternate version of Chesnutt's "The Negro in Art" from *Essays and Speeches*. The typescript is slightly more ironic than the published text.

3. Perhaps Chesnutt's pessimism about fiction as an agent of social change was generated, in part, by his conception of fiction, which originated with his awareness as a young man of the best-sellers of Stowe and Tourgée and his awareness in the years during which he published his novels of the best-sellers of Page and Dixon. This attitude toward fiction contrasts with what he articulated in his essay "Race Prejudice," where he said that in his "discussion of race prejudice I am seeking the long-time remedy" (*Essays* 234). In his fiction, he always wanted to have an immediate effect on his white audience.

4. Edmund Wilson agrees that Cable's novel is "serious" but sees that as its central problem: "The novel is completely synthetic, and it was most unfortunate that Cable, in attempting so serious a book, should have played into the hands of his critics by producing so thorough a bore" (584). In my experience, the novel is excruciatingly painful to read. Wilson says that the "slow strangulation of Cable as an artist and a serious writer is surely one of the most gruesome episodes in American literary history" (579). In particular, Cable was unable to write the book that he wanted to write because of Richard Watson Gilder, the editor of the *Century*. Cable sent Gilder several drafts of the novel, all of which Gilder rejected. In response to the first draft, Gilder wrote in August 1890, "I could weep for disappointment. . . . Here are gleams of the delightful old art—but [it is] a tract, not a story,—to my mind. Instead of a return *to* literature; an attempt to fetch everything into literature save & except literature itself" (quoted in Rubin 218). One would like to know whether Cable recalled Gilder's response only a few months earlier (in May 1890) to Chesnutt's "Rena Walden."

5. Chesnutt did read *John March, Southerner* and tactfully wrote to Cable that he thought it a "great book, but [it] does not appeal to me, for obvious reasons, quite as much as *The Grandissimes* or *Old Creole Days*" (*Letters* 83). In a 1916 lecture, "The Negro in Books," Chesnutt referred to the novel, saying that "Mr. Cable's later conception of the

reconstructed Negro in the character of Cornelius Leggett, the grafting mulatto politician, in his *John March, Southerner,* is less happy and less convincing" (*Essays* 433).

6. This conversation echoes one in Dixon's *The Clansman,* where Abraham Lincoln says, "There is no room for two distinct races of white men in America, much less for two distinct races of whites and blacks. . . . We must assimilate or expel" (46), and since assimilation is unimaginable in the racist imaginary, only expulsion is possible, something that Walter Benn Michaels calls "a kind of visceral or emetic anti-imperialism" ("Souls" 186).

7. It is interesting that in speaking to the white foreman he fires, French insists on his absolute right to be "master," while here he seems to imply that being a "master" of any sort is a double enslavement. Chesnutt sees connections between both kinds of masters—of slaves or of employees—but French does not.

8. In his 1894 pamphlet "Why Is The Negro Lynched?" Douglass wrote, "With a few noble exceptions, just enough to prove the rule, the upper classes of the South seem to be in full sympathy with the mob and its deeds. There are but few earnest words ever uttered against either. Press, platform and pulpit are generally either silent or they openly apologize for the mob and its deeds" (494). It is as if up to the time of *The Colonel's Dream,* Chesnutt wanted to believe in the idea of the silent South. As he wrote in 1903, "There is a silent white South, uneasy in conscience, darkened in counsel, groping for the light, and willing to do the right" (*Essays* 191). Although he might cling to this idea as a utopian hope, the novel demonstrates that at least in Colonel French's typical small southern town, the voice of the silent South would never be raised against macabre outrages like the exhumation of Peter's coffin.

Chapter 7

1. The final letter in the microfilm edition of the Chesnutt-Cable letters is dated March 7, 1921. While working on *Paul Marchand,* Chesnutt apparently wrote to ask Cable some questions about details of historical accuracy regarding New Orleans. The last sentence of Cable's response to Chesnutt is quite moving: "I think we might as well call our acquaintance 'present' as 'forever'" (7 March 1921).

2. Chesnutt uses the word *caste* eighteen times in *Paul Marchand.*

3. Toni Morrison has written in *Playing in the Dark* that one of the "common linguistic strategies employed in fiction to engage the serious consequences of blacks" (67) is fetishization. "This is especially useful in evoking erotic fears or desires and establishing fixed and major difference where difference does not exist or is minimal. Blood, for example, is a pervasive fetish: black blood, white blood, the purity of blood; the purity of white female sexuality, the pollution of African blood and sex. Fetishization is a strategy often used to assert the categorical absolutism of civilization and savagery" (68).

Chapter 8

1. In his review, DuBois wrote that the novel "is a blow in the face. It is an affront to the hospitality of black folk and to the intelligence of white" (173). He concludes his review by saying, "I cannot for the life of me see in this work either sincerity or art, deep thought, or truthful industry. It seems to me that Mr. Van Vechten tried to do something bizarre and he certainly succeeded" (174). In contrast, Chesnutt says in "The Negro in Present Day Fiction" that when *Nigger Heaven* appeared, he criticized it—"the title was the most offensive feature"—but the novel was "the pioneer of a flood of such books" (518). Chesnutt wrote to Van Vechten, who praised Chesnutt highly in *Nigger Heaven,* and in "a particularly complimentary letter," said, "As to the literary quality of the works, it is done with your usual vividness and sparkle." Chesnutt concluded by "hoping it may have the success which its brilliancy and obvious honesty deserve" (quoted in Pfeiffer xxx).

2. When living in Cleveland, Donald was never "called . . . 'nigger' or 'Negro.' Only once could he recall in later years was his race mentioned" (52).

3. Those cultural accomplishments, as Scott Malcomson has pointed out in *One Drop of Blood,* conjured up a vision of a "usable culture" that found its sources in a "blues culture" (232) that could be traced back to slavery. And the problem with slavery "was that the most abject, miserable period of black life in America also seemed the most authentically black" (233). African Americans such as Chesnutt (and his character, Donald Glover) worked hard to attain high Euro-American cultural capital, and the acknowledgment of blues culture as a source of authenticity would also entail an examination of middle-class African Americans' disjunction from that culture.

4. DuBois published *Dark Princess* in 1928, and it is remarkable for its internationalist focus. The princess of the title is from India, and at the end of the novel she marries the main African American character. Their child will be "Messenger and Messiah to the Darker Worlds!" (310). Although Chesnutt's character is resolutely national, both Chesnutt and DuBois still believed in the concept of the representative race leader. Chesnutt read *Dark Princess* and said, somewhat cryptically, that the main character was "somewhat unbalanced" (*Essays* 523).

5. In his 1905 speech, "Race Prejudice," Chesnutt stated, "There is no magic wand which we can wave and make [race prejudice] vanish in a night. There is no panacea we can take and cure it" (219). Here, we are meant to believe that Glover has discovered such a panacea.

Postscript

1. In *Cultures of Letters,* Richard Brodhead has said that "although Chesnutt wanted very badly to be a writer, it is only fair to admit that he wanted other things more. His 1899 toting-up of his savings makes clear that Chesnutt needed to be able to live securely in the

style of success before he would risk himself to writing; and when his career showed itself unprofitable, he reverted to surer ways to wealth. In this sense the peculiar worldly requirement Chesnutt had placed on authorship from the beginning helped make his career unviable in the long run" (210). If one rehistoricizes Chesnutt, his commitment to his family must be seen as more than a kind of "*peculiar* worldly requirement" he placed on authorship. The grandson (on his father's side) of a slave owner and his slave, Chesnutt had to balance his desire for literary success against his desire for his children's success. Their success as graduates of elite colleges signified as much for him as a resounding literary success would have.

Works Cited

"1898 Education—What Happened in 1898?" *1898 Foundation. Wilmington, North Carolina.* 17 Nov. 2000. <http://www.spinnc.org/spinsites/1898/education/chapter4.htm>

Andrews, William L. Foreword. Chesnutt, *Mandy* ix–x.

———. Introduction. *Collected Stories of Charles W. Chesnutt.* By Chesnutt. Ed. William L. Andrews. New York: Mentor, 1992. vii–xvii.

———. *The Literary Career of Charles W. Chesnutt.* Baton Rouge: Louisiana State UP, 1980.

———. "William Dean Howells and Charles W. Chesnutt: Criticism and Race Fiction in the Age of Booker T. Washington." *American Literature* 48 (1976): 327–39.

Athenaeus. *The Deipnosophists.* Trans. Charles Burton Gulick. Vol. 6. Cambridge: Harvard UP, 1937.

Atherton, Gertrude. *Senator North.* 1900. Ridgewood, NJ: Gregg, 1967.

Ayers, Edward L. *The Promise of the New South: Life after Reconstruction.* New York: Oxford UP, 1992.

Bay, Mia. *The White Image in the Black Mind: African-American Ideas about White People, 1830–1925.* New York: Oxford UP, 2000.

Bargainnier, Earl F. "*Red Rock:* A Reappraisal." *Southern Quarterly* 22 (1984): 44–53.

Barrett, James R., and David Roediger. "Inbetween Peoples: Race, Nationality, and the 'New Immigrant' Working Class." *Journal of American Ethnic History* 16 (1997): 3–44.

Bederman, Gail. *Manliness and Civilization: A Cultural History of Gender and Race in the United States, 1880–1917.* Chicago: U of Chicago P, 1995.

Bentley, Nancy. "White Slaves: The Mulatto Hero in Antebellum Fiction." *Subjects and Citizens: Nation, Race, and Gender from* Oroonoko *to* Anita Hill. Eds. Michael Moon and Cathy N. Davidson. Durham: Duke UP, 1995. 195–216.

Bewley, Marius. *The Eccentric Design: Form in the Classic American Novel.* New York: Columbia UP, 1963.

Blight, David W. *Race and Reunion: The Civil War in American Memory.* Cambridge: Harvard UP, 2001.

Bloomfield, Maxwell. "Dixon's *The Leopard's Spots:* A Study in Popular Racism." *American Quarterly* 16 (1964): 387–401.

Boas, Franz. *Anthropology and Modern Life.* 1928. Mineola: Dover, 1986.

———. "The Real Race Problem." *The Crisis* 1 (1910): 22–25.

Bold, Christine. "Popular Forms I." Elliot 285–305.

Bourke, Charles Francis. "The Committee of Twenty-Five." *Collier's Weekly.* 26 Nov. 1889: 5+.

Brodhead, Richard. *Cultures of Letters: Scenes of Reading and Writing in Nineteenth-Century America.* Chicago: U of Chicago P, 1993.

———. Introduction. *The Journals of Charles W. Chesnutt.* By Chesnutt. Durham: Duke UP, 1993.

Brown, William Wells. *Clotel; or, The President's Daughter: Three Classic African-American Novels.* Ed. Henry Louis Gates Jr. New York: Vintage, 1990.

Bruce, Dickson D. *Black American Writing from the Nadir: The Evolution of a Literary Tradition, 1877–1915.* Baton Rouge: Louisiana State UP, 1989.

Bynner, Witter. Letter to Charles W. Chesnutt. 6 Sept. 1903. Charles W. Chesnutt Papers, Special Collections, Fisk University Library, Nashville.

Cable, George Washington. *John March, Southerner.* 1894. New York: Scribner's, 1899.

———. Letter to Charles W. Chesnutt. 12 June 1889. George W. Cable Correspondence, 1889–98. Mf#4. Tennessee State Library and Archives. Nashville.

———. Letter to Charles W. Chesnutt. 25 Sept. 1889. George W. Cable Correspondence, 1889–98. Mf#4. Tennessee State Library and Archives. Nashville.

———. Letter to Charles W. Chesnutt. 7 March 1921. George W. Cable Correspondence, 1889–98. Mf#4. Tennessee State Library and Archives. Nashville.

———. *Lovers of Louisiana.* New York: Scribner's, 1918.

———. *The Negro Question: A Selection of Writings on Civil Rights in the South.* Garden City: Doubleday, 1958.

Cawelti, John G. *Adventure, Mystery, and Romance: Formula Stories as Art and Popular Culture.* Chicago: U of Chicago P, 1976.

Chamstzky, Jules. *Our Decentralized Literature: Cultural Meditations on Selected Jewish and Southern Writers.* Amherst: U of Massachusetts P, 1986.

Chesnutt, Charles W. "A Business Career." Charles W. Chesnutt Papers, Special Collections, Fisk University Library, Nashville.

———. *Charles W. Chesnutt: Essays and Speeches.* Eds. Joseph R. McElrath, Robert C. Leitz III, and Jesse S. Crisler. Stanford: Stanford UP, 1999.

———. *The Colonel's Dream.* 1905. Miami: Mnemosyne, 1969.

———. "Evelyn's Husband." Charles W. Chesnutt Papers, Special Collections, Fisk University Library, Nashville.

———. *An Exemplary Citizen: Letters of Charles W. Chesnutt, 1906–1932.* Eds. Jesse S. Crisler, Robert C. Leitz III, and Joseph R. McElrath Jr. Stanford: Stanford UP, 2002.

————. *Frederick Douglass*. Boston: Small, Maynard, 1899.

————. *The House Behind the Cedars*. 1900. New York: Penguin, 1993.

————. *The Journals of Charles W. Chesnutt*. Ed. Richard Brodhead. Durham: Duke UP, 1993.

————. *Mandy Oxendine*. Ed. Charles Hackenberry. Urbana: U of Illinois P, 1997.

————. *The Marrow of Tradition*. 1901. New York: Penguin, 1993.

————. "No Color Line in Literature." Charles W. Chesnutt Papers, Special Collections, Fisk University Library, Nashville.

————. *Paul Marchand, F.M.C.* Ed. Matthew Wilson. Jackson: UP of Mississippi, 1998.

————. *The Quarry*. Ed. Dean McWilliams. Princeton: Princeton UP, 1999.

————. "The Rainbow Chasers." Charles W. Chesnutt Papers, Special Collections, Fisk University Library, Nashville.

————. *The Short Fiction of Charles W. Chesnutt*. Ed. Sylvia Lyons Render. Washington: Howard UP, 1981.

————. *To Be an Author: Letters of Charles W. Chesnutt, 1898–1905*. Eds. Joseph R. McElrath Jr. and Robert C. Leitz III. Princeton: Princeton UP, 1997.

————. "To B. G. Brawley." 29 July 1914. Charles W. Chesnutt Papers, Special Collections, Fisk University Library, Nashville.

Chesnutt, Helen M. *Charles W. Chesnutt: Pioneer of the Color Line*. Chapel Hill: U of North Carolina P, 1952.

Cleman, John. *George Washington Cable Revisited*. New York: Twayne, 1996.

Rev. of *The Colonel's Dream,* by Chesnutt. *Richmond Leader* 30 Sept. 1905: n.p. Charles W. Chesnutt Papers, Special Collections, Fisk University Library, Nashville.

Conrad, Joseph. *Heart of Darkness*. Ed. Robert Kimbrough. 1899. New York: Norton, 1988.

Cook, Raymond A. *Thomas Dixon*. New York, Twayne, 1974.

Crane, Gregg D. *Race, Citizenship, and Law in American Literature*. New York: Cambridge UP, 2002.

"A Crime against the Ballot." *The Independent* 17 Nov. 1898: 1433–34.

Davenport, F. Garvin, Jr. "Thomas Dixon's Mythology of Southern History." *Journal of Southern History* 36 (1970): 350–67.

Davis, F. James. *Who Is Black? One Nation's Definition*. University Park: Pennsylvania State UP, 1991.

Dixon, Thomas. *The Clansman*. 1905. Lexington: U of Kentucky P, 1970.

————. *The Leopard's Spots*. New York: Doubleday, 1902.

Donaldson, Susan. *Competing Voices: The American Novel, 1865–1914*. New York: Twayne, 1998.

Donnelly, Ignatius. *Doctor Huguet*. 1891. New York: Arno, 1969.

Douglass, Frederick. "Introduction to *Why the Colored American Is Not in the World's Columbian Exposition*." Foner, *Life* 6:469–77.

————. "Why Is the Negro Lynched?" Foner, *Life* 6:491–523.

DuBois, W. E. B. "Books." Rev. of *Nigger Heaven*, by Carl Van Vechten. *Crisis* 33 (December 1926): 81–82. Rpt. in *The Critics and the Harlem Renaissance*. Ed. Cary D. Wing. New York: Garland, 1996. 173–74.

———. *Dark Princess: A Romance*. 1928. Jackson: UP of Mississippi, 1995.

———. "Strivings of the Negro People." *Atlantic Monthly* 80 (1897): 194–98.

Dunbar, Paul Laurence. *The Love of Landry*. 1900. New York: Negro Universities P, 1969.

Durso, Patricia Keefe. "The 'White Problem': The Critical Study of Whiteness in American Literature." *Modern Language Studies* 32 (2003): 1–3.

Edwards, Laura F. "Captives of Wilmington: The Riot and Historical Memories of Political Conflict, 1865–1898." Tyson and Cecelski, *Democracy* 114–40.

Elliott, Emory, ed. *The Columbia History of the American Novel*. New York: Columbia UP, 1991.

Elliott, Sarah Barnwell. *An Incident and Other Happenings*. 1899. Freeport: Books for Libraries P, 1969.

Ellison, Ralph. "The World and the Jug." *Shadow and Act*. New York: Random House, 1964. 107–43.

Farnsworth, Robert M. Introduction. *The Marrow of Tradition*. By Chesnutt. Ann Arbor: U of Michigan P, 1970.

Fauset, Jessie. *There Is Confusion*. New York: Boni and Liveright, 1924.

Ferguson, SallyAnn H. "Rena Walden: Chesnutt's Failed 'Future American.'" *Southern Literary Journal* 15 (1982): 74–82.

Fick, Thomas, and Eva Gold. "Race, Region, and the Reconstruction of the Southern Gentleman: The American Race Melodrama in Buckner's *Towards the Gulf*." *Southern Quarterly* 35.3 (1997): 29–41.

Fikes, Robert. "Escaping the Literary Ghetto: African American Authors of White Life Novels, 1946–1994." *Western Journal of Black Studies* 19 (1995): 105–12.

Finseth, Ian. "How Shall the Truth Be Told? Language and Race in *The Marrow of Tradition*." *American Literary Realism* 31.3 (1999): 1–20.

Fisher, Philip. *Hard Facts: Setting and Form in the American Novel*. New York: Oxford UP, 1985.

Foner, Eric. *Reconstruction: America's Unfinished Revolution, 1862–1877*. New York: Harper, 1988.

———. *Nothing but Freedom: Emancipation and Its Legacy*. Baton Rouge: Louisiana State UP, 1983.

———, ed. *The Life and Writings of Frederick Douglass*. New York: International, 1955.

Frederickson, George M. *The Black Image in the White Mind: The Debate on Afro-American Character and Destiny, 1817–1914*. Hanover: Wesleyan UP, 1971.

Gaston, Paul M. *The New South Creed: A Study in Southern Matchmaking*. New York: Knopf, 1970.

Gayle, Addison. "Literature as Catharsis: The Novels of Paul Laurence Dunbar." *A Singer in the Dawn: Reinterpretations of Paul Laurence Dunbar*. Ed. Jay Martin. New York: Dodd, Mead, 1975. 139–51.

Gilder, Richard Watson. "To William Dean Howells." 18 Feb. 1885. *The Rise of Silas Lapham.* By William Dean Howells. Ed. Don L. Cook. New York: Norton, 1982. 339.

———. Letter to George Washington Cable. 28 May 1890. George W. Cable Correspondence, 1889–98. Mf#4. Tennessee State Library and Archives. Nashville.

———. "The White City." *The Century* 46 (May 1893): 22.

Gillman, Susan. "The Mulatto, Tragic or Triumphant? The Nineteenth-Century American Race Melodrama." *The Culture of Sentiment: Race, Gender, and Sentimentality in Nineteenth-Century America.* Ed. Shirley Samuels. New York: Oxford UP, 1992. 221–43.

Gilmore, Glenda E. "Murder, Memory, and the Flight of the Incubus." Tyson and Cecelski, *Democracy* 73–93.

Gleason, William. "Jokes at the Nadir: Charles Chesnutt and David Bryant Fulton." *American Literary Realism* 24 (1992): 22–41.

Glover, Katherine. "News in the World of Books." McElrath, *Critical Essays* 84–85.

Godbold, E. Stanly, Jr. "The Battleground Revisited: Reconstruction in Southern Fiction, 1895–1905." *South Atlantic Quarterly* 73 (1974): 99–116.

Gross, Theodore. *Thomas Nelson Page.* New York: Twayne, 1967.

———. *Albion Tourgée.* New York: Twayne, 1963.

Hackenberry, Charles. Introduction. Chesnutt, *Mandy* xi–xxviii.

———. "Meaning and Models: The Use of Characterization in Chesnutt's *The Marrow of Tradition* and *Mandy Oxendine*." *American Literary Realism* 17 (1984): 193–202.

Haley, John. "Race, Rhetoric, and Revolution." Tyson and Cecelski, *Democracy* 207–24.

Haller, John S. *Outcasts from Evolution: Scientific Attitudes of Racial Inferiority, 1859–1900.* Urbana: U of Illinois P, 1971.

Harper, Frances E. W. *Iola Leroy; or, Shadows Uplifted. Three Classic African-American Novels.* Ed. Henry Louis Gates Jr. New York: Vintage, 1990.

Harris, Susan K. "Problems of Representation in Turn-of-the-Century Immigrant Fiction." *American Realism and the Canon.* Ed. Tom Quirk and Gary Scharnhorst. Newark: U of Delaware P, 1994. 127–42.

Hart, James D. *The Popular Book: A History of America's Literary Taste.* New York: Oxford UP, 1950.

Hattenhauer, Darryl. "Racial and Textual Miscegenation in Chesnutt's *The House Behind the Cedars*." *Mississippi Quarterly* 47 (1993–94): 27–45.

Honey, Michael. "Class, Race, and Power in the New South: Racial Violence and the Delusions of White Supremacy." Tyson and Cecelski, *Democracy* 162–84.

hooks, bell. *Black Looks: Race and Representation.* Boston: South End, 1992.

Hopkins, Pauline E. *Contending Forces: A Romance Illustrative of Negro Life North and South.* 1900. New York: Oxford UP, 1988.

———. *Hagar's Daughter. The Magazine Novels of Pauline Hopkins.* Ed. Hazel V. Carby. New York: Oxford UP, 1988.

Howells, Mildred, ed. *Life in Letters of William Dean Howells*. Vol. 2. Garden City: Doubleday, Doran, 1928.

Howells, William Dean. "An Exemplary Citizen." Rev of *Up from Slavery*, by Booker T. Washington, and *Frederick Douglass*, by Charles W. Chesnutt. *Booker T. Washington Papers, 1901–1902*. Ed. Louis R. Harlan and Raymond W. Smock. Vol. 6. Urbana: U of Illinois P, 1977. 195–96.

———. "The New Historical Romance." *North American Review* Dec. 1900: 935–48.

———. "Mr. Charles W. Chesnutt's Stories." *Atlantic Monthly* 85 (1900): 699–701.

———. "A Psychological Counter-Current in Recent Fiction." McElrath, *Critical Essays* 82–83.

———. *The Shadow of a Dream, and An Imperative Duty*. Ed. Edwin H. Cady. New York: Twayne, 1963.

———. "To Henry B. Fuller." 10 Nov. 1901. M. Howells 149.

Hughes, Langston. "The Negro Artist and the Racial Mountain." *Nation* 122 (23 June 1926): 692–94. Rpt. in Wing 166–68.

Jauss, Hans Robert. *Toward an Aesthetic of Reception*. Trans. Timothy Bahti. Minneapolis: U of Minnesota P, 1982.

Johnson, James Weldon. *The Autobiography of an Ex-Colored Man*. Ed. William L. Andrews. 1912. New York, Penguin: 1990.

———. "The Dilemma of the Negro Author." *American Mercury* 15 (Dec. 1928): 477–81. Rpt. in Wing 247–51.

Kaplan, Amy. "Black and Blue on San Juan Hill." In *Cultures of United States Imperialism*. Eds. Amy Kaplan and Donald E. Pease. Durham: Duke UP, 1993. 219–36.

———. "Nation, Region, and Empire." Elliot 240–66.

———. "Romancing the Empire: The Embodiment of American Masculinity in the Popular Historical Romance Novel of the 1890s." *American Literary History* 2 (1990): 659–90.

———. *The Social Construction of American Realism*. Chicago: U of Chicago P, 1988.

Kawash, Samira. *Dislocating the Color Line: Identity, Hybridity, and Singularity in African-American Narrative*. Stanford: Stanford UP, 1997.

Kirshenbaum, Andrea Meryl. "'The Vampire That Hovers over North Carolina': Gender, White Supremacy, and the Wilmington Race Riot of 1898." *Southern Culture* 4 (1998): 6–30.

Knadler, Stephen P. "Untragic Mulatto: Charles Chesnutt and the Discourse of Whiteness." *American Literary Realism* 8 (1996): 426–48.

Knight, Grant C. *The Critical Period in American Literature*. Chapel Hill: U of North Carolina P, 1951.

Kolchin, Peter. "Whiteness Studies: The New History of Race in America." *Journal of American History* 89 (2002): 154–73.

Leitz, Robert C. Rev. of *The Absent Man: The Narrative Craft of Charles W. Chesnutt,* by Charles Duncan. *American Literary Realism* 32 (2000): 272–74.

Lipsitz, George. *Time Passages: Collective Memory and American Popular Culture.* Minneapolis: U of Minnesota P, 1990.

"Literature." McElrath, *Critical Essays* 87.

López, Ian F. Haney. *White by Law: The Legal Construction of Race.* New York: New York UP, 1996.

Malcolm, Janet. "Justice to J. D. Salinger." *New York Review of Books* 21 June 2001: 16–22.

Malcomson, Scott L. *One Drop of Blood: The American Misadventure of Race.* New York: Farrar, 2000.

The Marrow of Tradition. Advertisement. Charles W. Chesnutt Papers, Special Collections, Fisk University Library, Nashville.

McElrath, Joseph R., Jr. "Charles W. Chesnutt's Library." *Analytical and Enumerative Bibliography* 8 (1994): 102–19.

———, ed. *Critical Essays on Charles W. Chesnutt.* New York: Hall, 1999.

———. "W. D. Howells and Race: Charles W. Chesnutt's Disappointment of the Dean." *Nineteenth-Century Literature* 51 (1997): 474–99.

———. "Why Charles W. Chesnutt Is Not a Realist." *American Literary Realism* 32 (2000): 91–108.

McGowan, Todd. "Acting without the Father: Charles Chesnutt's New Aristocrat." *American Literary Realism* 30 (1997): 59–74.

M'Kelway, A. J. "The Cause of the Troubles in North Carolina." *The Independent.* 24 Nov. 1889: 1488–1492.

McWilliams, Dean. *Charles W. Chesnutt and the Fictions of Race.* Athens: U of Georgia P, 2002.

———. "Charles Chesnutt and the Harlem Renaissance." *Soundings* 80 (1997): 591–606.

———. Introduction. *Paul Marchand, F. M. C.* By Charles W. Chesnutt. Princeton: Princeton UP, 1999. vii–xix.

———. Introduction. Chesnutt, *Quarry* ix–xvii.

Megivern, Jim. "A Tale of Three Documents." *1898 Foundation. Wilmington, North Carolina.* 17 Nov. 2000. <http://www.spinnc.org/spinsites/1898/resources/tale.htm>.

Mencke, John. *Mulattoes and Race Mixture: American Attitudes and Images, 1865–1918.* N.p.: UMI Research, 1979.

Metcalf, Ellison. *Charles W. Chesnutt: A Reference Guide.* Boston: Hall, 1977.

Michaels, Walter Benn. *Our America: Nativism, Modernism, and Pluralism.* Durham: Duke UP, 1995.

———. "The Souls of White Folk." *Literature and the Body: Essays on Populations and Persons.* Ed. Elaine Scarry. Baltimore: Johns Hopkins UP, 1988. 185–209.

Mixon, Wayne. *Southern Writers and the New South Movement, 1865–1913.* Chapel Hill: U of North Carolina P, 1980.

Moddelmog, William E. "Lawful Entitlements: Chesnutt's Fictions of Ownership." *Texas Studies in Literature and Language* 41 (1999): 47–69.

Moore, John Trotwood. *The Bishop of Cottontown.* Philadelphia: Winston, 1906.

Morrison, Toni. *Playing in the Dark: Whiteness and the Literary Imagination.* Cambridge: Harvard UP, 1992.

Mott, Frank Luther. *Golden Multitudes: The Story of Best Sellers in the United States.* New York: Macmillan, 1947.

———. *A History of American Magazines, 1885–1905.* Vol. 4. Cambridge: Harvard UP, 1957.

Najmi, Samina. "Janet, Polly, and Olivia: Constructs of Blackness and White Femininity in Charles Chesnutt's *The Marrow of Tradition.*" *Southern Literary Journal* 32 (1999): 1–19.

The Negro Problem: A Series of Articles by Representative American Negroes of To-Day. New York: Pott, 1903.

"Nineteen Negroes Shot to Death." *New York Times* 11 Nov. 1989: 1.

Norris, Frank. *Moran of the Lady Letty: A Story of Adventure off the California Coast.* 1898. New York: AMS, 1971.

Nowatzki, Robert. Rev. of *Mandy Oxendine,* by Charles W. Chesnutt. *African American Review* 33 (1999): 706–07.

Ouida. "The New Woman." *North American Review* 158 (1894): 610–19.

"Our Duty in Cuba." *Collier's Weekly* 26 Nov. 1898: 2–3.

Page, Thomas Nelson. *In Ole Virginia.* 1887. Ridgewood: Gregg, 1968.

———. *Red Rock: A Chronicle of Reconstruction.* 1898. Ridgewood: Gregg, 1967.

Painter, Nell Irvin. *Standing at Armageddon: The United States, 1877–1919.* New York: Norton, 1987.

"Peace in North Carolina." *The Independent* 10 Nov. 1898: 1349–50.

Pfeiffer, Kathleen. Introduction. *Nigger Heaven.* By Carl Van Vechten. Urbana: U of Illinois P, 2000. ix–xxxix.

Pickens, Ernestine Williams. *Charles W. Chesnutt and the Progressive Movement.* New York: Pace UP, 1994.

Pierpont, Claudia Roth. "Cries and Whispers." *New Yorker* 2 April 2001: 66–75.

Posnock, Ross. *Color and Culture: Black Writers and the Making of the Modern Intellectual.* Cambridge: Harvard UP, 1998.

———. "How It Feels to Be a Problem: Du Bois, Fanon, and the 'Impossible Life' of the Black Intellectual." *Critical Inquiry* 23 (1997): 323–49.

Prather, H. Leon, Sr. *We Have Taken a City: Wilmington Racial Massacre and Coup of 1898.* Cranbury: Associated U Presses, 1984.

———. "We Have Taken a City: A Centennial Essay." Tyson and Cecelski, *Democracy* 15–41.

Price, Kenneth M. "Charles W. Chesnutt, the *Atlantic Monthly,* and the Intersection of African-American Fiction and Elite Culture." *Periodical Literature in Nineteenth-Century America.*

Eds. Kenneth M. Price and Susan Belasco Smith. Charlottesville: U of Virginia P, 1995. 257–74.

Rabinowitz, Howard N. *The First New South, 1865–1920.* Arlington Heights: Harlan Davidson, 1992.

Rampersad, Arnold. "White Like Me." Rev. of *Paul Marchand, F. M. C.* By Charles W. Chesnutt. *New York Times* 25 Oct. 1998: sec. 7, p. 32.

Ramsey, William. "Family Matters in the Fiction of Charles W. Chesnutt." *Southern Literary Journal* 33 (2001): 30–43.

Renan, Ernest. "What Is a Nation?" *Nation and Narration.* Ed. Homi K. Bhabha. London: Routledge, 1990. 8–22.

Roe, Jae H. "Keeping an 'Old Wound' Alive: *The Marrow of Tradition* and the Legacy of Wilmington." *African American Review* 33 (1999): 231–43.

Roediger, David R. *Colored White: Transcending the Racial Past.* Berkeley: U of California P, 2002.

———. Introduction. *Black on White: Black Writers on What It Means to Be White.* Ed. David R. Roediger. New York: Schocken, 1998. 3–26.

Rosenblatt, Roger. *Black Fiction.* Cambridge: Harvard UP, 1974.

Rousseau, Jean-Jacques. *Émile.* Trans. Barbara Forley. London: Dent, 1993.

Rubin, Louis D., Jr. *George Washington Cable: The Life and Times of a Southern Heretic.* New York: Pegasus, 1969.

Saks, Eva. "Representing Miscegenation Law." *Raritan* 8 (1988): 39–69.

Scales-Trent, Judy. "Notes of a White Black Woman." *Critical White Studies: Looking behind the Mirror.* Ed. Richard Delgado and Jean Stefancic. Philadelphia: Temple UP, 1997. 475–81.

Scharnhorst, Gary. " 'The Growth of a Dozen Tendrils': The Polyglot Satire of Chesnutt's *The Colonel's Dream.*" McElrath, *Critical Essays* 271–80.

Schraufnagel, Noel. *From Apology to Protest: The Black American Novel.* Deland: Everett/Edwards, 1973.

Secor, Robert. "Puck." *American Humor Magazines and Comic Periodicals.* Ed. David E. E. Sloan. New York: Greenwood, 1987. 219–26.

Sedlack, Robert P. "The Evolution of Charles Chesnutt's *The House Behind the Cedars.*" *CLA Journal* 19 (1975): 125–35.

Smiley, Jane. "Say It Ain't So, Huck." *Harper's* Jan. 1996: 61–67.

Sollors, Werner. *Beyond Ethnicity: Consent and Descent in American Culture.* New York: Oxford UP, 1986.

"Some New Books." Rev. of *The Colonel's Dream,* by Chesnutt. Nashville *Banner* 29 Oct. 1905: n.p. Charles W. Chesnutt Papers, Special Collections, Fisk University Library, Nashville.

Starr, Kevin. Introduction. *The Octopus.* By Frank Norris. 1901. New York: Penguin, 1986.

Stepan, Nancy Leys, and Sander L. Gilman. "Appropriating the Idioms of Science: The Rejection of Scientific Racism." *The Bounds of Race: Perspectives on Hegemony and Resistance.* Ed. Dominick LaCapra. Ithaca: Cornell UP, 1991. 72–103.

Stowe, Harriet Beecher. *Uncle Tom's Cabin*. Ed. Elizabeth Ammons. 1852. New York: Norton, 1994.

Sundquist, Eric. *Faulkner: The House Divided*. Baltimore: Johns Hopkins UP, 1983.

————. Introduction. *The Marrow of Tradition*. By Charles W. Chesnutt. 1901. New York: Penguin, 1993. vii–xlvii.

————. *To Wake the Nations: Race in the Making of American Literature*. Cambridge: Harvard UP, 1993.

Tate, Claudia. *Domestic Allegories of Political Desire: The Black Heroine's Text at the Turn of the Century*. New York: Oxford UP, 1992.

Taylor, Walter Fuller. *The Economic Novel in America*. 1942. New York: Octagon, 1964.

Terrell, Mary Church. "Lynching from a Negro's Point of View." *North American Review* 178 (1904): 853–68.

Thomas, Brook. *American Literary Realism and the Failed Promise of Contract*. Berkeley: U of California P, 1997.

Tichi, Cecelia. "New Writers and the New Woman." *Columbia Literary History of the United States*. Ed. Emory Elliott. New York: Columbia UP, 1987. 589–606.

"To Shed a Light on the Race Problem." *Cleveland Press* n.d.: n.p. Charles W. Chesnutt Papers, Special Collections, Fisk University Library, Nashville.

Tourgée, Albion. Letter to Charles W. Chesnutt. 8 Dec. 1888. Charles W. Chesnutt Papers, Special Collections, Fisk University Library, Nashville.

————. "The South as a Field for Fiction." *Forum* 6 (1888): 404–13.

Towards the Gulf: A Romance of Louisiana. 1887. Freeport: Books for Libraries, 1972.

Twain, Mark. *Pudd'nhead Wilson*. Ed. Sidney E. Berger. 1894. New York: Norton, 1980.

Tyson, Timothy B., and David S. Cecelski. Introduction. Tyson and Cecelski, *Democracy* 3–13.

————, eds. *Democracy Betrayed: The Wilmington Race Riot of 1898 and Its Legacy*. Chapel Hill: U of North Carolina P, 1998.

Van Vechten, Carl. *Nigger Heaven*. 1926. Urbana: U of Illinois P, 2000.

Waddell, Col. Alfred M. "The Story of the Wilmington, N. C., Race Riots." *Collier's Weekly* 26 Nov. 1898: 4–5.

Washington, Booker T. "The Awakening of the Negro." *Atlantic Monthly* 78 (1896): 322–28.

————. "Industrial Education." *Negro Problem* 7–29.

Wegener, Frederick. "Charles W. Chesnutt and the Anti-Imperialist Matrix of African-American Writing, 1898–1905." *Criticism* 41 (1999): 465–93.

"The 'Wellington' Revolution." Rev. of *The Marrow of Tradition*, by Chesnutt. *Wilmington (North Carolina) Standard* 7 Jan. 1902: n.p. Charles W. Chesnutt Papers, Special Collections, Fisk University Library, Nashville.

West, Henry Litchfield. "The Race War in North Carolina." *Forum* Jan. 1899: 578–91.

Williams, Kenny J. "The Masking of the Novelist." *A Singer in the Dawn: Reinterpretations of Paul Laurence Dunbar*. Ed. Jay Martin. New York: Dodd, Mead, 1975. 152–207.

Williamson, Joel. *The Crucible of Race: Black/White Relations in the American South since Emancipation*. New York: Oxford UP, 1984.

———. *New People: Miscegenation and Mulattoes in the United States*. New York: New York UP, 1984.

Wilson, Edmund. *Patriotic Gore: Studies in the Literature of the American Civil War*. New York: Oxford UP, 1962.

Wilson, Matthew. "The African American Historian: David Bradley's *The Chaneysville Incident*." *African American Review* 29 (1995): 97–107.

———. "The Advent of the 'Nigger': The Careers of Paul Laurence Dunbar, Henry O. Tanner, and Charles W. Chesnutt." *American Studies* 43 (2002): 5–50.

Wing, Cary, ed. *The Politics and Aesthetics of "New Negro" Literature*. New York: Garland, 1996.

Wolkomir, Michelle J. "Moral Elevation and Egalitarianism: Shades of Gray in Chesnutt's *The Marrow of Tradition*." *CLA Journal* 36 (1993): 245–59.

Woodward, C. Vann. *Origins of the New South, 1877–1913*. Baton Rouge: Louisiana State UP, 1951.

Wright, Gavin. *Old South, New South: Revolutions in the Southern Economy since the Civil War*. New York: Basic, 1986.

Yarborough, Richard. "Violence, Manhood, and Black Heroism: The Wilmington Riot in Two Turn-of-the-Century African American Novels." Tyson and Cecelski *Democracy* 225–51.

Index